TABLOID
JOURNALISM

TABLOID JOURNALISM

An Annotated Bibliography of English-Language Sources

GERALD S. GREENBERG

Bibliographies and Indexes in Mass Media
and Communications, *Number 10*

GREENWOOD PRESS
Westport, Connecticut • London

Library of Congress Cataloging-in-Publication Data

Greenberg, Gerald S.
   Tabloid journalism : an annotated bibliography of English-language
sources / Gerald S. Greenberg.
     p. cm.—(Bibliographies and indexes in mass media and
communications, ISSN 1041–8350 ; no. 10)
   Includes indexes.
   ISBN 0–313–29544–1 (alk. paper)
   1. Sensationalism in journalism—Bibliography. 2. Sensationalism
in television—Bibliography. 3. Tabloid newspapers—Bibliography.
I. Title. II. Series.
Z6944.S45G76   1996
[PN4784.S4]
016.30223—dc20   96–8942

British Library Cataloguing in Publication Data is available.

Library of Congress Catalog Card Number: 96–8942
ISBN: 0–313–29544–1
ISSN: 1041–8350

First published in 1996

Greenwood Press, 88 Post Road West, Westport, CT 06881
An imprint of Greenwood Publishing Group, Inc.

Printed in the United States of America

The paper used in this book complies with the
Permanent Paper Standard issued by the National
Information Standards Organization (Z39.48–1984).

10 9 8 7 6 5 4 3 2 1

CONTENTS

PREFACE

This bibliography lists and briefly summarizes English-language books; scholarly journal, popular magazine, and trade journal articles; as well theses/dissertations which comment upon the practice of sensationalizing news reporting, commonly referred to as tabloid journalism.

While the compilation emphasizes U. S. print practitioners of the genre—especially the supermarket tabloids—chapter three is devoted to American tabloid television, the pervasiveness of which, some analysts believe, presents special problems. Similarly, the tabloid journalist's quest for the sensational has tested the legal boundaries protecting personal privacy. The ongoing debate surrounding this issue comprises chapter four. The final chapter surveys other nations' varied experience with this phenomenon, from England's lengthy history to the recent emergence of tabloidism in Eastern Europe.

The difficulty encountered by researchers seeking to locate archival collections of the very publications which most perfectly represent the genre—the supermarket tabloids and their spiritual forbearers, the phototabloids of the 1920's,—is briefly discussed in the opening chapter.

All sources listed in this compilation have been personally examined and evaluated by the compiler. It is hoped that this volume will be of assistance to researchers interested in the manner in which sensationalism impacts communications, popular culture and law as well as journalism.

I would like to thank Eleanor Block, Librarian at Ohio State University's Journalism Library, and Melanie Putnam, Librarian at Ohio State University's College of Law Library, for their research assistance as well as the staff of Ohio State University's Undergraduate Library for serving as a receptive audience, and providing suggestions. The service provided by David Tuffs and the Ohio State University Interlibrary Loan Department is also greatly appreciated.

INTRODUCTION

Tabloid journalism is not a recent phenomenon. Indeed, sensationalism has been a feature of news reporting for as long as news has been reported, as evidenced by the luridness of early English broadsides and news ballads. In America, the colonial news sheet, *Public Occurrences* was banned after one issue due to the scandalous innuendo it contained. However, the pervasiveness and influence of the genre has steadily increased in the past twenty years, beginning with the debut of the *National Enquirer* at America's supermarket checkout stands. The process was greatly assisted by the advent of tabloid television in the early 1980's. The call for censorship which accompanied the rise of yellow journalism in the nineteenth century and jazz-age tabloids of the 1920's are heard once more as critics insist that the electronic media's unique ability to influence the intellect of its audience threatens us all with the death of discourse.

This compilation, while emphasizing English-language journal articles and monographs discussing tabloid journalism during the period 1975-1994, also provides an historical overview of the genre by listing sources which comment upon sensational journalism of earlier eras: the penny press, yellow journals, the phototabloids, and exposé magazines. Certainly sources which criticize sensationalism—sometimes viciously—predominate, because such journalism is provocative in its exaggerated appeal to the emotions, continually calling into question whether anything remains of what was once termed "good taste" (and, if so, if it is capable, any longer, of being offended). Well represented, however, are scholarly studies which explain, defend and champion tabloid journalism from historical, sociological, anthropological and political viewpoints. These works place tabloid journalism within age-old folklore traditions or Rabelaisian carnival culture which gives voice to society's underclass. Analysts of the genre disagree over whether the supermarket tabloids serve to reinforce the status quo by encouraging the readership to believe that anyone can become a cultural icon (or destroy one), or if popular culture as embodied in the tabloids is, in reality, a Neo-Marxist thrust at the establishment.

Tabloid television has thoroughly obscured the boundaries of information and entertainment as sensation-heavy newscasts join reality-TV programs and tabloid talkshows in providing viewers with cheaply-produced "infotainment" which consistently attracts large audiences. Sources analyze the manner in which televised news creates a reality for the viewership and express concern over the effect which violent/sexual/scandalous programming has upon the passive viewer.

The legal boundaries of intrusive journalism have never been clearly drawn, although a right to privacy has frequently been asserted. Case law and law review essays debate the efficacy of defamation suits as remedy for the excesses of tabloid journalism. How can we reconcile freedom of the press with a right to be let alone? Complicating matters is our culture's obsession with celebrity. Does the public figure's image constitute a creative property deserving protection against an aggressive press anxious to publicize scandal? Sources debate such issues and offer alternatives to traditional legal remedies.

Finally, sensational news reporting is international in scope. Whenever a nation's press has been able to break free from the control of government and political parties, a popular press aimed at mass readership has developed. England pioneered such newspapers in the nineteenth century, and produced the first tabloid early in the twentieth. Emerging nations are finding that commercialization of news reporting entails adoption of many tabloid-type features so popular in the west.

I

PRIMARY SOURCES

Research collections of popular penny press newspapers, such as James Gordon Bennet's *New York Herald* and Benjamin Day's *New York Sun*, are found in libraries across the country. The same is true of the yellow press publications of Joseph Pulitzer and William Randolph Hearst. However, when the researcher investigates the supermarket tabloids of today and their direct predecessors, the phototabloids of the 1920's, the task is much more difficult. Only three research libraries collect such material, and their holdings are incomplete.

001   Bowling Green State University Popular Culture Collection. Bowling Green, Ohio.
Among this library's Genre Periodical Collection can be found several of the supermarket tabloids (partial runs) as well as representative exposé magazines including *Confidential* (1953-1968) and *True Confessions* (1927, 1929).

002   The Library of Congress. Independence Avenue at First St. SE, Washington D.C.
Collects many of the supermarket tabloids (partial runs), and the *New York Daily News* (1919-   ).

003   The New York Public Library Research Library. Fifth Avenue & 42nd St., New York, N.Y.
Collects several of the supermarket tabloids (partial runs). Features complete holdings of Bernarr Macfadden's *New York Evening Graphic* (1924-1932), the *New York Daily Mirror* (1924-1972), and the *New York Daily News* (1919-   ).

2

U.S. PRINT JOURNALISM

GENERAL WORKS

004   Bleyer, Willard Grosvener. *Main Currents in the History of Ameri-can Journalism.* Boston: Houghton Mifflin, 1927. 464 pgs.
Traces the influences, both English and American, which gave rise to the modern popular/sensational press. Separate chapters cover emergence of the penny papers; James Gordon Bennett and the *New York Herald*; E. L. Godkin and the reaction to sensational journalism; Charles Dana and the *New York Sun*; Joseph Pulitzer and the *New York World*; and William Randolph Hearst and the *New York Journal*. Chapter 16, "The Development of the Present-Day Newspaper" (pp. 389-429) includes discussion of the tabloids *New York Mirror* and *New York Evening Graphic*.

005   Cohen, Stanley and Jock Young, eds. *The Manufacture of News: Social Problems, Deviance and the Mass Media.* London: Constable, 1981. 506 pgs.
Examines how the news media presents stories of social deviance and what such presentation reveals about their views of society. Media behavior is seen in the light of two variant theories — the Mass Manipulative and the Market/Commercial models that regard the audience either as victims of a political conspiracy or willing consumers of cultural products. Chapters address media presentation of crime, sexuality, mental illness, political extremism, industrial conflict, women, and drug use, but come to no real conclusions.

006   Emery, Michael and Edwin Emery. *The Press and America: An Introspective History of the Mass Media*. Englewood Cliffs: Prentice Hall, 1992. 7th edition. 715 pgs.

Chapter 6, "A Press for the Masses" (pp. 95-117) discusses the rise of penny papers, highlighting Day's *Sun* and Bennett's *Herald*. Chapter 9, "The New Journalism" (pp. 169-206) focuses on the sensationalism of Pulitzer and Hearst. Chapter 13, "The Twenties: Radio Movies, Jazz Journalism" (pp. 265-299) includes discussion of the tabloids (New York's *Daily News*, *Evening Graphic*, and *Mirror*).

007   Fiske, John. *Understanding Popular Culture*. Boston: Unwin Hyman, 1989. 206 pgs.

Enunciates a theory of popular culture in capitalist societies characterized by the struggle between dominant and subordinate ideologies. Popular culture is formed in reaction to the dominant norm. Describes tabloid journalism as constructively excessive and obvious, enabling the reader to mock convention through parody. Sees the sensational as "excessive failure of the normal."

008   Gans, Herbert J. *Popular Culture and High Culture*. New York: Basic Books, 1974. 149 pgs.

A sociological study of popular vs. high culture in American society. Argues that regular culture expresses at least in part, the values and needs of a segment of Americans, and is not purely an invention of the commercial media. Champions the causes of cultural democracy and pluralism. Offers analysis, definition, and criticism of popular cultures, and public policy implications of popular culture analysis.

009   Green, Ward. *Star Reporters and 34 of Their Stories*. New York: Random House, 1948. 402 pgs.

A collection of some of the best remembered, most popular and highly-regarded newspaper stories of the period 1869-1934. The stories, mostly human interest in style—many of them sensational—are reproduced as they appeared originally, preceded by an introductory commentary from compiler Ward. Included are: "A Sob Sister" (Winifred Black); "Annie Laurie" (covering a tidal wave in Galveston, Texas); "A Woman Tells" (Irving S. Cobb on Evelyn Nesbitt's testimony at the murder trial of Harry Thaw); "Remember the Pig Woman?" (Dudley Nichols on Jane Gibson's testimony at the Hall-Mills murder trial); and "A Woman Burns" (Gene Fowler covering the electrocution of murderess Ruth Brown Snyder).

010   Hughes, Helen MacGill. *News and the Human Interest Story*. Chicago: The University of Chicago Press, 1940. 313 pgs.

Celebrates the human interest story as a form of popular literature which has been largely responsible for the commercial success of the newspaper industry. Chapter 9, "Sensationalism and the Yellow Press" (pp. 217-255), traces the history of the Pulitzer and Hearst publications and the tabloids of the 1920's. Covers in detail the invention, application, and reception of Emil Gauvreau's composograph as employed by MacFadden's *Evening Graphic*.

011   Kobre, Sydney. *Development of American Journalism*. Dubuque: Wm. C. Brown, 1969. 767 pgs.
The history of American journalism as a social institution. Part 3, "Popular Penny Press (1830-1865)" (pp. 197-345), chronicles the rise of the first sensational press. Chapter 18, "New York Press: The Innovators" (pp. 364-393), covers the contributions of Joseph Pulitzer, Charles Dana, and William Randolph Hearst. Chapter 34 "Tabloids: Kisses, Bullets, and Liberals" (pp. 605-615) relates the advent of the sensational photo tabloids of the 1920's beginning with the *New York Daily News*.

012   Lee, Alfred McClung. *The Daily Newspaper in America: The Evaluation of a Social Instrument*. New York: Macmillan, 1937. 797 pgs.
Standard history of American journalism, topically-arranged. Discusses each aspect of the industry. Chapter 16, "The Editorial Staff" (pp. 603-641), covers the role played by sensationalism in journalistic policy.

013   Lippmann, Walter. *Public Opinion*. New York: The Free Press, 1949.
Reprint of the 1922 classic study that investigates how we form our notions, ideas, and attitudes concerning the world about us, and why they so often mislead us. Part 7 (pp. 201-230) deals with the newspapers, consisting of chapters 21-24: "The Buying Public," "The Constant Reader," "The Nature of News," and "News, Truth, and a Conclusion." Sees the press as a frail institution shouldering the burdens of popular sovereignty and truth, the instincts for which democratic theorists hoped were inborn. People prefer "the curious trivial as against the dull important" and "hunger for sideshows and three-legged calves" because we have failed to create a machinery of knowledge that would permit people to transcend casual experience and prejudice.

014   Mott, Frank Luther. *American Journalism: A History: 1690-1960*. Toronto: Macmillan, 1962, 901 pgs.
Third edition of the 1941 comprehensive history of American journalism. Includes informative chapters on the penny press of the 1830's, Joseph Pulitzer and the *New York World*, as well as the tabloid newspapers of the 1920's

015   Ross, Ishbel. *Ladies of the Press: The Story of Women in Journalism by an Insider.* New York: Harper, 1936. 622 pgs.
Comprehensive examination of women's role in American journalism. Highlights the contribution of women reporters such as Nellie Bly and Annie Laurie during the rise of the sensational press. Separate chapters are devoted to the "Sob Sisters," Dorothy Dix's coverage of the Hall-Mills murder trial; and Julia Harpmann's career in tabloid journalism beginning with the *New York Daily News* in 1919. While most of the book is arranged topically, part four (pp. 481-600) surveys women's contributions by geographical regions.

016   Saltzman, Joe. "Tabloid Hysteria." *USA Today* (May, 1994): 21.
Demonstrates that tabloid journalism, or its historical equivalent, has existed for over 300 years. Offers excerpts of English and American articles complaining about the very same excesses we now associate with "tabloidism." Provides various definitions of the term "tabloid," and suggests that it is the responsibility of the reading public to pass final judgement on the phenomena.

017   Schiller, Dan. *Objectivity and the News: The Public and the Rise of Commercial Journalism.* Philadelphia: University of Pennsylvania Press. 1981, 222 pgs.
Examines the concept of objectivity as a journalistic standard. Attempts to reconcile the emergence of the objective standard with the sensationalism of the penny press. Pays tribute to Michael Schudson's *Discovering the News* (see entry #019), while differing with the sociological characterization of the penny press's reading public in the earlier work.

018   Schilpp, Madelon Golden and Sharon M. Murphy. *Great Women of the Press.* Carbondale: Southern Illinois University Press, 1983, 248 pgs.
Surveys the contribution of 18 American women journalists, each afforded her own chapter, spanning the 18th to 20th centuries. Included are muckraker Ida Tarbell, columnist Dorothy Dix, and reporter Annie Laurie, all key figures of the popular/sensational press.

019   Schudson, Michael. *Discovering the News: A Social History of American Newspapers.* New York: Basic Books, 1978, 228 pgs.
Addresses the concept of objectivity in journalism by examining the nature of the profession as it evolved in American society. Traces sensationalism in news coverage to the birth of the penny press in the 1830's. The *New York Sun* and its successors were perceived as sensational because they covered all the news, including events which were

considered immoral (murder trials, e.g.). Joseph Pulitzer wedded sensationalism to style in the 1880's by glorifying self-promotion in the *New York World* through the use of illustrations and banner headlines. Places sensational news coverage within the context of competing journalistic traditions: objectivity, literary tradition, and muckraking/investigative reporting. The author sees no new journalistic ideal to replace that of objectivity, but stresses that because perceptions are subjective, there needs to be a greater appreciation for different ways of reporting.

020   Stephens, Mitchell. *A History of the News: From the Drum to the Satellite*. New York: Viking, 1988, 400 pgs.
Demonstrates that sensationalism is a feature of news reporting as old as newspapers themselves, citing Roman emperor Commodus (A.D. 180-192) who ordered the city gazette to report anything he did that was typical of a gladiator or procurer. Discusses a 16th century handwritten German newssheet describing an execution and many instances where supernatural phenomena were reported. Expresses surprise that television journalists have not been as graphic in their portrayal of the sensational as their tabloid newspaper counterparts. Concludes that human nature has always been and will always be attracted by the bizarre and the gruesome.

021   Stevens, John D. *Sensationalism and the New York Press*. New York: Columbia University Press, 1991, 210 pgs.
Examines New York City's history of sensational newspapers in three different eras: the penny press of the 1930's, the yellow press of Pulitzer and Hearst in the 1880's-90's, and the pictorial tabloids of the 1920's Modern supermarket tabloids are briefly surveyed in chapter 14, pp. 155-161. Issues addressed include the nature of tabloid readership, actual newspaper content, and contemporary critical commentary of the publications.

022   Stevens, John D. "Sensationalism in Perspective." *Journalism History* 12 (1985): 78-79.
Historical overview of sensational news coverage throughout the ages and citizen reaction/evaluation of the same. Introduces special issue on sensationalism (see entries #034, 044, 103 for other articles contained in this number.)

023   Tebbel, John. *The Compact History of the American Newspaper.* New York: Hawthorn Books, 1963, 286 pgs.
Briefly surveys the roles played by the newspaper throughout the history of the American press: instrument of propaganda, personal expres-

sion, and commerce. Highlights the penny press innovator James Gordon Bennett in "The Giants of New York" (pp. 93-124). Details William Randolph Hearst's *San Francisco Examiner* in "The Sensational West" (pp. 155-173). "Passing of the Old Order" (pp. 209-229) touches upon the 1920's tabloids.

024   Weaver, Paul H. *News and the Culture of Lying.* New York: The Free Press, 1994, 243 pgs.
Argues against the manner in which professional journalists create their own reality and present it to the public as actuality. By transforming so much news into stories of crisis and emergency, society is trained to react in an authoritarian rather than a democratic/constitutional manner. Chapter 2, "Pulitzer's Revolution" (pp. 33-67), places the responsibility for crisis journalism and the changes that ensued on Joseph Pulitzer's sensationalizing of the news. Chapter 6, "Traitors to Their Experience" (pp. 141-171), includes a discussion of the first American tabloid newspaper, Joseph Medill Patterson's *New York Daily News*, which is seen as an overreaction against the manipulations of respective journalism. Concludes by calling for a less sensational form of journalism reported by journalists who are less like professional experts and more like responsible citizens.

HISTORICAL OVERVIEW

The Penny Press

025   Bode, Carl. "The Rampant Press." In *Anatomy of American Popular Culture 1840-1861.* 250-265. Berkeley: University of California Press, 1959.
Lauds the penny press and its practitioners in America, James Gordon Bennett (*New York Herald*) and Ben Day (*New York Sun*) for their championing popular causes, while intimating that their emphasis on "robbery, riot and rape" was less than praiseworthy. Also addresses the journalistic contributions of Horace Greely, Henry Peterson, Robert Bonner, Louis Godey, and James De Bow.

026   Brown, Lee. *The Reluctant Reformation: On Criticizing the Press in America.* New York: David McKay, 1974, 244 pgs.
Brief survey of the history and nature of press criticism in America. Chapter 1, "Power, the Press, and Criticism" (pp. 1-20), contrasts penny press sensationalism with Walter Lippmann's standard of public inter-

est/objectivity. Chapter 2, "The Fabric of Press Criticism: Unbroken Threads" (pp. 21-49), chronicles the press criticism of E. L. Godkin and Charles Dickens. Extensive appendices include codes of ethics, reports considering a national press council, surveys on newspapers' image, and newspaper use of internal criticism.

027   Bruce, John. *Gaudy Century: The Story of San Francisco's Hundred Years of Robust Journalism.* New York: Random House, 1948. 302 pgs.
Anecdotal history of San Francisco's first hundred years as seen by its many newspapers. The excitement of the gold rush and the frontier violence it spawned is all reported in their pages. Chapter 12, "The Scandal Sheets" (pp. 78-80), discusses papers such as *Our Mazeppa* and *Sunday Varieties* which practiced "keyhole reporting," publicizing the sins of selected citizens.

028   Capehart, Charles. "The Beginnings of American Journalism." *The Editor and Publisher and Journalist* (26 April 1913): 27-44, 46, 48, 50, 52, 54.
Chronicles the history of news reporting in America including *Publick Occurrences* (1690), banned by colonial authorities after one issue. Surveys a multitude of noteworthy publications throughout the country over the years, including representatives of the penny press and the new sensational journalism of Charles Dana and Joseph Pulitzer. (Special issue of the publication).

029   Carlson, Oliver. *The Man Who Made News: James Gordon Bennett.* New York: Duell, Sloan and Pierce, 1942.
Biography which stresses Bennett's independence from the political powers of his day, how such freedom enabled Bennett to tell the real news in his paper, and the praise and scorn which accompanied this journalistic revolution. Part III, "The *New York Herald* (pp. 121-223), recounts the founding and development of the *New York Herald* including its ground breaking coverage of crime news as evidenced in the paper's investigation of the "Ellen Jewitt Murder Mystery" (pp. 143-167).

030   Carvalho, S. S. "James Gordon Bennett, The Elder, Possessed Rare Genius as a Newspaper Maker." *The Editor and Publisher* (25 May 1918): 9.
Hails Bennett Sr. for inventing many of the features newspapers now take for granted (financial reports, weather reports, shipping news, special correspondent, e.g.), and, above all, for gathering and printing all the news, a sensational and unconventional notion before the advent of the penny press.

031   Coleman, Albert Evander. "New and Authentic History of the 'Herald'
          of the Bennetts." *The Editor and Publisher* (5 April 1924): 9-10.
       Second installment in a series which tells the story of James Gordon
       Bennett and his penny press sensation, the *New York Herald*. Covers the
       founding of the newspaper in 1835 and Bennett's bitter rivalry with
       Benjamin Day's penny press pioneer, the *Sun*.

032   Cooper, James Fenimore. "On the American Press." In *The American
          Democrat,* edited by George Dekker and Larry Johnston.
          180-186. Baltimore: Penguin Books, 1969.
       First published in 1838, the famed American novelist and social critic
       condemns "press tyranny" which rules over the individual's private, as
       well as his public life. Describes the contemporary ("penny") press as
       untruthful, unintelligent, and ruthless—in brief, "a great agent of mis-
       chief."

033   Crouthamel, James L. *Bennett's New Herald and the Rise of the Popu-
          lar Press.* Syracuse: Syracuse University Press, 1989.
       A scholarly study of Bennett's major journalistic achievement—estab-
       lishment of a cheap, popular, mass circulation newspaper in America.
       Chapter 2, "Sensationalism and the Newspaper Revolution" (pp. 1942),
       details how Bennett expanded upon the *Sun's* successful experiment in
       sensationalism by featuring stories about the tragedies and scandals of
       others.

034   Francke, Warren. "Sensationalism and the Development of 19th
          Century Reporting: The Broom Sweeps Sensory Details." *Jour-
          nalism History* 12 (1985): 80-85.
       Concentrates on the relationship between the news reporter and sensa-
       tional detail, asking the question whether sensationalism increased dur-
       ing the penny press era because more reporters gained greater access to
       more news subjects. Discusses application of news reporting tech-
       niques—observation and interview—to sensational news coverage.
       Stresses the importance of news availability and journalistic style in
       determining the degree of sensationalism present in a newspaper. Con-
       tains excerpts of nineteenth-century sensationalism.

035   Harding, William. "The One Cent Paper." *The Editor and Publisher*
          (24 April 1909): 11.
       Article based on James Parton's *Life of Horace Greely* which credits
       Greely's associate, Horatio Davis Sheppard, with the idea for the first
       metropolitan penny paper. Sheppard and Greely sold the experimental
       New York Morning Post for three days in January, 1833, eight months
       before the appearance of Benjamin Day's *Sun*. Describes how Sheppard's

idea for "a small, spicy daily paper" was conceived after watching street merchants hawking their wares.

036   Lee, James Melvin. "Growth and Development of American Journalism: Beginning of Party Organs, First Dailies, and Penny Press." *The Editor and Publisher* (8 December 1917): 11, 22.
Third installment of an historical overview recounting the progress of American journalism. This entry discusses the birth of an independent penny press, opposed by the political parties but beloved by the workingman. Notes the success of the penny press in uncovering municipal scandals.

037   Lee, James Melvin. "O'Brien Retells 'Story of the Sun.' " *The Editor and Publisher* (25 February 1928): 11, 54.
Reviews and discusses Frank O'Brien's new edition of *The Story of the Sun* (see entry #041), chronicling the history of the landmark penny paper.

038   Mann, Helen Scott. "When Dana Ruled the New York Sun." *The Editor and Publisher, The Fourth Estate* (23 May 1931): 13.
Reviews Charles I. Rosebault's new biography of *New York Sun* editor Charles A. Dana (see entry #110). Discusses personal and professional relationship between author and subject, and describes the book's treatment of Dana's personality and career. Highlights Dana's personal style of popular journalism.

039   Nerone, John C. "The Mythology of the Penny Press." *Critical Studies in Mass Communication*. 4 (1987): 376-404.
Challenges commonly held presumptions concerning the nature of the American penny press by arguing that it did not represent a journalistic revolution, but was rather an evolutionary step toward modernity. Does not regard the commercial penny press as necessarily more democratic than its predecessors which circulated popularly in a society that deferred to privilege. Contends that the penny press was not sensational by modern standards, and the sensationalism present was distinctly moralistic in tone. Also addresses method of sales, price, audience, partisanship (maintaining the penny press was impartial but not objective), politics, and the nature of the news.

040   Nordin, Kenneth D. "The Entertaining Press: Sensationalism in Eighteenth Century Boston Newspapers." *Communication Research* 6 (1979): 295-320.
Contends that the colonial press, especially Boston's, stressed sensation, human interest, and scandal long before the penny press appeared

on the scene. Content analysis of Boston newspapers, 1704-1784 supports thesis. Reasons for this development: inherited tradition from the English press; sensational events were common on the frontier; and Massachusetts's mass literacy.

041   O'Brien, Frank. *The Story of the Sun.* New York: D. Appleton and Co., 1928. 305 pgs.
Recounts the establishment of the first permanent penny newspaper, the *New York Sun* by Benjamin H. Day in 1833. Chapter 4, "Day Finds a Rival in Bennett" (pp. 59-72), traces the *Sun/Herald* competition for popular press supremacy in nineteenth century New York.

042   Peebles, Paul. "James Gordon Bennett's Scintillations." In *Highlights in the History of the American Press*, edited by Edwin H. Ford and Edwin Emery. 150-159. Minneapolis: University of Minnesota Press, 1954.
Pays tribute to penny press pioneer James Gordon Bennett and his *New York Herald* which debuted in 1835. Characterizes Bennett's publication as one of the first "news" papers—impudent, incisive, and witty. It was regarded as sensational because it reported all the news as it occurred.

043   Pray, Isaac Clark. *Memoirs of James Gordon Bennett and His Times by a Journalist.* New York: Stringer & Townsend, 1855. 488 pgs.
Pioneering biography of the man who built the *New York Herald* into an independent, popular penny newspaper, a forerunner of the later sensational publications of Pulitzer and Hearst. Chapter 14 (pp. 186-196) covers the founding of the *Herald*, and discusses the reputation of the penny press.

044   Shaw, Donald L. and John W. Slater. "In the Eye of the Beholder? Sensationalism in American Press News, 1820-1860." *Journalism History* 12 (1985): 86-91.
Maintains that the sensationalism of the penny press consisted primarily of style (abbreviated) and news diffusion (widespread due to railroad and telegraph) rather than content, which was little different than human interest stories in earlier decades (and quite tame by modern standards).

045   Tannenbaum, Percy H. and Mervyn D. Lynch. "Sensationalism: The Concept and Its Measurement." *Journalism Quarterly* 37 (1960): 381-392.
Describes development of an empirical approach to measuring journalistic sensationalism—the "Sendex" or semantic differential index.

Briefly reviews arguments for and against sensational content in journalism, and discusses problems related to defining and measuring sensationalism. Includes statistical tables.

046   Tannenbaum, Percy H. and Mervyn D. Lynch. "Sensationalism: Some Objective Method Correlates." *Journalism Quarterly* 39 (1962): 317-323.
Describes development of a method for objectively identifying characteristics of written news messages which cause them to be regarded as sensational. Builds on the authors previous investigation of journalistic sensationalism, and its measurement through use of their "Sendex" technique (see entry #045).

047   Tucker, Andie. *Froth & Scum: Truth, Beauty, Goodness, and the Ax Murder in America's First Mass Medium*. Chapel Hill: University of North Carolina Press, 1994. 257 pgs.
Investigates the manner in which the penny press covered two sensational murders, analyzing the extent to which objectivity prevailed. The murders of Ellen Jewitt (1836) and Samuel Adams (1841), as portrayed in the penny press, involve societal factors which make it difficult to arrive at the truth. Argues that, ultimately, the readership decides on the type of coverage its press will deliver.

048   Wilmer, Lambert A. *Our Press Gang, Or A Complete Exposition of the Corruptions and Crimes of the American Newspapers*. Philadelphia: J. T. Loyd, 1860. 404 pgs.
Detailed, protracted indictment of the American press, charging corruption of law, justice, morality, civil order, and the "American way." Views the penny press's appeal to the masses as subversive and degrading, and its methods of news gathering an invasion of privacy. Section 15, "Newspaper Slanders" (pp. 251-268), attacks the "vile habit" of scandal-mongering. Contains many illustrations of newspaper sensationalism to which the author objects.

Yellow Journalism

049   "Accuse Newspapers." *The Editor and Publisher and Journalist.* 1 July 1911: 1.
Discusses charge by the committee of The American Academy of Medicine that the press causes suicides by reporting instances of such tragedy in detail. News editors respond that, regardless of the validity of the charge, newspapers must report the news.

050   Alger, George W. "Sensational Journalism and the Law." *The Atlantic Monthly* 91 (1903): 145-151.
Criticizes yellow journalism for utilizing intimidation rather than persuasion in order to influence public opinion. Similarly, believes the popular press has won favored court decisions with its crusading tactics, which the author finds offensive. The public's belief in judicial integrity is being undermined. Distinguishes between journalistic charges of prejudice (which may be warranted), and corruption (which are insupportable).

051   "American Reporters." *The Editor and Publisher and Journalist* (20 April 1912): 7.
Discusses article which appeared in the *London Newspaper Owner* complementing the aggressiveness of the American news reporter and the cleverness of its yellow journals for providing great amusement as well as insight. Finds yellow journalism an accurate reflection of the American character.

052   Barrett, James Wyman. *Joseph Pulitzer and His World.* New York: Vanguard Press, 1941. 449 pgs.
The *World's* last city editor depicts Pulitzer as a sensational crusader for a new activist school of journalism. Chapter 3, "New York *World*" (pp. 55-82), recounts Pulitzer's acquisition of the *World*, and his revitalization of the newspaper by application of sensational populist principles. Chapter 7, "Turn of the Century" (pp. 180-214), includes description of Alfred Harmsworth's (later Lord Northcliffe) tabloid version of the *World* issued (at Pulitzer's invitation) 1 January 1901 as an experiment in futuristic journalism.

053   Bent, Silas. *Newspaper Crusaders: A Neglected Story.* New York: Whittlesey House, 1939. 313 pgs.
Celebrates the leadership role played by prominent journalists in social reform. Chapter 2, "Pulitzer: Past Master" (pp. 20-42), examines the accomplishments of Joseph Pulitzer's *New York World.* Chapter 7, "Hearst: Playboy and Prodigy" (pp. 43-59), highlights the positive influences of William Randolph Hearst's newspapers.

054   Brisbane, Arthur. "As in a Mirror." *The Editor and Publisher.* 9 July 1910: 8.
Reprint of Brisbane's article in the *New York Evening Journal* which seeks to explain why prize fights and conflagrations monopolize most newspaper space while great thinkers are ignored. Brisbane asserts that newspapers are mirrors reflecting their times and the interests of their readership.

055   Brisbane, Arthur. "Yellow Journalism." *The Bookman.* 19 (1904): 400.
Declares that yellow journalism is war on hypocrisy and class privilege. It is the journalistic creed of the activist, reformist newspaper in its ascendancy. Success breeds satisfaction and complacency, conservatism and decline. Hearst's competitive triumph over Pulitzer illustrated the cycle. Yellow journalism's defects are insignificant in comparison to its merits.

056   "Brisbane Buys Washington Times From Munsey and Adopts Hearst Features." *The Editor and Publisher* (30 June 1917): 3, 22.
Reports that longtime Hearst-associate, Arthur Brisbane, master of human-interest reporting, has purchased the *Washington Times* and plans to institute changes which will cause it to resemble Hearst's *New York Evening Journal.*

057   Brooks, Sidney. "The American Yellow Press." *The Living Age.* 272 (1912): 67-76.
Assesses both the accomplishments and shortcomings of America's yellow press in a balanced manner, beginning with a tribute to the career of the innovative Joseph Pulitzer and his *New York World.* Praises the populist advocacy of the yellow press while criticizing the overemphasis on sensationalism which takes liberties with the truth. Believes that the worst excesses of the yellow press are in the past. [First published in the *Fortnightly Review,* 96 (1911): 1126.]

058   Brooks, Sidney. "The Yellow Press: An English View." *Harper's Weekly* (23 December 1911): 11.
Appreciates the achievements of the yellow press: success in convincing many non-reading immigrants to read, assisting the public health movement, championing the underdog, and distributing classic literature (as inserts in its holiday editions, e.g.). Its sins are understandable in the absence of strict British-type libel laws. England has a yellow press as well, but it is less spectacular.

059   Budd, Louis J. "Color Him Curious About Yellow Journalism: Mark Twain and the New York City Press." *Journal of Popular Culture* (Fall 1981): 25-33.
Examines Mark Twain's relationship with the New York newspapers of his day, and his stance on the high vs. low culture nature of the publications. States that although Twain preferred Godkin's establishment *Evening Post,* he repeatedly accommodated the more sensational *World* and *Journal* (of Pulitzer and Hearst, respectively) for a combination of economic, political, and cultural reasons.

060   Cohen, Anne B. *Poor Pearl, Poor Girl!: The Murdered Girl Stereotype in Ballad and Newspaper.* Austin: University of Texas Press, 1973. 131 pgs.
Maintains that nineteenth-century newspaper stories and ballads about murdered girls conform to traditional folklore formulas and themes. Moral stance, character and story details are examined. The murder of Pearl Bryan in 1896 and its newspaper coverage forms the basis of the study.

061   "Col. Watterson's Alarm About Newspaper Sensationalism." *The Editor and Publisher* (27 November 1909): 8.
Editorial which argues that sensational journalism is a guarantor of democracy rather than a violation of privacy, as charged by Col. Henry Watterson in his address to the National Press Club in Washington. Claims that the public should rightly judge the nature of the news to be reported. Praises popular editorialists like Arthur Brisbane for secularizing morality, thereby educating the masses.

062   Crawford, Remsen. "Wilbur Storey Launched Yellow Journalism as Editor of Old *Chicago Times.*" *The Editor and Publisher* (3 April 1920): 7-8.
Chronicles the career of Wilbur F. Storey who adopted the motto, "Raise Hell and Sell Newspapers!" when he assumed half ownership of the *Chicago Times* in 1861. Called "the first yellow journalist of America," Storey pioneered coverage of sensational stories with oversized lurid headlines. (The hanging of a criminal who protested his innocence by predicting his ascension to heaven was headlined "Jerked to Jesus.") Includes information on suppression of the *Times* during the Civil War, and its destruction by fire in 1871.

063   "Crime Publicity." *The Editor and Publisher* (22 October 1910): 1.
Reports address of Illinois State Attorney John E. W. Wayman who favors factual reporting of crime and scandal in newspapers, because such publicity deters crime and protects the public. Warns against falsifying or exaggerating in order to enhance stories.

064   "Criticizes American Press." *The Editor and Publisher* (19 November 1910): 2.
Reports that G. M. Simons, editor of the *Amsterdam* (Holland) *Telegraph* faults American papers for sensationalizing street crimes and ignoring important foreign news. Crime and scandal receive scant coverage in Holland.

065   "Do the Newspapers Make Children Criminals?" *The Editor and Publisher* (16 December 1911): 6.

Editorial which asserts that children do not commit crimes merely because they read criminal accounts in newspapers. Argues that most newspapers are decent and intended for adults. Contends that newspapers are actually instruments for the prevention of crime by virtue of their publication of evil for the purpose of facilitating its elimination.

066   "Dr. Butler Attacks Yellow Journalism." *The Editor and Publisher* (17 February 1917): 16.
Reports the remarks of Columbia University president Nicholas Murray Butler to alumni charging the press with practicing "inflammatory journalism" in its inaccurate chronicling of his activities. Includes response from the *New York World* labeling Butler's remarks as irresponsible sensationalism.

067   Duggan, Lisa. "The Trials of Alice Mitchell: Sensationalism, Sexology, and the Lesbian Subject in Turn-of-the-Century America." *Signs* 18 (1993): 791-814.
Examines sensational treatment of the Alice Mitchell Murder case (1892), perhaps the first same sex love-murder story publicized in America. Focuses on what contemporary newspaper coverage reveals of national attitudes and understanding of lesbianism. Sample newspaper accounts include *New York World* coverage.

068   "The Falsification of the News." *The Independent* 84 (1915): 420.
Complains that New York's leading newspapers ignore the essential content of news events in order to sensationalize marginal aspects of a story. Similarly, it is argued that the papers are adopting a yellow journalism approach to the European conflict, clamoring for American involvement in the war.

069   "The Faults of the Press." *The Editor and Publisher and Journalist* (10 August 1912): 8.
Editorial which responds to Rev. Charles Sheldon's attack on the press (see entry #112). Argues that modern newspapers conform to a higher ethical standard than those in the past. "Vicious newspapers" exist, but are gradually being rejected by the public. Refutes Sheldon's assertions regarding distasteful advertising as well.

070   Garnsey, John Henderson. "The Demand for Sensational Journals." *The Arena* 18 (1897): 681-686.
Argues that there is no demand for sensational newspapers aside from that which is artificially created by such newspapers themselves. Includes discussion of the libel laws, and the possible suppression of the newspapers. Predicts the ultimate failure of sensational journalism.

071   Gilbert, Simeon. "The Newspaper as Judiciary." *The American Journal of Sociology* 12 (1906).
Views the newspaper as judgemental voice of the populace in each nation, making and changing history throughout the world. Regards "the yellow-sheet monstrosities" as guilty of "criminal journalistic offenses." Such papers, however, will themselves be judged and made to answer for their transgressions by the enlightened element in the journalistic community.

072   [Godkin, E. L.] "Excitability." *The Nation* 66 (1898): 160.
Attributes the success of the yellow press to the excitability of the American character. Analyzes the reasons for such excitability, citing general prosperity and optimism which resulted after the American Revolution. Predicts that the excesses of sensational newspapers coupled with increasing national problems will produce a more moderate press.

073   [Godkin, E. L.] "The Rights of the Citizen. IV - To His Reputation." *Scribner's Magazine* 8 (1890): 58-67.
Essay which seeks to establish the importance of one's reputation: it affords comfort in communal living; grants influence among one's peers; and is an essential prerequisite for acquiring business capital or credit. Recounts and analyzes the history of libel and slander law in western society leading to establishment of the privacy concept. Discusses the role played by newspapers in privacy intrusion, concluding that society is mistaken when it condones such intrusion merely because the gossip business has become a profitable industry.

074   [Godkin, E. L.] "The Unfortunate Press." *The Nation* 62 (1896): 355-356.
Deplores the childishness and unprincipled levity of the popular press. Calls for greater maturity and gravity. Discusses increasing competition and cost associated with newspaper ownership; responsibility of the readership for the state of American newspapers; and proposes newspaper boycotts to force an end to sensationalism.

075   Gorn, Elliot J. "The Wicked World: The *National Police Gazette* and Gilded-Age America." *Media Studies Journal* Winter 1992: 1-15.
Views the graphically-violent *National Police Gazette* of late nineteenth century New York as a forerunner of modern tabloid journalism. Appealing primarily to lower class white males, the publication offered sensational coverage of violent crime, sports (especially illegal blood sports), and sex—all in a personal, chatty style. Includes discussion of the publication's misogyny, racism, and anti-semitism.

076   "The Gossip About King Manuel and the Stage Dancer." *The Editor and Publisher* (15 October 1910): 8.
Editorial which argues that newspapers are justified in covering scandals as long as such stories are factual—not mere gossip.

077   "A Great Mystery." *The Nation* 57 (1893): 301-302.
Questions the existence of an audience for sensational newspapers which exaggerate societal evils and ignore all that is good. Includes a letter that appeared in the *London Spectator* in which an English visitor to Chicago attests to the false impression of America conveyed by sensational newspapers.

078   Grinnell, Charles E. "Modern Murder Trials and Newspapers." *Atlantic Monthly* 88 (1901) 662-673.
Asserts that newspapers' sensational reporting of criminal trials—omitting involved, subtle testimony and exaggerating the emotional—still does more good than harm by lawfully publicizing the entire affair. Such publicity strengthens our legal system. The alternative — censorship — is unacceptable.

079   Holt, Hamilton. *Commercialism and Journalism.* Boston: Houghton and Mifflin, 1909. 105 pgs.
Discusses the threat to journalism which is posed by commercialism. Concludes that while the influence of advertisers menaces press freedom, recognition of this danger will mobilize the community to act effectively against it. Characterizes the yellow press (pp. 86-91) as a combination of typography and theatrics which is the journalistic equivalent of Tammany Hall, simultaneously serving, representing, and exploiting the masses. (The author—managing editor of the *Independent*—contributed this essay as part of the "Barbara Weinstock Lectures on the Morals of the Trade" series.)

080   "Huge Head-Lines." *The Editor and Publisher* (24 April 1926): 74.
Editorial which attests to the commercial success of oversized "boxcar" headlines by discussing their past popularity with the newsboys who found such sensational displays easier to hawk to customers. Today, first pages are tailored to the readers, not the newsboys.

081   "The Influence of Headlines." *The Editor and Publisher* (15 July 1922): 24.
Supports the views of Walter S. Meriwether, editor and publisher of the *Charleston Mississippi Sun,* who maintains that screaming headlines greatly influence behavior of the readership, and that such a technique

should be used to promote civil well being rather than sociopathic activity. Theorizes that crime waves have been initiated by sensational headlines; virtuousness could be fostered in a similar manner.

082   Ireland, Alleyne. "Joseph Pulitzer on Practical Newspaper Ethics." In *Interpretations of Journalism,* edited by Frank Luther Mott and Ralph D. Cassy. 462-463. New York: F. S. Crofts & Co., 1937.
Excerpt from Ireland's biography of Pulitzer in which the journalist defends sensationalism as long as it is moral and accurate. Views uncovering vice as essential in a democracy.

083   Irwin, Will. "Yellow Journalism." In *Highlights in the History of the American Press,* edited by Edwin H. Ford and Edwin Emery. 267-283. Minneapolis: University of Minnesota Press, 1954.
Recounts the rise and reign of yellow journalism from the 1880's—1911, explaining the roles played by commercialism and technology in making possible the new journalistic form. Surveys the roles played by Pulitzer, Hearst, Morill Goddard, and Arthur Brisbane.

084   "Journalism's Great Debt to Joseph Pulitzer." *The Editor and Publisher and Journalist* (4 November 1911): 8.
Editorial praising Joseph Pulitzer's revolutionary journalistic style marked by greater sensationalism, aggressiveness, and advocacy. He revived the *World* with yellow journalistic techniques but abandoned the practice when hysteria resulted. Includes favorable comment upon Pulitzer's philanthropy.

085   "Journalistic Dementia." *Nation* 60 (1895): 195-196.
Decries the puerility and vulgarity of the "blackguard newspapers" which invade the privacy of family and bedroom in search of "copy." Laments that these subjects may well be an accurate barometer of popular taste. Blames the economic status of the industry for the problem: the unstable, insecure nature of the work attracts irresponsible youth, while management purposely recruits the unscrupulous who will pry into the private lives of their subjects.

086   Juergens, George. *Joseph Pulitzer and the New York World.* Princeton: Princeton University Press, 1966. 362 pgs.
Examines the journalistic techniques employed by Joseph Pulitzer in resurrecting the *New York World.* Chapter 2, "Sensationalism" (pp. 43-92) details how Pulitzer updated the journalistic techniques pioneered by James Gordon Bennett and Benjamin Day in appealing to the masses. The components of a sensational journalistic style are discussed: human interest stories including gossip/scandal; relegation of statecraft stories to the back pages; and use of slangy/personal prose.

087   Lee, James Melvin. "Growth and Development of American Journalism: Period of Reconstruction and Adjustment." *The Editor and Publisher* (5 January 1918): 8, 23, 26.
Fifth installment in a series narrating the development of American journalism. Covers the period 1865-1900 including the reformist/muckraking activities of the popular newspapers, the influence of commercialization, and the practice of yellow journalism during the Spanish-American War.

088   Lundberg, Ferdinand. *Imperial Hearst: A Social Biography.* Westport, Connecticut: Greenwood Press, 1960. 406 pgs.
Reprint of 1936 biography which casts Hearst as a political reactionary and fascist. Chapter 3 (pp. 49-82) describes Hearst's exploitation of sex and sensation, and his eager adoption of yellow journalism as a circulating-building strategy. Includes preface by Charles A. Beard.

089   Martin, Edward S. "Terrestrial Troubles, Men, and Tabloids." *Harpers Monthly Magazine* 154 (1927): 661-664.
Recalls newspaper competition of the 1880's when Pulitzer brought his *World* from St. Louis to New York. Sees the tabloids as both a reflection of the public's appetite for the sensational, and a cause for it's increased craving (because they feed it).

090   Marzolf, Marion. *Up From the Footnote: A History of Women Journalists.* New York: Hastings House, 1977. 310 pgs.
Examines the increasingly expanding role played by women in American journalism. Chapter 2, "Sob Sister to War Correspondent" (pp. 32-73), chronicles the rise of women reporters and columnists for the yellow press, producing "sob sister" stories (such as the reports produced at the 1907 trial of Harry Thaw for the murder of New York architect, Stanford White) which boosted circulation. The contribution of sensational reporters; Beatrice Fairfax, Dorothy Dix, Winifred Black Bonfils, Ada Patterson, Nixola Greely-Smith, and Mildred Gilman are included.

091   Mencken, Henry L. "Newspaper Morals." *The Atlantic Monthly* 113 (1914): 289-297.
Praises constructive journalism—a necessity when communicating ideas to the masses—as a progressive force. Journalism facilitates social and ethical reform by exaggerating evil in order to mobilize its readership: "You must have a good show to get a crowd..."

092   Millis, Walter. "Hearst" *The Atlantic Monthly* 148 (1931): 696-709.
Recaps the career of William Randolph Hearst, a practitioner of the maxim: "Give the public what it wants." Intelligent, courageous, and

wealthy, Hearst understood the principle underlying the success of Joseph Pulitzer's *World:* utilization of sensationalism to secure the popularity necessary in waging populist battles. Considers the tabloid newspapers of the 1920's too vulgar to be in the Hearst tradition. A laudatory evaluation not entirely lacking in criticism of the man.

093   "Modern Journalism." *The Editor and Publisher and Journalist* 14
          (1915): 565, 567.
       Reports on *New York Times* editor Charles R. Miller's address to the American Conference of the Teachers of Journalism in which the speaker announced the death of the sentimental human interest story. Miller states that due to the commercial nature of society, the public wants practical stories about the accumulation of wealth instead. Still, says Miller, the most popular kind of news printed is invariably about contests or fights.

094   Montgomery-M'Govern, J. B. "An Important phase of Gutter Journalism: Faking." *The Arena* 19 (1898): 240-253.
       Castigates sensational newspapers for reportedly fabricating stories. Cites example of newspaper-created story assigned to a reporter who was charged with recruiting an expert to attest to its veracity. Discusses similar practice of enhancing cable dispatches with imaginary detail.

095   Nevins, Allen. *The Evening Post: A Century of Journalism.* New York:
          Boni and Liveright, 1922. 590 pgs.
       Describes English/American journalist E. L. Godkin's objections to the nineteenth century sensational journalism found in the *New York Sun, World,* and *Journal.* Founder of the *Nation,* and later editor of the *Evening Post,* Godkin's journalistic ideals are presented in chapter 25 "News, Literature, Music, and Drama, 1880-1900" (pp. 546-567).

096   "The New York Horror and the Press." *The Editor and Publisher*
          (1 April 1911): 8.
       Editorial which defends graphic newspaper descriptions of the carnage which resulted from the Triangle Shirt Waist Company fire. Critics of such coverage need to realize that necessary industrial and social reforms will not occur unless the press is free to portray such unpleasantness.

097   "Newspaper Delusions." *The Editor and Publisher and Journalist* 47
          (1915): 1060.
       Excerpts from a paper read by John A. Sleicher, editor of *Leslie's Weekly,* at the University of Missouri during Journalism Week, May 3-7. Deplores the fact that the public wants newspapers which serve as

"theater and circus as well as school and pulpit." Argues for professionalization of journalism and less—but more accurate— news.

098   "Newspaper Essentials." *The Editor and Publisher* (15 October 1910): 6. Quotes Dean Joseph French Johnson of the New York University School of Commerce, Accounts, and Finance who maintains newspaper success depends on satisfying the human instincts for contests, sex, and humor.

099   "Newspaper Makers at Work: Arthur Brisbane." *The Editor and Publisher* (14 April 1917): 9, 45.
       Profiles Hearst editorialist Arthur Brisbane covering his early years with Charles Dana and the *New York Sun,* his talent for reporting the human interest story, his tenure with Joseph Pulitzer's *World,* and his association with William Randolph Hearst. Discusses Brisbane's journalistic innovations: oversized type for "big scare heads," and editorials written to be read by the common man.

100   "The Newspaper Must Print Criminal News." *The Editor and Publisher and Journalist* (1 July 1911): 6.
       Editorial which argues in favor of clear, factual, reporting of crime including suicide. Maintains that publication of such acts aids in uncovering their causes. Favors omitting lurid details which are so popular with the yellow press.

101   Noguchi, Yone. "A Japanese on American Journalism." *The Editor and Publisher* (26 August 1916): 10.
       Applauds the decline of yellow journalism which reached its height after victory in the Spanish-American War, during which time newspapers sensationalized Associated Press reports to suit their own purposes. Prefers the stateliness of the *New York Times* to the sensationalism and sarcasm of the *Sun.*

102   Ogden, Rollo, ed. *Life and Letters of Edwin Lawrence Godkin.* New York: Macmillan, 1907. 2 volumes.
       The British/American journalist expresses his distaste for the vulgar new journalism of Bennett's *Herald* and Dana's *Sun* in numerous passages from his correspondence. A bibliography of Godkin's books and magazine articles is found in volume 2 preceding the index.

103   Olasky, Marvin. "Late 19th Century Texas Sensationalism: Hypocrisy or Biblical Morality?" *Journalism History* 12 (1985): 96-100.
       Attempts to explain why Texas newspaper editors continually condemned sensationalism at professional conferences while practicing

sensational journalism in their newspapers, 1880-1900. Concludes that hypocrisy does not explain the situation, finding rather that anti-sensationalist rhetoric coexists comfortably with sensational reporting. Maintains that context and underlying morality are more important than surface sensationalism in evaluating journalism's value.

104   "100th Anniversary of Charles A. Dana, 'Who Created Journalism in America.' " *The Editor and Publisher* (14 August 1919): 50.
Celebrates the one hundredth anniversary of the birth of longtime *New York Sun* editor and owner Charles Dana. Recounts his career, highlighting the personal control he exercised over the *Sun* from 1867-'97, during which time, "the *Sun* was Mr. Dana, and Mr. Dana was the *Sun*."

105   Park, Robert E. "The Natural History of the Newspaper." *The American Journal of Sociology* 29 (1923): 273-289.
Chronicles the history of the newspaper in America viewing the yellow press as a means by which the working class could be captured as readers, greatly increasing newspaper circulation. Credits Dana and Pulitzer with taking preliminary steps along this line. Discusses Walter Lippmann's analysis of newspapers and methods for their improvement.

106   Park, Robert E. "The Yellow Press." *Sociology and Social Research* 12 (1927): 3-11.
The yellow press is viewed as democracy in action, making reading the news easy and popular for the masses. Benjamin Day, Joseph Pulitzer, and William Randolph Hearst are seen as courageous innovators who greatly increased the circulation of newspapers by stressing love/romance (for women) and sports/politics (for men) in their publications.

107   "Penny Dreadfuls." *The Independent* 62 (1907): 507-509.
Editorial which maintains that the sensational news stories and serialized fiction featured by the yellow press are virtually indistinguishable. Ironically, gruesome details of actual crimes receive more complete coverage in the traditional newspapers which devote less space to sensationalism and fiction.

108   Pilgrim, Tim A. "Privacy and American Journalism: An Economic Connection." *Journalism History* 14 (1987): 18-25.
Hypothesizes that Warren and Brandeis asserted a right to privacy (see entry #606) in response to the aggressiveness of the nineteenth-century reporters who were economically motivated to obtain sensational stories. Traces the evolution of the privacy concept in American society.

109   Roosevelt, Theodore. "The Public Press." In *Interpretations of Journalism,* edited by Frank Luther Mott and Ralph D. Casey. 471-473. New York: F. S. Crofts & Co., 1937.
Excerpt from a speech before the Press Club in Milwaukee, 7 September 1910, in which the President argued against the notion that journalists ought to provide the public with whatever it wants to read in the newspapers. Honesty and truthfulness must be first considerations.

110   Rosebault, Charles J. *When Dana Was the Sun* Westport Conn.: Greenwood Press, 1931. 294 pgs.
Biography of *New York Sun* editor Charles Dana, emphasizing his personification of "Personal Journalism" (pp. 175-186), describes Dana's style, at times partisan and vitriolic, sensational in its coverage of virtually all the news as it occurred. Chapter 34, "Dana Talks About the Education and Training of Newspaper Men, and the Ethics of Journalism" (pp. 286-294), discusses Dana's credo which combined journalistic thoroughness with competition and fair play.

111   Seitz, Don C. *Joseph Pulitzer: His Life and Letters.* New York: Simon & Schuster, 1924. 478 pgs.
Relies heavily on correspondence in depicting Joseph Pulitzer as the "Liberator of Journalism." Chapter 6 "The New *World*—1883-1885" (pp. 129-154) recounts Pulitzer's acquisition of the *New York World* from Jay Gould, and establishment of his populist/journalist principles. Pulitzer's rivalry with Dana's *Sun* and Bennett's *Herald* is detailed.

112   "Sheldon Attacks the Newspapers." *The Editor and Publisher and Journalist* (10 August 1912): 6.
Reprints and comments on an article by Rev. Charles M. Sheldon, author and former newspaper editor who finds fault with the press in several areas: uncivilized advertising (patent medicines, e.g.); invasion of privacy (which he equates with robbery); inaccuracy; and a poor sense of proportion (accentuating the trivial).

113   Smith, F. Hopkinson. "The Muck-Rake as a Circulation Boomer." *The Critic* 48 (1906): 511.
Castigates the yellow press as subversive, whose aim it is to defame honorable persons and institutions (the United States Senate, e.g.) while sowing the seeds of anarchy among the gullible lower classes.

114   Stone, Candace. *Dana and The Sun* New York: Dodd, Mead, and Company, 1938. 431 pgs.
Biography of Charles A. Dana, editor of the *New York Sun*, 1868-1897.

Adhering to the motto "The Sun Shines for All," Dana is viewed as champion of personal/sensational journalism in stark contrast to the more conservative journalistic concepts of E. L. Godkin and Adolph Ochs. Chapters 2, "Dana Recreates the *Sun*" (pp. 29-55) and 5, "Sensational Attacks of the *Sun*" (pp. 115-134) illustrate Dana's technique.

115   Swanberg, W. A. *Citizen Hearst.* New York: Charles Scribner's Sons, 1961. 555 pgs.
Comprehensive biography of William Randolph Hearst. Book Three, "The War Maker," (pp. 79-169) highlights the yellow journalism of Hearst's *New York Journal*, while Book Five, Chapter 9, "Influences Malign and Benign" (pp. 425-434) details Hearst's tabloid venture, the *New York Mirror.*

116   Swanberg, W. A. *Pulitzer.* New York: Charles Scribner's Sons, 1967. 462 pgs.
Comprehensive biography of the nineteenth-century populist/journalist and his sensational *New York World*. Part 2, "Sensationalist" (pp. 47-62) details Pulitzer's plans to revolutionize his newspaper, while part five, "War With Hearst" (pp. 205-255), covers his rivalry with Hearst's *New York Journal.*

117   "Symposium: Giving the Public What It Wants." In *The Coming Newspaper*, edited by Merle Thorp. 223-247. New York: Henry Holt, 1915.
Journalists of the day respond to the proposition that the newspaper should cater to the tastes of the readership. Issues discussed include the newspaper as educator, differentiating between "highbrow" and "lowbrow" news; creation of demand vs. response to demand and distinguishing between sensational appeal to the masses and pandering to criminals.

118   "The Tendency to Big Headlines." *The Editor and Publisher* (6 August 1910): 8.
Editorial which complains about exaggerated, oversized headlines assigned to trivial news items. Such a circulation ploy depreciates news values and undermines public confidence in the paper.

119   "Theology and Yellow Journalism: The Bane of the Headline." *The Biblical World* 33 (1909): 363-366.
Editorial which complains that religion cannot receive proper treatment from a press that sensationalizes and misrepresents all it reports. Religious stories are covered by reporters unschooled in theology. Scientific news suffers a similar fate. All is "sacrificed to the Moloch of sensationalism."

120   Thomas, W. I. "The Psychology of the Yellow Journal." *The American Magazine* 65 (1908): 491-497.

Asserts that the sensational aspect of yellow journalism appeals to man's primal violent nature. Yellow journalism is immoral, because it is an obstacle to social control, speaking to man's worst instincts. Moreover, it is worse than its readers because it cynically exploits their taste for the lurid. Detects, however, a movement toward self-reform evidenced by a moderation of sensationalism.

121   " 'Thumped Over News Values.' " *The Editor and Publisher* (4 September 1926): 40.

Reports that *New York World* columnist Heywood Broun objects to the manner in which newspaper reporters continue to harass composer Irving Berlin, demanding that he continue to offer comments on his recent marriage.

122   "Wants to Be Yellow." *The Editor and Publisher* (9 December 1911): 5.

Reports address by Arthur Brisbane to the Genesee Valley Hunt Club (N.Y.) in which he alluded to his use of huge, sensational headlines to sell Hearst newspapers. Includes discussion of the importance of condensing and marketing news to the public.

123   Watterson, Henry. "The Personal Equation in Journalism." *The Atlantic Monthly* 106 (1910): 40-47.

Predicts that the process of social evolution will doom sensational journalism as the masses become increasingly educated and discriminating. Decency and accuracy will become the journalistic standards which ensure profitability. Discusses the personal journalism of the bygone days which produced journalistic giants like Greely who dominated the profession.

124   "Yellow Journalism." *The Editor and Publisher and Journalist* (17 May 1913): 15.

Comments upon a new English novel, *The Prosperous Yankee* by "Ponsonby" which characterizes yellow journalism as a deceitful enterprise which employs reporters as dishonest detectives in order to obtain slanderous secrets for publication. Maintains much of the information contained in the novel is obviously false and the book should not have been published.

125   " 'Yellow Journalism' Defined." *The Editor and Publisher* (20 January 1917): 14.

Notes *New York Evening Journal* editor Arthur Brisbane's definition of the term "yellow journalism," supplied to luncheon attendants at the

Brooklyn Civic Club on January 11. Brisbane maintains the phrase is applied to anything new or successful in the journalism field.

126   "Yellow Journalism Evils." *The Editor and Publisher and Journalist* (19 August 1911): 8.
Editorial which argues that the lying and misrepresentation associated with the yellow press do great harm to individuals and communities, far outweighing any good which comes from such sensationalism. Predicts an early end to the journalistic style.

Jazz Journalism

127   Alexander, Jack. "Profiles: Vox Populi-II" *The New Yorker* (13 August 1938): 19-24.
The second installment in a three-part profile of *New York Daily News* publisher Joseph Medill Patterson, this article details the founding of the pioneer American tabloid, stemming from Patterson's meeting with Lord Northcliffe whose *London Daily Mirror* had caused a sensation in England. Recounts Patterson's personal history and includes discussion of subsequent competing tabloids: Hearst's *New York Mirror*, and Macfadden's *New York Evening Graphic*. The first installment in the series (*The New Yorker* 6 August 1938: 16-21) focused on Patterson's temperament and style while the third (*The New Yorker* 20 August 1938: 19-23) discusses the recent respectability of the once-sensational *Daily News*.

128   "Announce *New York Illustrated News*." *The Editor and Publisher* (19 June 1919): 1, 39.
Reports that the Chicago Tribune Company will start publication of a daily illustrated newspaper in New York called the *Illustrated Daily News*, patterned on the *London Daily Graphic* and *London Daily Mirror*. Describes a "dummy" of the first issue featuring sensational news in brief which lends itself to illustration: love stories, human interest news, and curiosities. Tabloid dimensions are noted.

129   Barber, Solon R. "Rise of Pictorial Journalism Seen by New York Editor in 1875." *The Editor and Publisher* (30 July 1927): 44.
Discusses the prophetic views of David G. Croly of the *New York Daily Graphic* who declared in 1875 that cities would have illustrated daily newspapers devoted to reporting the news photographically. Crimes, scandals, and accidents must all be illustrated. Includes comments by Charles Dana, James Gordon Bennett, Whitelaw Reid, E. L. Godkin,

and William Cullen Bryant on the state of journalism in the late nineteenth century.

130   "Beck Blames Press for Triviality of Modern Thinking." *The Editor and Publisher* (22 December 1923): 4.
Reports that James M. Beck, Solicitor General of the U.S., has charged newspapers with creating interest in conflict and sensation among the public by emphasizing violence and scandal in their reporting. Beck also argues against the trend of briefly covering a multitude of stories rather than writing about a few important issues in depth.

131   Bennet, William Rose. "The Phoenix Nest." *The Saturday Review of Literature* (15 June 1946): 46-47.
Eulogizes *New York Daily News* publisher Joseph Medill Patterson as a "lesser Hearst," someone who exploited vulgarity and abandoned his earlier vision of helping improve the lives of America's workingmen. Argues that, although Patterson frequently associated with the "man in the street," his newspaper provided him with "sensational muck" instead of useful education.

132   "Bent Assails, Stern Defends, Newspapers." *The Editor and Publisher, The Fourth Estate* (23 February 1929): 61.
Reports debate between Silas Bent, reporter and lecturer, and J. David Stern, publisher of the *Philadelphia Record.* Debate occurred before the Philadelphia Contemporary Club after Bent called for revocation of press freedoms due to the manner in which newspapers trivialized important news while exploiting sex and crime. Stern claimed for newspapers the same freedom of expression extended to literature everywhere.

133   Bent, Silas. *Ballyhoo: The Voice of the Press.* New York: Horace Liveright, 1927. 398 pgs.
A study of the state of American newspapers in the 1920's Characterizes the press (and the American people) as "unstable mentally and emotionally" due to the absence of a guiding written and oral tradition in America. ("Ballyhoo" is the author's preferred term for sensationalism.) Finds the press guilty of libelous behavior, but views the new journalistic form as a natural outgrowth of its predecessors, "the daily printed folklore of the factory age." Frontispieces depict an *Evening Graphic* "composograph" of Rudolph Valentino and Enrico Caruso meeting in "the spirit world."

134   Bent, Silas. "The Hall-Mills Case in the Newspapers." *The Nation* 123 (1926): 80-81.

Documents the voluminous press coverage extended to the sensational murder trial, originally investigated by Hearst's tabloid *Mirror*. The *New York Times* devoted the most words to the story, the *Daily News*, the most pictures. Bent praises the *Mirror* for reviving a noble journalistic tradition in its investigation of the murder.

135   Bent, Silas. "The I's Have It." *The Independent* 120 (1928): 135-136, 144.

Contrasts the personal journalism of Horace Greely and Charles Dana, whose editorials impacted on national policy, with the sensational trivia which permeates all pages of newspapers circa. 1928. Argues that such modern personal journalism featured most glaringly in the tabloids, is directly descended from the early commercialism of James Gordon Bennett. Maintains that the increasing puerility of the press results from advertisers' need for mass readership. Outlines a number of concepts developed more fully in *Ballyhoo* (see entry #133).

136   Bent, Silas, "Roller Coaster Journalism." *Saturday Review of Literature* 4 (1928): 884-885.

Maintains that the popularity of the tabloids does not indicate popular demand for them. Rather, the public takes what it can get in herdlike fashion. Calls for a newspaper aimed at the intelligent reader, but doubts it will be heeded.

137   Bessie, Simon Michael. *Jazz Journalism: The Story of the Tabloid Newspapers*. New York: Russell & Russell, 1966. 247 pgs.

A reissue of the 1938 classic history of the tabloid newspaper, the author focuses on the first modern example of the genre in America—the *New York Daily News* and Bernarr Macfadden's *New York Evening Graphic*. The tabloid is seen as more accurately reflective of America's vitality during the 1920's (and sorrow during the Depression) than the establishment press, because it was more closely in touch with the common people. Concludes that the tabloid is a natural and happy outgrowth of the nation's industrial democracy making its contribution to American folklore.

138   Bliven, Bruce. "Graphic Realist." *The New Republic* 49 (1926): 167-169.

Satirical essay honoring "Maestro (Bernarr) Macfadden" whose "romantic - satiric - realistic" vision is presented in the pages of the *New York Evening Graphic* daily. Recounts the tabloid's coverage of the Peaches Browning scandal in order to highlight what the author regards as its unparalleled depiction of American life and culture.

139   Brand, E. Byron. "Ministers Declare Crimeless Dailies Would Quickly Bore Readers." *The Editor and Publisher, The Fourth Estate* (22 December 1928): 19.
Reports that Ministers in Mount Clemens, Michigan, given the opportunity to report the news, included crime prominently in their stories because it is news of an exceptional variety.

40   "Brisbane Puts News First, Comics Second." *The Editor and Publisher, The Fourth Estate* (3 October 1931): 9, 19.
Reports on Arthur Brisbane's radio broadcast on the occasion of the *New York Evening Journal's* thirty-fifth anniversary. Discusses the nature of news to different audiences, elements of a successful newspaper (news, comics, sports, fiction, editorials, respectively), and the manner in which the newspaper reflects society. Maintains that newspapers should not be blamed for reflecting society's sensational nature.

141   "Brisbane Sees Big Opportunities for Newspaper Publishers Now." *The Editor and Publisher, The Fourth Estate* (17 October 1931): 8.
In an interview, Arthur Brisbane, Hearst editor and executive, discusses mass circulation, advertising, and sensational journalism. Brisbane responds to Walter Lippman's prediction of the demise of journalistic sensationalism by maintaining that sensationalism will continue because the world about which newspapers report is sensational.

142   Burt, Struthers. "Tabloids and Truthful Tales." *Saturday Review of Literature* (10 March 1928): 661-662.
Compares those who condemn the tabloids for printing filth with the aristocrats who carried scented bottles to ward off smallpox. Asserts it is better to attack the cause (surroundings and circumstances that breed crime, vulgarity, and disease) than the agent. Agrees that it is better to read trash than not to read at all.

143   "Censorship or ——— ?" *The Editor and Publisher* (5 February 1927): 34.
Editorial which explores forsaking freedom of the press if it becomes the only alternative to the continued debauchery exhibited by elements of the New York press in the coverage of the Peaches Browning case. (Much of the criticism alludes to the composographs which Bernarr Macfadden's *Evening Graphic* created in order to depict the Browning's unorthodox sex life.) Advocates committing journalistic panderers to prison or the asylum before they succeed in leading the public to degeneracy.

144   "Censures Newspapers for Crime News." *The Editor and Publisher* (4 October 1928): 26.

Reports that O. S. Spillman, Nebraska Attorney General, attacked the manner in which newspapers report crime in an address to the National Association of Attorneys-General, July 24. Spillman accused newspapers of failing to condemn crime, sensationalizing sex appeal of female criminals, and failing to report corporate crime.

145   Chapman, John. *Tell It to Sweeny: The Informal History of the New York Daily News.* New York: Doubleday, 1961. 288 pgs.
Recounts the history of Joseph Medill Patterson's "gum-chewers rag," the tabloid *New York Daily News,* from 1919-1961. "New York's Picture Newspaper" is described as skillfully written and edited in addition to featuring a sensational style and convenient format, enabling the publication to outlive most competitors.

146   "The Chicago Murder." *The Editor and Publisher* (14 June 1924): 22.
Editorial which argues that most newspaper coverage of the Leopold-Loeb murder case is necessary and instructive, revealing the depravity of the "jazz age." Relatively few newspapers sensationalize the case by attempting to inject glamor or romance in order to maintain gains in circulation.

147   "Chorines Posed For Composograph of Famous 'Siamese Twins.'" *The Editor and Publisher* (18 August 1928): 19.
Describes how *New York Evening Graphic* editor-in-chief E. H. Gauvreau created a story featuring a composite photo about the impending surgical separation of Siamese twins Mary and Margaret Gibb. Two chorus girls posed on an operating table for creation of the "composograph." Includes reaction of other journalists to this controversial photographic technique as well as a description of the process.

148   Cohen, Lester. *The New York Graphic: The World's Largest Newspaper.* Philadelphia: Chilton Books, 1964. 241 pgs.
Relates the eight-year history (1924-1932) of Bernarr Macfadden's *New York Evening Graphic.* Credits the newspaper's brief success to its staff (particularly Emil Gauvreau and Walter Winchell), numerous contests, and the controversial composograph (composed photograph).

149   "Col. Lindbergh's Appeal." *The Editor and Publisher, The Fourth Estate* (20 August 1932): 26.
Editorial which recommends cooperation with the Lindbergh family's request for limiting publicity concerning their second son, but rejects implication that press sensationalism surrounding the first son led to the child's kidnapping and murder.

150   Covert, Cathy. "A View of the Press in the Twenties." *Journalism History* 2 (1975): 66-67, 92-96.
Excerpt from the author's book, *Fraud on the Front Page; The Dissemination of Freudian Ideas in the American Newspaper of the 1920's* Comments that 1920's journalism appealed to emotions as well as intellect, employing an approach that was Freudian in nature. Sees the 1920's tabloid as journalism's attempt to reach the lower class.

151   "Crime and the Press." *The Saturday Evening Post* (26 January 1935): 2.
Editorial which contends that sensationalizing is beneficial when it results in greater awareness of the problem and more frequent identification and apprehension of offenders. Acknowledges, on the other hand, that lurid reporting of crimes is a serious social problem, especially when it romanticizes criminals.

152   "Crime News Necessary Says Psychiatrist." *The Editor and Publisher* (24 April 1926): 54.
Reports that Topeka psychiatrist Karl Menninger regards the newspaper reporting of crime news as beneficial to society for two reasons: it provides "vicarious expression for the criminal tendencies of many readers" and it serves to publicize the causes of criminal behavior (some of which are subconscious compulsions). These factors outweigh the arguments of critics who oppose news coverage of crimes.

153   "Crime Publicity." *The Editor and Publisher* (18 February 1928): 24.
Editorial which responds to a Lansing, Michigan clergyman who contended that crime publicity produces new criminals. Argues that such an assertion is an absurd generalization, incapable of seriously addressing a complex issue.

154   "Crimson News." *The Editor and Publisher* (19 March 1921): 26.
Argues that while murders, divorces, and suicides have certain news value, such subjects must be treated by journalists who can create drama and romanticism out of sordidness—not pandered to the masses as filth. Objects to the amount of space devoted to sensationalism at the expense of more educational, edifying news. Several examples of recent sensational news stories are provided. Finds the motion pictures guilty of similar offenses.

155   Cummings, E. E. "The Tabloid Newspaper." *Vanity Fair* (December 1926): 83, 146.
Argues that the tabloid newspaper is symptomatic of America's infantile national mentality, offering "vicarious indulgence of the pomp and

vanities of this wicked world." Characterizes the tabloid as a dream-like, visual tribute to the present, supplanting older newspapers which provoked thought about the history of events. Provides a psychoanalytic interpretation of the tabloid newspaper and its readership.

156   "Daily Refutes Charge of 'Sensationalism.' "*The Editor and Publisher* (4 December 1926): 49.
Discusses charges of sensationalism leveled against the *Springfield Republican* after the newspaper published a report exposing existing safety hazards in Springfield, Mass. schools. Newspaper refutes the charge by contemplating the price of silence: inaction, and possible disaster in the event of a fire.

157   De Rochemont, Richard. "The Tabloids." *The American Mercury* 9 (1926): 187-192.
Recounts the history of tabloid newspapers, Lord Northcliffe's first efforts in 1903 London, and surveys the tabloid field in the U.S. Establishes that success depends heavily on sensationalism (which appeals to the masses and compensates for weak support by advertisers) and photography (which helped the *New York Daily News* prosper).

158   " 'De-Smut the News and Fiction' Hopwood Urges N.Y. Publishers." *The Editor and Publisher* (5 February 1927): 12.
Reports remarks of Erie C. Hopwood, president of the American Society of Newspaper Editors and editor of the *Cleveland Plain Dealer*, to the New York State Press Association. Hopwood maintained that some editors are insulting public taste in parading indecency on their front pages (citing the Peaches Browning case to be the epitome of such scandal). Calls for a balance between information and entertainment.

159   "Draper and Gauvreau Discuss Newspapers." *The Editor and Publisher, The Fourth Estate* (29 August 1931): 14.
Reports on radio broadcast featuring discussion between Arthur S. Draper, assistant editor of the *New York Herald Tribune* and Emil Gauvreau, managing editor of the *New York Daily Mirror.* Gauvreau portrayed the modern newspaper as entertainer and champion of the average man. Draper stressed character and dignity, shunning sensationalism as indicative of poor taste.

160   Ernst, Robert. *Weakness is a Crime: The Life of Bernarr Macfadden.* Syracuse: Syracuse University Press. 1991. 278 pgs.
Unauthorized biography of the *New York Evening Graphic* publisher which draws on new primary source material, earlier biographies, and the recollection of Macfadden's widow. Chapter 6, "The PornoGraphic"

(pp. 89-107), deals with Macfadden's sensational 1920's paper, which anticipated the supermarket tabloids.

161   "Fast and Fair News." *The Editor and Publisher, The Fourth Estate* (1 December 1928): 32.
        Editorial which credits one London newspaper correspondent with defusing the crisis which followed English charges of sensationalism leveled at the American press for its reporting of the sinking of the British steamer "Vestris" (see entry #253). Following the recommendation of the English journalist, nautical advisors joined the official inquiry into the tragedy and calmness prevailed. Asserts that testimony of survivors was sensational without embellishment, despite British claims to the contrary.

162   "Find News Is News." *The Editor and Publisher, The Fourth Estate.* (22 December 1928): 28.
        Editorial which lauds the experiment that permitted clergymen in Mount Clemens, Michigan to edit the day's news (see entry #140). The paper which was produced prominently featured crime news. Maintains that the exercise will result in greater understanding of the press by clergy, and increased public confidence in the press.

163   "Fit to Print?" *The Nation* 115 (1922): 492.
        Reflects on the journalistic space given by New York's newspapers to tawdry tales of murder and scandal. Personal human interest stories resonate most deeply in people. The newspapers are not to blame for devoting coverage to such stories, because the market place demands it.

164   "Four-Year-Old Crime Gives *Mirror* Beat." *The Editor and Publisher* (31 July 1926): 5.
        Details how the *New York Mirror*, working to solve the 1922 Hall-Mills murder case, succeeded in convincing authorities to arrest Frances Steven Hall, widow of the slain Rev. Edward W. Hall. Describes how the tabloid's detective work resulted in the paper's securing for itself a sensational scoop.

165   Gabler, Neal. *Winchell: Gossip Power and the Culture of Celebrity.* New York: Alfred A. Knopf, 1994. 681 pgs.
        Definitive biography of popular influential gossip columnist Walter Winchell. Argues that Winchell understood the subject of gossip—its ability to humanize and demystify the celebrated and powerful, a valuable leveling force in a democracy. Views Winchell as a prime mover in establishing a cult of celebrity which has effectively replaced the pe-

dantic culture of Walter Lippmann and E. L. Godkin. Covers in great detail Winchell's stint with Macfadden's *New York Graphic* and his long association with Hearst's *New York Mirror*. Debates Winchell's legacy: the simultaneous enlivenment and debasement of journalism.

166   Gauvreau, Emil. *Hot News.* New York: The Macaulay Company, 1931. 316 pgs.
An inside view of "Tabloidia," the author's name for "a world of emotions and sensations" where the innovative journalist makes excitement happen. Gauvreau presents a fictionalized version of his experiences as a tabloid journalist with Bernarr Macfadden's *New York Evening Graphic* (here reinvented as Mammoth City's *Evening Comet*).

167   Gauvreau, Emil. *My Last Million Readers* New York: E. P. Dutton, 1941. 488 pgs.
Memoir by former editor of Bernarr Macfadden's *New York Evening Graphic* and William Randolph Hearst's *New York Mirror* which relates Gauvreau's experience in tabloid journalism. Book III, "Muscling In," chapters 1 through 3 (pp. 99-135) describe the author's experiences with Macfadden's *Graphic.* Chapters 4 through 11 covers Gauvreau's relationship with William Randolph Hearst who hired him as editor of the *Mirror.* Book IV, "The Great Illuminist" (pp. 203-305) discusses Arthur Brisbane's ascendancy at the *Mirror.*

168   "Ghoulish Trading." *The Editor and Publisher* (20 November 1926): 26.
Editorial condemning the practice of persons associated with the Hall-Mills murder trial selling confidential information to the newspapers. Characterizes as "journalistic monstrosities" the newspaper stories written by the husband and daughter of the accused. Offers theories to explain the public's acceptance of such vulgarity.

169   "Gigolo Journalism." *The Editor and Publisher* (23 January 1932): 22.
Editorial which attacks gossip columns, characterizing them as libelous invasions of privacy which cynically sneer at life's most important relationships. Contains examples of gossip items appearing in such columns. Predicts gossip will alienate many readers who will become intolerant of such sleaze.

170   "A 'Good' Murder," *The Editor and Publisher* 26 March 1927: 32.
Editorial which argues that newspaper coverage of murder acts as deterrent to such violence.

171   Harrington, H. F. "Readers Find Emotional Escape in Dailies." *The Editor and Publisher* (24 April 1926).

Praises the newspaper as offering "a gateway of emotional escape" to readers through engaging human interest stories. Several excerpts of such articles dubbed "little masterpieces" of the reporters art are provided. Discusses the attraction of stories about celebrities and heroes. Maintains that newspaper inaccuracies are unintentional, caused by the pressure of deadlines.

172   "A Haunting Picture." *The Editor and Publisher* (21 January 1928): 24.
Editorial which criticizes publication of photo depicting the electrocution of Ruth Snyder, maintaining that there was no justification for violating a journalistic principle by blatantly disobeying the instructions of the prison's warden.

173   "Hits Papers Leading 'Maudlin Parade.' " *The Editor and Publisher, The Fourth Estate* (12 April 1930): 22.
Reports that editorial in the *Red Bluff* (CA) *News* scolds the press for its preoccupation with the fate of a sheep-killing dog where the widespread misery caused by the Depression receives scant attention. Accuses the press of puerility and sensationalism.

174   "How Shall Press Treat Crime News?" *The Editor and Publisher* (23 January 1926): 7-8.
Provides excerpts of a debate concerning the propriety of newspaper crime reporting held at an open forum of the Society of American Newspaper Editors. Included are remarks of Harvey Ingham (*Des Moines Register*), C. H. Dennis (*Chicago Daily News*), James T. Williams (*Boston American*), Tom Wallace (*Louisville Carrier-Journal*), Marvin Creager (*Milwaukee Journal*), Grove Patterson (*Toledo Blade*), and Verne Marshall (*Cedar Rapids Evening Gazette*). A wide variety of opinions are expressed.

175   " 'Human' Newspaper Is Only Sound Type, Hopwood Tells Indiana Group." *The Editor and Publisher* (23 April 1927): 52.
Reports on address by *Cleveland Plain Dealer* editor Erie C. Hopwood to American Society of Newspaper Editors in which newspapers were classified as either "conservative", "human" or "sensational". Hopwood maintained that only the human paper will ultimately succeed because it prints stories with which the readership can most readily identify. Tabloids were characterized as "an infectious disease" which could precipitate government censorship.

176   "Jazz-Age Baby, Patterson's Tabloid Tops Them All on Its 25th Birthday." *Newsweek* (3 July 1944): 60, 62.

Celebrates the twenty-fifth anniversary of New York's photo-tabloid patterned after Lord Northcliffe's *London Daily Mirror.* Guesses at reasons for its success: contests, sex appeal, photographs which appealed to non-English speaking immigrants. Includes information on founders Joseph M. Patterson and Robert R. McCormick.

177   "Jazzed-up News." *The Quill.* (November 1987): 33.
Reprint of January 1926 article warning that the "news fiction" school of reporting which is becoming so popular leads to disregard for the truth.

178   "Joe Patterson of the *News.*" *Life* (10 June 1946): 47-48, 50.
Assesses the career of Joseph Patterson, founding publisher of the *New York Daily News*, on the occasion of his death. Concludes that Patterson's instinct for tastes of the common man was responsible for the tabloid's success. Includes overviews of Patterson's career, reproductions of sample front pages, and cartoon panels (political and otherwise).

179   Johnston, Alva. "The Great Macfadden." *The Saturday Evening Post* (21 June 1941): 9-11, 97-98, 100; (28 June 1941): 20-21, 90-93.
Complete account of Bernarr Macfadden's career to age seventy-three. The article's second installment (28 June) covers the *New York Evening Graphic,* Macfadden's experiment in sensational journalism, and suggests the paper might have succeeded had Macfadden concentrated his efforts on it.

180   Jones, Weimer. " 'Lurid' Story Given Bigger Play Telegraph Editor's Story Shows." *The Editor and Publisher, The Fourth Estate* (18 July 1931): 26.
Maintains that the average American newspaper presents its news in a sensational manner based on a survey conducted of twenty southern newspapers. The survey compared the manner in which the papers treated two stories—the execution of a man and women convicted of murder, and the death of a world -renowned singer (Dame Nellie Melba). Analysis revealed that the executions received much greater journalistic attention. Statistical details provided.

181   "Joseph Patterson, 1879-1946." *Newsweek* (3 June 1946): 62-63.
Reports the death of the *New York Daily News* founder, recounting Patterson's career which was highlighted by establishment of the popular illustrated tabloid in 1919. Discusses the more sensational era in the 1920's, reporting on sex and murder. Quotes Patterson on the paper's gradual move toward relative respectability.

182   Kandel, Aben. "A Tabloid A Day." *Forum* 77 (1927): 378-384.
       Charges the tabloids with taking unfair advantage of "the mentally help-
       less." Photography, sex, and sensationalism explain their success. Blames
       the tabloids for lowering the general level of the press and corrupting
       school children. Indicts tabloids in detail for their many sins. Includes
       discussion of New York's *Daily News, Mirror* and *Evening Graphic,*
       and cites sample headlines for contempt.

183   Kingsbury, Susan M. and Hornell Hart. *Newspapers and the News: An
       Objective Measurement of Ethical and Unethical Behavior by
       Representative Newspapers.* New York: G. P. Putnam's Sons, 1937.
       238 pgs.
       Employs an original research instrument, the "Spectrum of News Inter-
       ests," in order to measure the degree of sensationalism present in promi-
       nent American newspapers for the year 1929 (pre-Depression). Chap-
       ters also deal with political bias, ethical codes, social service of news-
       papers, and previous studies of newspaper readers and content. Includes
       statistical charts and tables.

184   Klurfield, Herman. *Winchell: His Life and Times.* New York: Preager
       Publishers, 1976. 211 pgs.
       Biography of journalist Walter Winchell by his longtime ghostwriter.
       Chapter 4, "The Byline Opiate" (pp. 23-38), recounts Winchell's years
       with Bernarr Macfadden's sensational *New York Evening Graphic.* In-
       cludes Winchell's long tenure at the *New York Daily Mirror.*

185   Lawrence, Raymond D. "Why News Is News, Analyzed By Professor."
       The Editor and Publisher (21 May 1927): 11-12.
       Discusses which news stories have the greatest appeal to readers and
       why. Individually addresses a variety of human instincts to which suc-
       cessful news stories appeal: conflict, love/romance/sex, adventure, pity/
       sympathy, play/pleasure, fascination/fear, and recognition/fame/celeb-
       rity.

186   Lee, James Melvin. "Our Own World of Letters." *The Editor and
       Publisher* (26 June 1926): 34.
       Includes comments from N. A. Crawford, Director of Publications, U.S.
       Department of Agriculture, who opposes suppression of luridly sensa-
       tional tabloids because they represent a social safety valve for certain
       individuals who would likely turn to violence without the opportunity
       for such a release.

187   Levy, Newman. "Justice Goes Tabloid." *The American Mercury* 34
       (1935): 385-392.

Castigates the newspaper publicity frenzy which accompanied coverage of the trial of Bruno Hauptmann, charged with the kidnapping and murder of the Lindbergh baby. Charges that "all sense of proportion and much of decency was lost." Includes discussion of the practice of "trying a case in the newspapers," journalistic ethics, and the need for legal limits to journalistic excess. Ultimately, argues for the type of press restrictions instituted in England to protect personal privacy.

188   Liebling, A. J. "The Wayward Press: Mamie and Mr. O'Donell Carry On." *The New Yorker* (8 June 1946): 90, 92, 95-98.
Hypothesizes about the future of the *New York Daily News* after the death of founding publisher Joseph Patterson. Surveys opinions from the *New York Times* and the tabloid *PM*. Provides an overview of Patterson obituary columns from the *Washington Times-Herald,* Chicago *Tribune,* and the *Daily News* itself. Ends by observing that Patterson's paper appears to have recovered its equilibrium after losing its captain.

189   Lippmann, Walter. "Two Revolutions in the American Press." *The Yale Review* 20 (1931): 433-441.
Analyzes tabloid journalism, "the first politically independent press the world has known." Sees the genre as a type of romantic fiction which sows the seeds of its own destruction by overemphasizing amusement and excitement at the expense of providing information. Eventually, such papers either become more sober or fail.

190   "Lippmann Sees Passing of Popular Press." *The Editor and Publisher, The Fourth Estate* (17 January 1931): 10, 41.
Discusses Walter Lippmann's address at Yale University regarding the evolution of American journalism from government control to political party control to commercial independence. Lippmann credits yellow/tabloid journalism with liberating newspapers from hidden controls. Sensationalism, however, is self-destructive, producing a jaded boredom. Predicts the tabloids must moderate or fail commercially. Liberal quotes from Lippmann's speech provided.

191   Lofton, John. "Trial By Fury." *The Nation* 193 (1961): 415-419.
Faults both the press and the criminal justice system for catering to the public's vigilante mentality. Injustice results when selling newspapers and reelecting judges/prosecutors assumes paramount importance. Includes historical overview of the press's sensational coverage of criminal trials such as the Hall-Mills murder case in 1926 (see entries #134, #164).

192   Macfadden, Mary and Emil Gauvreau. *Dumbbells and Carrot Strips: The Story of Bernarr Macfadden.* New York: Henry Holt and Company. 1953. 405 pgs.
Bernarr Macfadden's third wife recounts her life with the physical culture enthusiast and publisher of the *New York Evening Graphic,* sensational 1920's tabloid. Provides background on the establishment of Macfadden Publishing with information on *True Story* and *Midnight,* sensational magazines which preceded the *Graphic.* Pages 375-405 focus on the newspaper.

193   "Macfadden's Daily to Appear Soon." *The Editor and Publisher* (19 July 1924): 34.
Reports the imminent debut of Bernarr Macfadden's new daily tabloid which will dramatize the news and employ sensationalism to effect moral uplifting of the readership. Notes that Emil Gauvreau will serve as managing editor.

194   "Macfadden's Family: He Wages War on Weakness: How a Puny Orphan Through His Own Winning Fight for Strength, Developed the World's Most Vital Editorial Technique." *Time* (21 September 1936): 44-46.
Recounts Bernarr Macfadden's career in physical culture and magazine/newspaper publishing. Asserts that Macfadden's tabloid the *Evening Graphic* "set all time journalistic marks for sensational incoherence".

195   Mallen, Frank. *Sauce for the Gander.* White Plains, New York: Baldwin Books. 1954. 243 pgs.
Complete history of Bernarr Macfadden's sensational tabloid, the *New York Evening Graphic* (1924-1932). Includes a "Composite Gallery" of *Graphic* "composographs" (composite photographs), and a biographical section featuring a dozen *Graphic* alumni such as Walter Winchell and Ed Sullivan ("Alumni Cum Laude." pp. 147-201).

196   Miller, Charles Grant. "Living Journalism and Poison that Kills." The *Editor and Publisher* (15 May 1920): 7, 34.
Sixth installment in a series, this entry lambastes free publicity afforded cultural icons by newspapers who help to create false gods for the public to worship. Details the actual space devoted to such idol worship. Includes objections to the manner in which philanthropic and civic organizations use the press as well.

197   Moore, Samuel Taylor. "Those Terrible Tabloids." *The Independent* 116 (1926): 264-266.
Condemns tabloid journalism, as practiced in New York City, as "an

unholy blot on the fourth estate," due to its sordidness and distortions. Opines that the genre's success is due either to mankind's "Rabelaisian sense of humor" or its stupidity. Sees danger in the possibility that traditional papers will copy the tabloids in order to achieve the same commercial success. Includes examples of tabloid reporting methods, exaggerations/inaccuracies, and use of photography. Reproduces a sampling of tabloid front pages.

198   "More Static." *The Editor and Publisher* (3 April 1926): 26.
Brief editorial which opposes the plan of tabloids to publish the text of popular speeches delivered on radio. Maintains that the tabloids are out of their element—speeches should be published in standard newspapers, and the tabloids should stick to their usual frivolousness.

199   Mosedale, John. *The Men Who Invented Broadway: Damon Runyon, Walter Winchell, and Their World.* New York: Richard Marek Publishers, 1981. 321 pgs.
Recalls New York City's popular culture in the 1920's as experienced by two of its most famous journalists. Chapter 8 (pp. 132-152) describes two of the most sensational scandals of the decade, both created and promoted by the tabloids: the *New York Mirror's* Hall-Mills murder case and the *New York Evening Graphic's* Peaches-Browning affair. The careers of the paper's owners—William Randolph Hearst and Bernarr Macfadden, respectively—are also discussed.

200   "Mr. Macfadden Defines News." *The New Republic* (8 October 1924): 133-135.
Critiques Bernarr Macfadden's sensational tabloid the *New York Evening Graphic* after the appearance of its first few issues. Comments that while Macfadden's emphasis on the sensational human interest story is similar to the approach adopted by the other urban tabloids, his abandonment of the journalist's civic duty to report on public events is reprehensible. Likens the *Graphic* to a daily *True Story* magazine.

201   Nathan, George Jean. "Clinical Notes: The Tabloids." *The American Mercury* 7 (1926): 363-364.
Credits photography for the success of the tabloids. Maintains that the yellow press, successful for many years, failed when the public began to disbelieve its many fantastic claims. Tabloids succeed because—for the present—the readership believes that pictures don't lie. Includes discussions of the tabloid's many other reputed attractions, such as sensationalism.

202   "Obnoxious Pictures." *The Editor and Publisher* (1 September 1928): 26.

Editorial which argues against publication of newspaper photographs which invade the subject's privacy and/or offend standards of decency. It is not sufficient to proclaim, as the editor of the *Raleigh (NC) Times* did, that the public demands such photographs. Warns that supplying such pictures could lead to government censorship of all newspapers.

203   "An Offensive Picture." *The Editor and Publisher* (21 May 1927): 32.
Editorial which criticizes newspaper photograph depicting a distraught mother grieving over the body of her murdered daughter.

204   "Our Lying Press." *The Nation* 135 (1932): 547.
Criticizes the misuse of photographs by the tabloid press, sympathizing with English complaints regarding the practice. Cites *New York Evening Graphic's* "composite" picture ("composograph") as an extreme example of such abuse.

205   Oursler, Fulton. *The True Story of Bernarr Macfadden.* New York: Lewis Copeland, 1929. 281 pgs.
Laudatory biography of the publisher and physical culturist, by the *New York Evening Graphic's* executive editor. Chapter 9, "The Story of the Graphic" (pp. 242-264) defends the sensational tabloid against its many critics by stressing the newspaper's health and moral values.

206   Partridge, S. "Are Tabloid Newspapers a Fifth Estate?" *The Editor and Publisher* (30 April 1927): 140.
Discusses the importance of style in all news reporting. Argues that skilled tabloid reporting prints sensational word pictures similar to those created in literature. Tabloids lacking style, and dull newspapers will both suffer from decreasing circulation and advertising. Maintains that standard papers incorporate much sensational news.

207   "Passing of a Giant." *Time* (3 June 1946): 87-91.
Recounts the career of *New York Daily News* publisher Joseph Patterson. Depicts the tabloid as "the ribald historian of the flapper-speakeasy-whoopee 20's", competing with Hearst's *Mirror* and Macfadden's *Evening Graphic* to provide the quickest news on the era's scandals and murders. Credits Patterson with printing the era's most gruesome photograph—convicted murderess Ruth Snyder in Sing Sing's electric chair.

208   "Perhaps The Public Has Been Maligned." *The Christian Century* 49 (1932): 901.
Celebrates the end of the *New York Evening Graphic*, Bernarr Macfadden's sensational tabloid (frequently dubbed the "Pornographic.") Hopes the *Graphic's* failure may be attributed to the fact that the public

possesses a stronger sense of decency than the tabloid journalists believe. Mentions scandals popularized by the *Graphic*.

209   Pew, Marlen. "Shop Talk at Thirty." *The Editor and Publisher, The Fourth
       Estate* (8 December 1928): 52.
       Recaps charges of sensationalism initiated by British journalists after
       reading American press coverage of the "Vestris" sinking (see entry
       #253). Maintains that the first stories could be nothing other than sen-
       sational, based on survivor's harrowing accounts. Discusses Anglo-
       American differences in reporting styles. Included: implications for
       the British and American shipping industries.

210   "Picture Ethics." *The Editor and Publisher* (16 August 1924): 20.
       Editorial which argues against the taking of photographs for newspaper
       publication without the permission of the subject. Maintains that news-
       paper editors normally exercise good judgement in selecting photos for
       inclusion in their papers, rejecting those with no legitimate news value.

211   Price, Jack. "Trailing Big News with the Cameraman." *The Editor and
       Publisher* 57 (1924): 254, 256.
       New York World photographer relates methods employed to obtain pho-
       tos of politicians, celebrities, and crime victims. Discusses tricks used
       to obtain photos in difficult circumstances; including hidden cameras,
       decoys, and subterfuge. Article features a picture of former New York
       Mayor William Gaynor at the moment a would-be assassin's bullet struck
       him.

212   "Printing Crime News Means Facing Facts." *The Editor and Publisher*
       (29 May 1926): 8.
       Reports that Henry Justin Smith, Managing Editor of the *Chicago Daily
       News*, argues that barring crime news from newspapers is an ostrich-
       like policy. Smith refers to principles adopted by the American Asso-
       ciation of Newspaper Editors which denounce "deliberate pandering to
       vicious instincts" in condemning overly-sensational crime coverage.
       (Contains extensive excerpts from speech to the Illinois Federation of
       Women's Clubs.)

213   "Printing Crime News a Necessity, Philadelphia M.E. Declares." *The
       Editor and Publisher* (13 June 1925): 4.
       Reports on address by Melvin F. Ferguson, Managing Editor of the
       Philadelphia Record, entitled "The Functions of a Newspaper." Crime
       must be reported because the public wants information, says Ferguson.
       Publications which sensationalize and exaggerate crime and scandal,
       however, violate the best journalistic traditions. Crime reporting should
       occupy a subordinate position in the newspaper.

214   " 'Professor Prophet' Acquires Another Sanatorium." *Newsweek* (29 June
            1935): 27-28.
        Derides Bernarr Macfadden's controversial notions regarding health and
        physical culture as well as the value of his publications. Characterizes
        Macfadden's *New York Evening Graphic* as "America's outstanding ex-
        ample of sleazy, vulgar journalism." Also comments on the propriety
        of the composograph (composed photograph).

215   "Ralph Pulitzer Flays 'Hang-Dog' Press." *The Editor and Publisher* (16
            April 1921): 32.
        Son of Joseph Pulitzer condemns purveyors of "hangdog journalism"
        which focuses on the lust and morbidness in the news rather than re-
        porting the honesty of life in an evenhanded manner. Castigates the
        polite press as well, which avoids the life of the masses altogether.
        Praises his father for functioning not only as a chronicler of life but as
        a champion for reform. (From remarks made at the Pulitzer School of
        Journalism.)

216   "Reaction from Jazz Journalism Seen." *The Editor and Publisher* (5 May
            1928): 24.
        Reports remarks of Karl A. Bickel, president of the United Press, who
        declared that while sensationalism builds newspaper circulation, it dis-
        courages advertisers. Predicts a sounder journalistic period as the jazz
        age comes to a close.

217   "Refuses to Publish Murder Trial Dirt." *The Editor and Publisher, The
            Fourth Estate* (7 December 1929): 28.
        Reports that the *Chattanooga News* announced it will not publish sala-
        cious details of the Walter Ligget murder trial, because it is not willing
        to participate in a "parade of filth" in order to fully record court pro-
        ceedings.

218   "Return to Realism Urged on Modern Press." *The Editor and Publisher*
            (8 October 1927): 70-71.
        Reports on discussion which dominated the annual Newspaper Insti-
        tute held at Rutgers University, Oct. 3-4: realism vs. sensationalism in
        news reporting. Speakers addressed a variety of issues including the
        propensity for viewing events and persons as either all good or all bad;
        freedom of the press in the face of pervasive vulgarity; and the neglect
        of important news in favor of the sensational.

219   Roche, John F. "Bernarr Macfadden Tells Philosophy Behind His
            Newspaper Enterprises." *The Editor and Publisher, The Fourth
            Estate* (31 August 1929): 5-6.

Bernarr Macfadden, publisher of the *New York Evening Graphic*, defends his newspaper's emphasis on sensationalism in an interview. Characterizes most newspapers as cold, mechanical, and prudish. Discusses the importance of sensationalism to news presentation. Includes information on the financial status of Macfadden's publishing empire.

220   Roche, John F. "Broadway Overrated Says Hellinger." *The Editor and Publisher, The Fourth Estate* (1 February 1930): 9.
Interview with Mark Hellinger, gossip columnist for the *New York Daily Mirror*, who finds Broadway a great source of human interest stories. Gossip is described as "Broadway's coin of the realm." Discusses Hellinger's career as reporter for the *Daily News*; lawyers and prisoners as sources of human interest stories; and Hellinger's reminiscences of best stories.

221   Roche, John F. "Unparalleled Response by Press and Public Met Lindbergh Climax." *The Editor and Publisher, The Fourth Estate* (21 May 1932): 5-6, 40, 42.
Recounts journalistic orgy which accompanied revelation of the Lindbergh baby's death at the hands of kidnapper. As the self-imposed press silence which accompanied the seventy-two day search for the child proved incapable of securing safe return, newspapers turned to sensationally proclaiming the tragic resolution of the case. Details of coverage discussed.

222   Roche, John F. "Walter Winchell's 'Big Ear' Hears All Broadway Gossip and Slang." *The Editor and Publisher* (17 March 1928): 20.
Discusses Walter Winchell's talent for collecting celebrity gossip which is published in the *New York Evening Graphic*. Comments on the inventive slang expressions coined by Winchell in relating his tales of Broadway. Includes biographical data.

223   Rudd, Arthur Sarell. "The Development of Illustrated Tabloid Journalism in the United States." Master's thesis, Columbia University, 1925.
Early scholarly survey of the genre which includes the history of tabloid journalism (primarily Harmsworth's ventures); the status of tabloid newspapers in the 1920's (including New York's *Daily News; Daily Mirror* and *Evening Graphic*) and predictions for the future (continued growth and change). Discussion is limited to tabloids which featured photography. Consequently, the old *New York Daily Graphic* (1873) is included, but the sensational penny press and yellow journals are not.

224   Schneider, Walter E. "Fabulous Rise of *N.Y. Daily News* Due to Capt. Patterson's Genius." *The Editor and Publisher* (24 June 1939): 5-7, 45-48.

Traces the success of Joseph Medill Patterson's *New York Daily News* from "Peck's bad boy of journalism" to the more serious, economics-minded tabloid of the depression era. Discusses Patterson's management style and work habits. Includes statistical tables documenting the rise of the *News's* circulation, and a personal note by Patterson to *The Editor and Publisher* on the occasion of the paper's twentieth anniversary.

225   Schuyler, Philip. "Baring America's Classic Crime Mystery." The *Editor and Publisher* (4 September 1926): 7.
Presents and discusses the manner in which the *New York Mirror's* investigation of the Hall-Mills murder case resulted in the arrest and indictment of Frances Stevens Hall, former wife of the slain Reverend. Article is based on information provided by Philip A. Payne, Managing Editor of the *Mirror*. Includes reproduction of sensational *Mirror* front page displaying evidence being used to prosecute the case.

226   Schuyler, Philip. "Classic Vindication of Press As Safeguard Seen in New Jersey Murder Trial." *The Editor and Publisher* (6 November 1926): 3-4, 42.
Argues that the sensational nature of the Hall-Mills Murder case is not the primary reason for the unprecedented level of press coverage devoted to the trial. Rather, the high level of excitement is attributed to the fact that the *New York Mirror* succeeded in apparently solving the case after law enforcement authorities were unable to do so.

227   Schuyler, Philip. "Death Chair Picture Climaxes Press Coverage of Snyder-Gray Story." *The Editor and Publisher* (21 January 1928): 3-4, 39.
Discusses propriety of publishing photograph depicting the electrocution of convicted murderess Ruth Snyder obtained by *New York Daily News* photographer who concealed the camera beneath his trousers. Witnesses express opinions regarding capital punishment. Includes survey of newspapers that chose to run the photo and those that did not.

228   Schuyler, Philip. "Editors Analyze Selling Elements of Snyder-Gray Murder Story." *The Editor and Publisher* (14 May 1927): 4, 49.
Discusses reasons for the popularity of the Ruth Snyder-Henry Gray murder trial coverage as evidenced in record-setting newspaper sales. Editors point to the elements of sex (adultery leading to murder), identification with those charged (middle class), pity, and courtroom confrontation.

229   Schuyler, Philip. "Just What Is This Yellow Journalism?" *The Editor and Publisher* (27 February 1926): 9, 47.

Discussion with John K. Winkler, former reporter with the *New York American*, who maintains that sensational news is a commodity which appeals to ninety-five percent of newspaper readers. Touches upon newspaper coverage of the Dot King, Cathcart-Craven, and Hall-Mills cases.

230   Schuyler, Philip. "London Writers Decry 'Sensational' Play of Vestris Inquiry in U.S." The *Editor and Publisher, The Fourth Estate* (1 December 1928): 3-4.
Discusses the fact that London newspaper correspondents stationed in New York charged the American press with sensationalism for the manner in which Americans covered the sinking of the British ship "Vestris." British correspondents characterized as "yellow journalism" American charges of neglect and incompetence leveled at the English ship owners and captain. Included: harassment by American reporters, publication of falsehoods, and need for stronger libel laws in America. Examples of hysterical headlines and rumors (shark attacks, e.g.) are provided.

231   Schuyler, Philip. "Men Responsive to Human Interests Write Stories That Sell Papers." *The Editor and Publisher* (17 September 1927): 16.
Discusses characteristics of popular newspaper stories with Joseph Mulcahy, managing editor of the *New York Evening Journal*. Mulcahy cites human interest content and screaming headlines as important factors. Includes review of several outstanding human interest stories (Lindbergh crossing the Atlantic and the death of Rudolph Valentino, e.g.).

232   Schuyler, Philip. "Philadelphia Illustrates Two Ways of Getting Tabloid Readers." *The Editor and Publisher* (19 June 1926): 33.
Contrasts the style and appeal of two relatively new Philadelphia tabloids, the *Philadelphia Daily News* and the *Philadelphia Sun*. The former emphasizes sex, crime, and scandal, benefiting from a working relationship with the *New York Mirror*. The latter is somewhat less sensational, resembling the London —rather than the New York—tabloids. Circulation, advertising, and staffing is discussed.

233   "Scores Sensationalism." *The Editor and Publisher* (22 October 1927): 15.
Reports that William Preston Beazell, assistant managing editor of the *New York World*, declared today's "scarlet journalism"—which invades the privacy of its subjects—worse than the yellow journalism of the past. (Comment was made in address to University Press Club of the University of Michigan, Oct. 21.)

234   "Sensational Cry of Professor-Critic Attacked by Texas Editor." *The Editor and Publisher* (7 May 1927): 46.
Reports that Richard C. Bush, managing editor of the *Waco Times Herald* defended newspapers against charges of sensationalism, made by Dean W. S. Allen of Baylor University, during Journalism Week activities held at the university. Bush referred to sensationalism contained in biblical tales in maintaining that such sensationalism is not offensive when well-written and edited.

235   " 'Sensational' News Not Essential to His Paper, Publisher Finds." *The Editor and Publisher, The Fourth Estate* (6 June 1931): 42.
Discusses the success of *Berkeley* (CA) *Daily Gazette* publisher Charles E. Dunscomb's non-sensational journalistic style. The newspaper has prospered despite the fact that it sanitizes murder accounts; rejects sex stories, horse racing and prize fights; and barely mentions divorces. Banner headlines are also rarely employed. Attributes success to family appeal and the paper's proximity to the University of California, the state's cultural center.

236   "Sensationalism." *The Editor and Publisher* (30 August 1924): 20.
Brief editorial which notes G. K. Chesterton's remarks that distinguish beneficial—or benign—sensationalism which stimulates thought (the murder stories of Hamlet or Macbeth, e.g.) and detrimental—or malignant—sensationalism in which emotion overruns thought.

237   "Shallow Critics." *The Editor and Publisher* (22 October 1927): 30.
Editorial which refutes the contentions of press critics who proclaim today's journalism unsurpassed in salaciousness. Argues that modern journalism's openness and honesty permits investigation of social problems which were ignored previously. Such truthfulness invites criticism.

238   Spivak, John L. "The Rise and Fall of a Tabloid." *The American Mercury* 32 (1934): 306-314.
Discusses the eight-year history of Bernarr Macfadden's sensational tabloid, the *New York Evening Graphic*, emphasizing the role played by managing editor Emil Gauvreau. Highlights various strategies employed to boost circulation and compensate for a lack of advertisers (who sought to avoid association with the newspaper): beauty contests, scandals, politics, and the composograph.

239   Stevens, John D. "Social Utility of Sensational News: Murder and Divorce in the 1920's." *Journalism Quarterly* 62 (1985): 53-58.
Asserts that sensational news, though much maligned, forces the audi-

ence to confront (and perhaps redefine) its own values. Draws parallels
between times of social upheaval and periods in which the press is
undergoing heaviest attack for its sensationalism. Discusses coverage
of the Hall-Mills murder case and the Edward Browning-"Peaches"
Heenan scandal.

240   "Suggests Press Might be Slighting Crime." *The Editor and Publisher
           The Fourth Estate* (19 April 1930): 40.
       Reports that New York Municipal Court Justice Nathan Sweedler be-
       lieves the press does not devote enough attention to crime news, a sur-
       vey having revealed that only two percent of all news relates to crime.
       Sweedler theorizes that some crime news is not sensational enough to
       satisfy the press. Regards crime reporting as a deterrent to future crime.

241   Sullivan, R. B. "The Classy Allusion." *Esquire* December 1936: 94-95,
           278, 280.
       Disagrees with critics who proclaim the ignorance of tabloid readers.
       Cites the many allusions to classical literature contained in tabloid head-
       lines (Borgia, Adonis, Casanova, and Godiva, e.g.) in order to demon-
       strate the level of sophistication required of the tabloid readership.
       Humorous tone.

242   Sullivan, R. B. "Torso, The Tenth Muse." *Esquire* March 1937: 42, 199-201.
       Contends that murder, treated in formulaic manner by newspapers, is
       "a tedious and sordid business" not worth the readers attention. Lists
       many of the standard categories by journalists to pigeonhole such crimes
       (axe murder, torch murder, *American Tragedy* murder, e.g.).

243   " 'Surprising,' Says Macfadden of New Daily." *The Editor and
           Publisher* (30 August 1924): 5.
       Bernarr Macfadden reveals the nature of his new daily tabloid, the
       Evening Graphic: no crime news; constructive sensationalism to be
       utilized; and no information without entertainment. Discusses the
       publisher's tendency to "Macfaddenize" all his publications. Includes
       details of the newspaper's financial structure.

244   "Surveys Tabloid Journalism." *The Editor and Publisher* (30 May 1925): 32.
       Reports the completion of the first comprehensive survey of tabloid
       journalism—Arthur S. Rudd's "the Development of Tabloid Journal-
       ism in the United States," accepted as a graduate thesis by the Colum-
       bia University School of Journalism (see entry #223). The thesis covers
       history, analysis, opinions, and predictions associated with the genre.
       The tabloids of Vanderbilt, Scripps-Howard, and Hearst are discussed.
       (This thesis is currently located at Northwestern University.)

245   "Tabloid Poison." *The Saturday Review of Literature* 3 (1927): 589.
      Views tabloid journalism with its sensationalism and cynical distortion
      of the news as the new exploiter of the masses' minds. The tabloid is
      variously described as the "new black plague" and "this poison liquor."
      Includes brief overview of how the working class freed itself from bodily
      exploitation only to fall victim to this new enslavement.

246   "Tabloids Censured by State Dailies." *The Editor and Publisher* (26 June
         1926): 44.
      Reports that the Associated Dailies of New York State has adopted a
      resolution censuring newspapers which publish salacious news or act
      irresponsibly in identifying victims of crime. The New York tabloids
      were noted as prime offenders.

247   " 'Tabloids in Gutter,' Says Villard; 'Tabloids Inevitable,' Says
         Weyrauch." *The Editor and Publisher* (19 March 1927): 12.
      Reports of radio debate between *Nation* editor Oswald Villard, and *New
      York Evening Graphic* assistant managing editor Martin Weyrauch on
      the question whether the tabloid press is a public nuisance. Text of the
      speakers' arguments is provided.

248   "Tabloids: Hearst Points His Biggest Gun at the *Daily News.*" *News-
         week* (24 November 1934): 18-19.
      Reports on circulation war between Hearst's *New York Daily Mirror*
      and Joseph Patterson's *New York Daily News*, the city's leading tabloid
      newspapers. Recounts history of the tabloid from Lord Northcliffe's
      London Daily Mirror, which began as an attempt to reformat Joseph
      Pulitzer's *World.* Included: biographical account of Hearst editor Arthur
      Brisbane.

249   "They Made Quick Decision in Launching N.Y.'s Newest Daily." *The
         Editor and Publisher* (17 July 1919): 13.
      Profiles Robert McCormick, Joseph Patterson, and William Field of
      the *Chicago Tribune* on their launching of the *New York Illustrated Daily
      News*, now in its sixth week of publication. Pronounces the paper "light-
      hearted" and "youthful," and continuing to improve in quality.

250   Thomas, Bob. *Winchell* Garden City, N. Y.: Doubleday, 1971. 288 pgs.
      Biography of controversial gossip/celebrity journalist Walter Winchell,
      including his five year association with Bernarr Macfadden's *New York
      Evening Graphic* (recounted in chapter four, pp. 15-34), and his thirty-
      four years with the *New York Daily Mirror.*

251   "The New Dailies Launched in New York." *The Editor and Publisher*
         (28 June 1924): 6.

Announcing the debut of Hearst's *New York Daily Mirror* and Frederick W. Enwright's *New York Bulletin*. Comments on the *Mirror's* stated aim of providing ninety percent entertainment, ten percent news, noting the tabloid's similarity to the *New York Daily News*. Enwright's *Bulletin* vowed to avoid any "highbrow" tendencies, and demonstrated a taste for the salacious in its coverage of a story involving Harry Thaw.

252   "Two N. Y. Executives Denounce 'Smut' Published in Tabloids." *The Editor and Publisher* (12 February 1927): 12.
Reports on the remarks of *New York World* executive editor Herbert Bayard Swope, and *New York Times* business manager Louis Wiley, condemning the "filth" published by tabloids in their coverage of the Browning affair. Such lewdness taints the entire industry and could lead to censorship.

253   " 'Vestris' Reporters Are Vindicated." *The Editor and Publisher, The Fourth Estate* (15 December 1928): 36.
Reports that preliminary findings absolve American reporters from charges of sensationalism involving their handling of the sinking of the British steamer "Vestris" (see entry #230).

254   "Vice Society Hales N. Y. *Graphic* to Court." *The Editor and Publisher* (12 February 1927): 5.
Reports that the New York society for the Suppression of Vice has charged Bernarr Macfadden's *Evening Graphic* with violation of the State penal code dealing with printed pornography for its coverage of the Peaches Browning case. Discusses Macfadden's defense of such coverage. Includes anti-*Graphic* actions of other New York dailies, notably the *New York Sun*.

255   Villard, Oswald Garrison. "Issues and Men." *The Nation* 146 (1938): 443.
Comments disparagingly upon the practice of giving the public what it wants, in this case sex exploitation by the newspapers. Analyzes an issue of the *New York World-Telegram* in this regard.

256   Villard, Oswald Garrison. "Tabloid Offenses." *The Forum* 77 (1927): 485.
Maintains that New York City's sensational tabloids degrade American journalism by pandering to the prurient. Refutes the argument that such newspapers inform those who otherwise would not read at all by asserting that tabloid growth is at the expense of the more responsible papers.

257   Walsh, Richard John. "The Ideological Undercurrents of the Jazz Age Tabloids: An Examination of Meanings in the Commercial Mass Media." Master's thesis, University of Washington, 1990. 129 pgs.

Views the tabloid newspapers of 1920's America as an interpretation of social reality. Concentrates on the meaning of the images conveyed to the public by the jazz age tabloids, concluding that due to commercialization of the newspaper industry, the messages received by the readers were detrimental to the concept of a truly free press and a democratic society. A content analysis of New York's *Daily News* is included.

258   Weiner, Ed. *Let's Go to Press: A Biography of Walter Winchell.* New York: G. P. Putnam's Sons, 1955. 270 pgs.
Standard biography of the controversial journalist. Chapter 4, "Time Step on a Typewriter" (pp. 38-50), details Winchell's tenure on Bernarr Macfadden's *New York Evening Graphic* (and his feuding with managing editor Emil Gauvreau). Includes Winchell's years with the *New York Daily Mirror.*

259   Wells, George Y. "Patterson and the Daily News." *The American Mercury* 59 (1944): 671-679.
Dismisses *New York Daily News* publisher's assertion that editorial policy is the reason for the tabloid's success. Instead, points to the paper's convenient size, sensational stories, photography, and comics. Recounts the twenty-five year history of the *News*, pointing to its coverage of the many sex and scandal stories featured in the 1920's.

260   Weyrauch, Martin. "The Why of the Tabloids." *The Forum* 77 (1927): 492-501.
Views criticism of the tabloids as conservative backlash against the creative liberalization of the American culture. Chronicles the rise of American tabloids: Patterson-McCormick's *New York Daily News*, Hearst's *Mirror,* Macfadden's *Evening Graphic.* Praises the tabloids' youthful, crusading spirit.

261   "What Is Progress?" *The Editor and Publisher* (22 December 1923): 28.
Editorial which argues against the assertions of *New Republic* editor Bruce Bliven that sensational news is antithetical to intelligent discussion of economic and social issues. Maintains that the root causes of many social problems are uncovered in stories which accurately investigate murders, suicides, and divorces. Includes discussion of Bliven's comments concerning motion pictures and radio.

262   "What Our Readers Say: 'Crimson News.' " *The Editor and Publisher* (2 April 1921): 32.
Letter from Tom Finty, Jr., editor of the *Dallas* (Texas) *Journal.* Concurs with *The Editor and Publisher* editorial critical of "crimson journalism" (see entry #154). Maintains that news wires are blocked for

hours, reporting stories unfit to be printed. Complains that younger readers accuse respectable papers of timidity for upholding standards of respectability.

263   "What They Are Saying: Abbott Scores Sensationalism." *The Editor and Publisher* (1 March 1924): 6.
Quotes Willis J. Abbott, editor of the *Christian Science Monitor*, who declares that clean journalism will triumph over the "menace' of sensationalism, because newspaper owners will be forced to choose between service to God or Mammon.

264   "Who Leads?" *The Editor and Publisher* (27 February 1926): 28.
Editorial which castigates New York dailies, especially the tabloids, which feature tales of sex and scandal prominently and regularly ignore the dictates of good taste. Such abdication of journalistic leadership threatens the very concept of a free press.

265   "Who Reads Tabloids?" *The New Republic* 51 (1927): 6-7.
States that most of the growth in tabloid circulation has not been at the expense of more traditional newspapers. The tabloids real influence lies in the fact that advertisers are flocking to them. In addition, newspaper publishers tend to imitate the tabloids, hoping to achieve the same success.

266   Williams, Michael. "Views and Reviews." The *Commonweal* (29 April 1938): 17.
Cites Oswald Garrison Villard's column in *The Nation* (see entry #255) to support the contention that newspapers rely on sex exploitation to an unprecedented degree in order to boost circulation. Complains that the press, in so doing, exhibits a blatant disregard for the basic traditions of Christianity.

267   Winchell, Walter. *Winchell Exclusive: "Things That Happened to Me—And Me to Them."* Englewood Cliffs, N. J.: Prentis -Hall. 1975. 332 pgs.
The noted reporter's anecdotal recollections of his journalistic escapades while working for Bernarr Macfadden's *Evening Graphic* and Hearst's *New York Mirror.*

268   "W. R. Hearst Notes Tendency Toward Tabloid Presentation of News." *The Editor and Publisher* (23 October 1926): 5.
Interview with William Randolph Hearst who discusses his perception of the public's preference for condensed entertaining news. Hearst traces the tabloid's lineage from Dana to Northcliffe to Hearst.

269   "W. R. Hearst Urges Editors to Adopt Tabloid Newspaper Principles."
          The Editor and Publisher, The Fourth Estate (17 August 1929): 16.
          Reports that William Randolph Hearst has urged the application of tab-
          loid newspaper principles—particularly, "brightness and brevity"—to
          all his newspapers, even the full-sized publications. Citing Lord
          Northcliffe as the originator of the tabloid style, Hearst argued that the
          entertainment value involved is of greater importance than the physical
          size of the newspaper.

270   Zwerin, Michael. "Flash!... Winchell Is a Reluctant Anach-
          ronism...(Ohmigahd!)." *Esquire* August 1968: 53-55, 122, 124.
          Profile of gossip columnist Walter Winchell at the end of his career.
          Recounts how Winchell rose to fame and power on the strength of his
          gossip/scandal journalism. Includes discussion of the birth of the gos-
          sip column genre based on celebrity worship, and Winchell's rhythmi-
          cally-paced tabloid language which punctuated his communication style.

Exposés

271   "Clean—And Otherwise." *Newsweek* (26 August 1957): 61.
          Surveys the manner in which newspapers covered the libel trial involv-
          ing *Confidential* magazine—from the sedate (*New York Times*) to the
          sensational (*New York Daily News* and *Mirror*).

272   Govoni, Steve. "Now It Can Be Told." *American Film* February, 1990:
          29-33, 43.
          Recounts the history of the 1950's scandal magazine *Confidential* from
          its founding by Robert Harrison until its demise due to a 1957 obscen-
          ity trial in Los Angeles. Included: featured writer Walter Winchell, the
          publication's sexism, homophobia and reactionary politics, and an ex-
          cerpt of a 1955 article about Joe DiMaggio and Marilyn Monroe.

273   "Sin, Sex and Sales." *Newsweek* (14 March 1955): 88.
          Describes the success of *Confidential*, the exposé magazine specializ-
          ing in scandal and crime. Includes circulation statistics and informa-
          tion on style, format, and imitators.

274   Sisk, John P. "The Exposé Magazines." *The Commonweal* 64 (1956):
          223-225.
          Analyzes the meaning and value of exposé literature in light of *Confi-
          dential* magazine's great popularity. Explanations for the popularity of
          such periodicals discussed include: envy, symbolic participation in ce-

lebrity and sin, revenge, and entertainment. The psychological implications of encountering corruption among the elite are investigated.

275   "Spreading the Smudge." *Newsweek* (9 September 1957): 64.
Reports on the manner in which the foreign press covers the *Confidential* libel trial. Also indicates that United Press and Associated Press
syndicates file two reports each—sensational and "laundered" versions.

276   Wolfe, Thomas K. "Public Lives: *Confidential* Magazine; Reflections
in Tranquility by the Former Owner, Robert Harrison, Who
Managed to Get Away With It." *Esquire* April 1964: 87-90, 152,
154, 155, 156-157.
Profile of, and interview with Robert Harrison, former publisher of
exposé magazine *Confidential*. Recounts Harrison's career in scandal
journalism beginning with a stint as copy boy on Bernarr Macfadden's
New York Evening Graphic. Includes information on methods for obtaining scandal stories, Walter Winchell's promotion of *Confidential*,
and Harrison's post-*Confidential* publication, *Inside News*.

277   "Women Are Exposé Fans." *America* 94 (1956): 520.
Expresses shock at learning that women comprise a substantial per-
centage of exposé magazine readership. Cites circulation figures for
Confidential, True Story, and *True Confession.*

MODERN PRACTICE

278   Alter, Jonathan. "America Goes Tabloid." *Newsweek* (26 December 1994):
34-36.
Sees the mid-1990's as the "golden age of tabloid news," when tabloid
television revived a sensationalism that was faltering with the traditional
print tabloids. Briefly recounts the history of sensational journalism. Included: the hypocrisy of tabloid TV viewers (who watch but complain
about too much coverage); negative effects of tabloidization on the news
industry; the tabloid phenomena as democracy in action; and tabloid
news as a nationally-shared experience which brings us closer together.

279   Apple Jr., R. W. "Gresham's Second Law." *Nieman Reports* (Summer,
1993): 66-68.
Washington Bureau Chief of the *New York Times* observes that British
tabloid journalism, imported to America, is degrading news coverage in
the U.S. Remarks are excerpted from a lecture delivered 8 April 1993.

280   Bain, George. "Sensational Sales for the Tabs." *Maclean's* (22 December 1986): 46.

Describes corporate organization and sales figures of the supermarket tabloids. Sensationalism is the tabloids' common denominator, but the *National Enquirer*, besieged by multiple celebrity lawsuits, is moving away from scandal.

281   Baker, Russell. "Keeping Ahead of the News." *New York Times Magazine* (23 March 1986): 16.
Humorous musings of why the supermarket tabloids' sensational stories cease to amaze after a while.

282   Barber, Simon. "The Boss Don't Like Robbery—Make it Swindle: Inside the *National Enquirer.*" *Washington Journalism Review* July/ August 1982: 46-49.
Author's account of the five months employment as articles editor at the *National Enquirer*. Comments on tyrannical control wielded by owner and publisher Generoso Pope.

283   Benensen, Lisa Ruppel. "The Tabloid That Would Not Die." *Brandweek* (26 June 1995): 46.
Discusses reasons for the continued survival of venerable tabloid *New York Daily News* despite strikes, bankruptcy, and falling circulation. Credits increased ad sales and the paper's ability to prevail over *New York Newsday*, a Long Island tabloid that refused to compete for the sensation-loving readership.

284   Berger, Jerry. "Damn the Facts—Roll the Presses." *The Editor and Publisher* (14 May 1994): 46, 56.
Blames erosion of journalistic standards on heightened competition for ratings/circulation ushered in by the birth of cable TV. Fairness and accuracy must be restored in order to recapture public trust.

285   Bernstein, Carl. "The Idiot Culture." *The New Republic* (8 June 1992): 22-28.
Laments the state of American journalism in the post-Watergate era. Finds fault with celebrity-distorted coverage, and replacement of news with gossip and sensationalism. Believes that popular culture at its lowest level (as represented by the Donahue/Rivera/Winfrey talk shows; "Hard Copy"; and Howard Stern), has effectively replaced real investigative journalism. Calls for return of responsible truth-seeking press which serves the public interest.

286   Bertrand, Claude-Jean. "Commercialism and U.S. Media Ethics." *The St. Louis Journalism Review* April 1988: 8.
Argues that journalism must serve the public—not just entertain it—in order to satisfy ethical requirements. Believes that the common ethical violations of journalists (distorting the meaning of a speech naming

rape victims, invading the privacy of grief-stricken families) pale in comparison to the transgressions of the corporations which own the media (blocking development of new technology to protect vested interests, and failure to cover news issues which might upset advertisers).

287   Bird, S. Elizabeth. *For Inquiring Minds: A Cultural Study of Supermarket Tabloids.* Knoxville: University of Tennessee Press. 1992. 234 pgs.
Places tabloid newspapers within the tradition of folk narrative by tracing sensationalist news reporting from its seventeenth century origins in news ballads and newsbooks. The penny press, yellow and jazz journalism are also discussed. The nature and structure of the supermarket tabloid industry as well as the content of the papers is examined. Separate chapters investigate how today's tabloids are written and read. Concludes that tabloids are popular with their readers for the same reasons they are disparaged by others—they are formulaic, sensational, and exaggerative. They do not, however, represent rebellion against the dominant culture. Rather, they offer temporary escape from—and ultimately accommodation to—existing society.

288   Bird, S. Elizabeth. "The Kennedy Story in Folklore and Tabloids: Intertextuality in Political Communication." In *Politics in Familiar Contexts: Projecting Politics Through Popular Media,* edited by Robert L. Savage and Dan Nimmo. 247-268. Norwood: Ablex Publishing, 1990.
Examines the depiction of John F. Kennedy as mythic hero by the tabloid press. Three recurring themes are cited: Kennedy is still alive, the Kennedy assassination conspiracy, and Kennedy as heroic womanizer. Compares tabloid structuring of the Kennedy myth with the constructs of oral folklore tradition.

289   Bird, S. Elizabeth. "Storytelling on the Far Side: Journalism and the Weekly Tabloid." *Critical Studies in Mass Communication* 7 (1990): 377-389.
Maintains that the supermarket tabloids tell their stories in much the same manner as the more conventional newspapers. Compares the two journalistic genres with respect to objectivity (both see the reporter as a neutral observer) and credibility (both call on experts to substantiate reporter observations). Minimizes the importance of distinguishing between information and entertainment.

290   Bird, S. Elizabeth and Robert W. Dardenne. "News and Storytelling in American Culture: Reevaluating the Sensational Dimension." *Journal of American Culture* Summer 1990: 33-37.
Argues that sensationalism is a necessary component of the news, with-

out which full information may not be communicated. Chronicles the long history of media criticism against sensationalism. Rejects the purely objective model of news reporting, asserting instead that storytelling which appeals to human interest contains a mythological quality which should be constructively incorporated in news reporting.

291   Blumenthal, Sidney. "Bill and Ted." *The New Republic* (17 February 1992): 13, 16.
Tracks the breaking Gennifer Flowers/Bill Clinton scandal story and the candidate's successful handling of it. Documents how the establishment press was driven by the tabloid *Star*'s decision to publicize the story. Claims television news parameters are set by "pseudo-news" tabloid shows.

292   Bonaduce, Danny. "My Life as a Has-Been." *Esquire* August 1991: 104-108.
The author, "Danny Partridge" of television's "The Partridge Family," looks sardonically at how the careers of ex-child stars are revived as tragic subjects in the tabloid media.

293   Boot, William. "Capital Letter: Getting High on Tower." *Columbia Journalism Review* May/June 1989: 18-20.
Pleads guilty to participating in press "rumor abuse" with regard to reporting of Secretary of Defense designate John Tower's alcohol problems. Sensationalism helped create negative public perception of the nominee which doomed his chances for confirmation.

294   Boulard, Garry. "Giving People What They Want to Read: *National Enquirer* Editor Talks About the Audience He Wants to Reach." *The Editor and Publisher* (4 May 1991): 46, 48.
Interview with *National Enquirer* editor Iain Calder, who discusses reasons for the tabloid's popularity, its publication style, and charges of unethical practices. Included is a brief history of the newspaper.

295   Brecker, Edward M. "Straight Sex, AIDS, and the Mixed-Up Press." *Columbia Journalism Review* March/April 1988: 46-50.
Faults the press for sensationally exaggerating the rate at which the AIDS epidemic was spreading to the heterosexual community. Contrasts such coverage with the under-publicized Center for Disease Control report released in December, 1987. Historically, the press has helped spread public health messages, but journalists also know that scare stories sell.

296   Brogan, Patrick. "Citizen Murdoch." *The New Republic* (11 October 1982): 19-23.

Assesses Rupert Murdoch as a throwback to the days of Hearst when newspaper tycoons were openly crass and manipulative in wielding their influence, and willing to take risks. Unfortunately, according to the author, the outcome of Hearst's and Murdoch's efforts is usually a newspaper like the *New York Post*—sensational and irresponsible in its appeal to the readership's basest instincts. Recaps Murdoch's career.

297   Brown, David. "Sound Effects." *Entertainment Weekly* (14 January 1994): 50-52.
Regrets that tabloid journalism's exposés of pop culture figures' personal lives make appreciation of their art rather difficult. In retrospect, for example, song lyrics take on unwanted, ironical connotations.

298   Brown, Jennifer E. "News Photographs and the Pornography of Grief." *Journal of Mass Media Ethics* Spring/Summer 1987: 75-81.
Argues for a balanced brand of photojournalism which carefully weighs the news value of a sensational photo against considerations of taste and privacy. Discusses why sensational photos often win prizes. Includes references to the National Press Photographers Association code of ethics.

299   Bruning, Fred. "Sleaze: Seductive, But Morally Grave." *Maclean's* (13 May 1991): 11.
Regrets that the *New York Times* stooped to the level of the tabloids in naming the alleged rape victim in the William Kennedy Smith case. Cites Kitty Kelly's exposé of the Regan White House as an example of scandal-mongering performing a public service. Also refers to Romanian-born writer Andrei Codrescu who related how quickly western-style tabloid diversions are replacing more sober interests (poetry, e.g.) in his native land.

300   Bruning, Fred. "A Zombie Nation Inhabiting Two Worlds." *Maclean's* (15 March 1993): 11.
Comments on the schizophrenic nature of the American society which we inhabit: the real world with its strides, risks, and crises, and the crazed realm of tabloid TV and talk radio where whatever feels or sounds good has replaced thought and analysis. Believes that tabloid entertainment is safe in small doses, but that overload can be dangerous.

301   Burkholder, Steve. "The *Lawrence Eagle-Tribune* and the Willie Horton Story." *Washington Journalism Review.* July/August 1989: 15-16, 18, 19.
Accuses Massachusetts newspaper of sloppy, biased reporting in its sensationalized coverage of the Willie Horton furlough story during the 1988 presidential campaign.

302   Byrne, John A. "Slugging It Out in the Supermarkets." *Forbes* (14

March 1983): 78-79.
Reports that Rupert Murdoch's *Star* and Canadian Mike Rosenbloom's *Globe* and *National Examiner* are making inroads in the supermarket tabloid trade, but Generoso Pope's *National Enquirer* remains atop the field. Recounts Pope's history with the *Enquirer* beginning in 1957.

303   Carlson, Margaret. "Should This Woman Be Named?" *Time* (29 April 1991): 28-29.
Relates the surprising decision of the *New York Times* and NBC to follow the lead of the tabloids (Britain's *Sunday Mirror* and the *Globe*, published in Boca Raton, Fla.) in publicizing the name of the alleged rape victim in the William Kennedy Smith case. Many news organizations—including *Time* magazine—adhered to tradition by refraining from such action. (Even the *National Enquirer* took the high road). Support is given to the view that the moral character of rape victims is still inevitably and unfairly called into question in such situations.

304   Case, Tony. "Covering Campaigns." *The Editor and Publisher* (25 July 1992): 12, 38.
Reports on panel of journalists, politicians and academics sponsored by Freedom Forum which met in conjunction with the Democratic National Convention to discuss whether media campaign coverage was "sleaze journalism" or merely democracy's watchdog doing its job. Includes comments from professor and author Larry Sabato (see entry #432), NBC News president Michael Gartner, ABC News correspondent Sandor Vanocur, *USA Today* columnist Barbara Reynolds, and talk-show host Larry King.

305   Case, Tony. "Health News With Tabloid Appeal." *The Editor and Publisher* (1 October 1994): 15, 37.
Conveys the opinions of David Satcher, Center for Disease Control director, concerning tabloid newspaper devotion to sensational disease stories (flesh-eating bacteria, e.g.), which pose little threat to the public, at the expense of more substantial, but less exotic, stories (successful immunization programs, e.g.) which need to be told.

306   Case, Tony. "Staged Journalism." *The Editor and Publisher* (25 March 1995): 11-12.
Discusses the practice of supermarket tabloids *National Examiner* and the *National Enquirer* creating their own crime scene photographs of Nicole Brown Simpson's body using models, makeup, and "computer enhancement." Mainstream journalists comment on the policy.

307   Clark, Mike. "The Crack Cocaine of Journalism." *The Editor and*

Publisher (7 March 1992): 7.

Maintains that the mainstream press should not have published Gennifer Flower's charges against Bill Clinton, first publicized by the tabloid *Sun*, because they do not meet the reasonable standards suggested by Political Science Professor Larry Sabato in his book *Feeding Frenzy* (see entry #432). (Sabato advises publicizing a politician's extramarital affairs only when they become compulsive, indiscreet and, therefore, dangerous.)

308   Clausen, Christopher. "Reading the Supermarket Tabloids." *The New Leader* (7 September 1992): 10-13.

Assesses the supermarket tabloid field, describing the format and topical specialization of each. Concludes that the stereotype of the typical tabloid reader is inaccurate. Rather each publication is carefully edited, and professionally produced for a distinctive audience. The tabloids cater to Americans' obsession with personality and distaste for politics.

309   Conroy, Mark. "From Tombstone to Tabloid: Authority Figured in *White Noise*." *Critique* 35 (1994): 97-110.

An analysis of Don Delillo's novel, *White Noise*, in which the only form of cultural transmission remaining to the principal character, a professor in a Midwestern college town, is the supermarket tabloid, "devotional tract" to the "saints of the mass media." The supermarket is seen as providing the bread of life for both the body (through consumption) and the spirit (through the tabloids).

310   Corkery, P. J. "Exclusive! Inside the *National Enquirer*." *Rolling Stone* (11 June 1981): 18-21.

Describes life as an articles editor from 1977-1979 with America's largest circulating newspaper.

311   Diamond, Edward. "Rupert Murdoch: Power Without Prestige: The Outsider Outbacker." *Washington Journalism review*. June 1980: 20-24.

Predicts the failure of Murdoch's *New York Post* because its lurid content repels advertisers. Discusses operational differences between British and American tabloids which mandate different paths to commercial success.

312   Dilucchio, Patrizia. "Elvis Sighted in Ancient Rome: Tabloids as Myth." *Whole Earth Review* Summer 1994: 89-93.

Argues that tabloids deal in non-literal truth, the type found in folk tales and myths. This type of truth is perceived as threatening by the fact-trained intelligentsia. Traces the focus of tabloids through the last several decades, mirroring the changes in American society and considers various interpretations of tabloid stories. Elizabeth Taylor's life is viewed as an "iconographic essay of our times."

313   "Doing the Devil's Work." *Columbia Journalism Review* January/
          February 1980: 22-23.
       Argues that Murdoch's sensationalism and social irresponsibility as manifested in his *New York Post* constitutes a genuine social evil by inciting hatred and encouraging intolerance. Discusses both journalistic and civic consequences of Murdoch's policies, and examines how Murdoch has altered his usual marketing techniques in order to appeal to New York's middle class readers.

314   Dorfman, Ron. "Peeping Watchdogs." *The Quill* June 1987: 14-16.
       Discusses the propriety of journalistic intrusion on the private lives of public figures. Included: staking out subject's home and asking subject whether he/she has ever committed adultery or used drugs. George McGovern's handling of the Eagleton affair in 1972 and the Gary Hart/ Donna Rice scandal are reviewed.

315   Douglas, Susan. "It's Howdy Doody Time." *The Progressive* October
          1994: 21.
       Criticizes the "infantilization" of political discourse by both politicians and media. Argues that "sandlot journalism"—stressing conflict and sensationalism—popularizes right-wing rhetoric which is equally simplistic.

316   Drushel, Bruce E. "Sensationalism or Sensitivity: Use of Words in
          Stories on Acquired Immune Deficiency Syndrome (AIDS) by
          Associated Press Videotext." *Journal of Homosexuality* 21. 1-2
          (1991): 47-61.
       Reports results of study which examined four weeks of stories on Associated Press videotext in order to determine whether AIDS stories contained sensationalist language which overemphasized the role of homosexuality in the spread of the disease. Concludes that while such language was largely not present in national AIDS stories, distortion and sensationalism may be fostered in the selection and editing process of newspapers. Includes statistical tables.

317   Ephron, Nora. "Media." *Esquire* March 1975: 12, 14, 47.
       Critiques Time Inc.'s *People* magazine. Finds fault with length of articles (too short); overemphasis on celebrity, indistinct photographs, and human interest (at the expense of mentioning any issues or ideas). Attributes style to the fact that the magazine must compete with the

National Enquirer at the checkout stand.

318   Evans, Harold. "A Typology of the Lurid." *Harper's* September 1984:
        56-59.
        Dissects Rupert Murdoch's journalistic style by examining several pages
        of his *New York Post*. Covered: Murdoch's appeals to fear and jealousy;
        his international press holdings; use of the "circus layout"; exploita-
        tion of greed and gore; and self-promotion.

319   Fairbank, Rosalyn D. "A Pro Takes You Inside the Fishbowl." *Tennis*
        July 1988: 53-54.
        A tennis pro reflects on the role of the press in light of the irresponsible
        sensationalism exhibited by the British tabloids at Wimbledon.

320   Farley, Christopher John. "Elvis Has Left the Supermarket." *Time*
        (3 May 1993): 19.
        Time's "Grapevine" columnist reports that a Harris Teeter supermarket
        in North Carolina has established a tabloid-free checkout lane in re-
        sponse to shopper requests.

321   Fisher, Marc. "The King of Sleaze." *Gentleman's Quarterly* April 1990: 185.
        Profile of Steve Dunleavy, tabloid television journalist on Fox's *The
        Reporters*. Covers Dunleavy's tabloid newspaper work for Rupert
        Murdoch's *Star* and *New York Post*. Credits Dunleavy with creation of
        what is widely considered to be the quintessential tabloid headline:
        "Headless Body in Topless Bar."

322   Fitzgerald, Mark. "Legitimate News Stories or Crap." *The Editor and
        Publisher* (2 July 1994): 50-57.
        Reports on discussion held by panelists at this years Investigative Re-
        porters and Editors Conference concerning the appropriateness of cov-
        ering sensational/scandalous news stories.

323   Flieger, Howard. "Investigative Trash." *U.S. News and World Report*
        (28 July 1975): 72.
        Editorial which excoriates the type of "investigative reporting" exhib-
        ited by a tabloid newspaper staff member who sifted through the gar-
        bage of Secretary of State Henry Kissinger in search of a story. The
        writer considers such behavior an invasion of privacy.

324   Fotheringham, Chris. "Is the Press Free to Lead or Free to Follow." *The
        Editor and Publisher* (15 April 1995): 41, 52.
        Criticizes "media melding" in which mainstream newspapers follow
        the lead of the supermarket tabloids, creating a mixture of good and

bad journalism. The result is mediocrity which confuses 'tabloid noise" with news.

325   Fox, Michael J. and Michael Pollan. "Michael J. Fox's Nuptials in Hell!" *Esquire* June 1989: 136-138.
The actor describes elaborate security tactics employed to guarantee the privacy of his wedding. Discusses a celebrity's obligation to fans and the press. Sample coverage of the event from disappointed, and vengeful tabloids provided.

326   Fox, Roy F. "Sensationspeak in America." *English Journal* March 1988: 52-56.
Analyzes the supermarket tabloids' use of language and logic in promoting their unlikely claims (Hitler masterminding Argentina's invasion of the Falkland Islands, e.g.). Considers tabloids relatively harmless, especially when compared to the more serious threats to our existence.

327   Francke, Warren. "An Argument in the Defense of Sensationalism: Probing the Popular and Historiographical Concept." *Journalism History* 5 (1978): 70-73.
Calls for a more precise definition of the "snarl word", "sensationalism," and a thorough examination of reporting methods, journalistic style and display before labeling a story sensationalist. Suggests that certain aspects of human existence are traditionally held as inferior to others, and therefore any reporting of them is derided as sensationalism. Maintains that absence of all sensationalism leads to lifeless journalism.

328   Friedman, Sharon M., Carol M. Gorny, and Brenda P. Egolf. "Reporting on Radiation: A Content Analysis of Chernobyl Coverage." *Journal of Communication* Summer 1987: 58-79.
Reports result of study which found that while the media did not sensationalize the Chernobyl nuclear accident in its coverage, there was not enough emphasis on the actual situation, nor was there adequate explanation provided for the disaster. Includes statistical tables.

329   "From Worse to Bad." *Newsweek* (8 September 1969): 79.
Reports on the *National Enquirer*'s change in style—from the lurid and salacious to the quirky and occult. Publisher Generoso Pope, Jr. aims for respectability, quality, and the highest sales figures of any publication.

330   Gamson, Joshua. "Incredible News: Tabloids Meet News." *The American Prospect* Fall 1994: 28-35.
Argues for a renewed, rebuilt vision of public service journalism to

counterbalance the pervasiveness of infotainment newsmagazines. Includes discussion of crime-sex-celebrity stories, the line between information and entertainment, the public complaint regarding sensationalism vs. the high ratings such programming receives.

331   Gannon, James P. "Warning: Entertainment Values Threaten Journalism's Health." *The Editor and Publisher* (27 August 1994): 48, 39.
Veteran journalist despairs over "new kind of food chain in journalism: if a sensational story appears anywhere, it appears everywhere." Cites naming of alleged rape victim in William Kennedy Smith case, Lorena and John Bobbitt, and the Gennifer Flowers incidents as evidence that newspapers are going the way of trash TV. Argues that newspapers are underestimating readers' taste for substantial, well-researched news coverage.

332   Garland, Francis P. "Tabloids vs. Standards: Is There a Difference?" Master's Thesis, West Virginia University, 1989. 35 pgs.
Describes study which determined that New York City area tabloids—*Daily News, Newsday,* and *Post*—use a significantly higher percentage of unattributed reports and opinion statements than standard newspapers.

333   Gelman, David. "Press Lord Captures Gotham!" *Newsweek* (17 January 1977): 48-52, 54-56.
Reports on Rupert Murdoch's acquisition of the *New York Post, New York, New West,* and the *Village Voice.* Discusses concern that Murdoch will convert his new properties to the same sleazy formula featured in his older ones. Highlights behind-the-scenes maneuvers involved in publishing takeovers.

334   Gergen, David. "Covering Public Citizens and Private Lives." *U.S. News and World Report* (13 May 1991): 13.
Rejects excuses given for "Kitty Kelly Journalism" in which journalists smear public figures with scandalous revelations of their private lives. Believes privacy is warranted unless compelling reason exists mandating disclosure. Claims current journalistic behavior compares unfavorably with that of campaign strategists who were lambasted for unethical tactics (Roger Aile's Willie Horton ads).

335   Gersh, Debra. "Alabama Tabloid Editor Fired." *The Editor and Publisher* (17 May 1986): 44.
Reports dismissal of the *Gadsden Free Times'*s editor one week after an article appeared describing the transformation of the newspaper into a tabloid featuring titillating headlines (see entry #336).

336   Gersh, Debra. "Racy Tabloid in the Bible Belt." *The Editor and Publisher* (10 May 1986): 14-15.
Describes how a direct mail broadsheet was transformed into a colorful tabloid with suggestive headlines (but conventional stories) in Gadsden, Alabama.

337   Gill, Mark Stuart. "The Shocking Truth About Tabloids." *McCall's* June 1992: 101-103.
Follows Janet Charlton, Beverly Hills correspondent for the tabloid *Star*, through a typical workday as she collects tips from informants in order to piece together her celebrity gossip column.

338   Giobbe, Dorothy. "No More O.J.-At Least in One Newspaper." *The Editor and Publisher* (13 May 1995): 15.
Reports that the Carollton, Ga. *Times-Georgian* newspaper will no longer run stories about the O.J. Simpson trial, labelling the event a 'farce', and its participants buffoons. Includes reaction of readers (mostly positive).

339   Gitlin, Todd. "Media Lemmings Run Amok." *Washington Journalism Review*. April 1992: 28-32.
Argues that the sleaze level is rising too high in campaign news coverage. Discusses whether Democrats and Republicans are given evenhanded investigational treatment; why the tabloids are setting the standard for news coverage; and the character question throughout U.S. political history.

340   Gleick, Elizabeth. "Leader of the Pack." *Time* (9 January 1995): 62.
Discusses legal and ethical questions raised by the *National Enquirer's* aggressive coverage of the O.J. Simpson case. Discusses checkbook journalism, pack journalism, and the practice of the traditional newspapers following the lead of the tabloids. Sample *Enquirer* cover pages included.

341   Glynn, Carroll Jr. and Albert R. Tims. "Sensationalism in Science Issues: A Case Study." *Journalism Quarterly* 59 (1982): 126-131.
Reports on a study that attempted to measure sensationalism in newspaper coverage of the Tellico Dam/Snail Darter environmental controversy. Concludes that sensationalism was evident in the manner in which peripheral issues, deemed more appealing to the readership, were afforded undue emphasis at the expense of more substantial legal/ political matters. Much of the sensational content is attributed to quotes employed by the newspapers analyzed, the *Knoxville News-Sentinel* and the *New York Times*.

342   Glynn, Kevin. "Reading Supermarket Tabloids as Menippean Satire."
       Communication Studies 44 (1993): 19-37.
       Analyzes the bizarre content of the supermarket tabloids such as the
       Weekly World News and the *Sun* in terms of Mikhail Bakhtin's notion
       of Menippean (carnivalesque) satire. Such analysis finds the tabloids
       under investigation productive of a type of discourse which "invents,
       undermines, and interrogates" cultural authority. Finds the tabloids
       encouraging incoherence, disruption, and antagonism to established
       institutions. Wishes such energy could be channelled more productively.
       Included: discussion of Pierre Bordieu's notion of cultural capital;
       Michael Foucault's theory of disciplinary powers; and John Fiske's
       understanding of the popular.

343   Gold, Victor. "Now It Can Be Told!" *Washingtonian* (April 1993): 27-29.
       Humorous look at the more bizarre stories which have appeared in the
       supermarket tabloids. (Adolf Hitler, age 103, helping Saddam Hussein
       plan the invasion of Kuwait, e.g.)

344   Goodwin, H. Eugene. *Groping for Ethics in Journalism.* Ames: Iowa
       State University Press, 1987. 411 pgs.
       Attempts to assist journalists in thinking through ethical problems re-
       lated to their profession. Chapter 9, "That's Shocking" (pp. 208-233)
       addresses the problems associated with use of sensational photos and
       language in news stories. Chapter 10, "Privacy" (pp. 234-265) discusses
       ethical guidelines to be observed by journalists when reporting about
       the private lives of persons in the news.

345   Gourley, Jay. "Beyond the Pail: The Theory and Practice of Garbage
       Journalism." *The Washington Monthly* October 1975: 45-51.
       The *National Enquirer* reporter who seized Henry Kissinger's trash to
       use as the basis for a story explains his methods and motives. Interpre-
       tation and evaluation of his findings included. Maintains the incident
       was meant as a lighthearted novelty, but was turned into a serious issue
       by overreacting national newspaper publishers.

346   Gourley, Jay. " 'I Killed Gig Young' and Other Confessions From
       Inside the *National Enquirer*." *The Washington Monthly* Septem-
       ber 1981: 32-38.
       Describes a contest staged by Generoso Pope of the *National Enquirer*
       in which teams of reporters compete ruthlessly in order to produce the
       most sensational story.

347   Gray, Paul. "The War of the Words." *Time* (17 January 1977): 60-61.
       Parodies the journalistic style of seven Rupert Murdoch-owned news-

papers by imagining the manner in which they would report a landing by Martians.

348   Greenfield, Meg. "In Defense of Sensationalism: The Media and the
        O. J. Simpson Case." *Newsweek* (26 September 1994): 72.
        Maintains that sensational news stories are important because they concern basic questions of good and evil, guilt and responsibility. There is no need to feel apologetic for devoting attention to them. News stories about trade pacts and legislative agendas, supposedly more deserving of our attention, are actually "more earnest than important."

349   Greenwell, J. Richard. "Message From the Editor." *ISC Newsletter*
        Winter 1983: 7.
        Editor of the International Society of Cryptozoology explains why the ISC does not believe it is worth the organization's time and effort to refute supermarket tabloids' claims regarding sightings of extinct animals. (See entry #456 for change in policy.)

350   Hansen, Elizabeth K. and Carmen Manning-Miller. "Supermarket
        Tabloids as Sources of Political Information." Paper presented to
        the Mass Communication and Society Division of the Association
        for Education in Journalism and Mass Communication, Kansas
        City, Missouri, 11-14 August, 1993.
        Reports on the results of a random telephone survey conducted after the 1992 presidential election which found that supermarket tabloids ranked lowest as a source of believable political information among all media sources listed. Concludes that supermarket tabloids serve primarily to entertain rather than inform. Includes statistical tables.

351   Hanson, Christopher. "How to Handle Dirty Stories (and Still Feel
        Clean)." *Columbia Journalism Review* March/April 1994: 14-16.
        Recommends down-playing sensational elements in stories concerning private conduct of public figures, and emphasizing issues which appear important to public policy. (Focuses on Arkansas state trooper's charge of President Clinton's sexual misconduct as an example.)

352   Hanson, Wes. "On the Record: Ethical Problems in the News Media."
        Ethics: Easier Said Than Done Issue 25 (1994): 30-47.
        A forum of prominent journalists, academics, and media critics address ethical questions concerning news coverage. Included: issues of bias, sensationalism, tabloid news and talk shows, celebrities' right to privacy, media hostility and cynicism, "gotcha" journalism, commercialization of the news, and checkbook journalism. Among the participants: Marvin Kalb, Howard Kurtz, Dan Rather, and Van Gordon Sauter.

353   Harris, Daniel. "Sex, Madonna, and Mia: Press Reflections." *The Antioch Review* 51 (1993): 503-518.
Criticizes sensational press coverage of Madonna's book, *Sex* and the Woody Allen/Mia Farrow controversy. Finds reviewers' bored reaction to Madonna's book disingenuous, a calculated pose intended to mask fear and prudery. Criticizes the hypocrisy of the tabloid press which condemned the Allen/Farrow journalistic feeding frenzy only to participate in it themselves.

354   Hausman, Carl. *Crisis of Conscience: Perspectives on Journalism Ethics.* New York: Harper Collins, 1992. 214 pgs.
Examines journalistic ethics as applied to a collection of conflicting principles in search of resolution. Chapter 5, "Fairness" (pp. 54-66) investigates use of language, story selection, and the news-gathering process in portrayal of subjects. Chapter 7, "The Right to Privacy v. the Public's Right to Know" (pp. 77-92) discusses the legal limits of sensational journalism.

355   Head, Allison Jane. "A Survey Analysis of Supermarket Tabloid Readership." Ph.D. dissertation, University of California at Berkeley, 1990. 146 pgs.
Describes study which investigated the characteristics of tabloid readers, how they differ from other readers, and what they like about tabloids. Concludes that tabloid readers are more likely to consider themselves knowledgeable about world affairs and collectors of useful information than other readers; tabloid readers are "information poor" (possessing high levels of information-seeking behavior but low levels of information-seeking skills); tabloid readership is more likely to occur among white women than any other race or gender group. Calls for further investigation of how information-seeking skills and behavior interact.

356   Henry III, William A. "Read All About Lolita!" *Time* (15 June 1992): 62.
Details the media's feeding frenzy surrounding the Amy Fisher/Joey Buttafuoco story. Comments on the hypocrisy of tabloid consumers suddenly inconvenienced by media coverage of a story in their own neighborhood.

357   Herbert, Suzanne Golubski. "Demented Tabloid Run By Aliens!" *M* April 1992: 43-44, 46, 48.
Reports that supermarket tabloid *Weekly World News* is achieving cult status by virtue of its bizarre irreverence. The publication is more profitable than the *National Enquirer* or the *Star* because it doesn't practice "checkbook journalism," and is virtually never sued. Instead, it specializes in the hysterically absurd ("Woman Killed By Fur Coat!;" "Heroic Mom Breast Feeds Orphan Elephant!," e.g.).

358   Hernandez, Debra Gersh. "O.J. Trial Coverage Hard to Avoid." *The Editor and Publisher* (22 April 1995): 42-43.
Reports on findings of survey conducted by the Times Mirror Center for the People and the Press which reported that 64% of the respondents who declared they were not interested in the O.J. Simpson case had nevertheless read, watched, or heard something about it in the previous 24 hours. Includes statistics on respondents' interest in other news stories as well (Tokyo subway gas attack, e.g.).

359   Herzog, Harold A. and Shelly L. Gavin. "Animals, Archetypes, and Popular Culture: Tales From the Tabloid Press." *Anthrozoös* 5 (1992): 77-92.
Analysis of the portrayal of human/animal relationships in the supermarket tabloid press. Argues that depictions of such relationships (either objects of affection, saviors, threats, victims, sex objects of wonder, or things to be used) represent psychological and cultural archetypes as old as mankind.

360   "Heterovisuwhat?" *Sports Illustrated* (13 March 1995): 14.
Expresses disapproval of the amount of attention which has been devoted to the Nancy Kerrigan/Tonya Harding story, while noting that academics convened in New York for a panel discussion entitled "Tabloid TV, Backstage Cameras, and Heterovisuality: Viewing Tonya and Nancy." Panelists discussed why Kerrigan was embraced by our popular culture and Harding scorned.

361   Hinkle, Gerald and William R. Elliot. "Science Coverage in Three Newspapers and Three Supermarket Tabloids." *Journalism Quarterly* 66 (1989): 353-358.
Reports on a study of three supermarket tabloids and three mainstream papers which compared coverage of science issues. Concludes that supermarket tabloids are more likely to report science stories, especially those concerning health. Fewer "pseudo-science" stories were found in the tabloids than the investigators expected. Includes statistical tables.

362   Hofstadter, Douglas R. "Metamagical Themas." *Scientific American* February 1982: 18, 20, 23, 24, 26.
Touts the Committee for the Scientific Investigation of Claims of the Paranormal and its common sense journal, *The Skeptical Inquirer*, as an antidote to the wild "scientific" claims of the tabloid press.

363   Hubbell, Sue. "Rare Glimpse Inside Tabloid World Reveals Editor is Mad Dog." *Smithsonian* October 1993: 71-80.

Traces historical background of tabloid press to its oral folklore traditions, recounting along the way, stories of the birth of the first modern tabloid newspapers; (Alfred Harmsworth's *London Daily Mail* and *Daily Mirror* in turn-of-the-century England); Americas first tabloid (Charles Patterson's *Illustrated Daily News* in 1919); Bernarr Macfadden's *True Story* and *New York Evening Graphic*; and Generoso Pope's transformation of a failing New York daily into the *National Enquirer*, the first supermarket tabloid. Also contains a revealing inside look at the daily operations of the *Weekly World News* and the *Globe*, (including interviews with their editors), as well as a description of the current state of the tabloid business. Comments upon the inaccessibility of supermarket tabloids to researchers.

364   "Into Battle." *The New Yorker* (26 July 1993): 29-30.
Reports on the hiring of Martin Dunn, editor of Rupert Murdoch's *Boston Herald*, to edit New York's *Daily News*. Notes the new pervasiveness of British personnel in the New York tabloid arena.

365   Ingram, Timothy. "Investigative Reporting: Is It Getting Too Sexy?" *The Washington Monthly* April 1975: 53-62.
Expresses concern that smaller newspapers with little tradition of investigative reporting will imitate Woodward and Bernstein's Watergate exposé by going after "easy fish"—scandal stories supported by questionable information obtained by reporters employing dubious methods. Notes tabloids like the *National Star* boasting of their new muckraking approach. Included: the thin line between aggressive reporting and deceit, coverage of public vs. private lives, conflict of interest, buying information, and malicious intent.

366   Johnson, Betty Kuhn. "Inquiring minds: Mythology Makes the Tabloids." *English Journal* (April 1990): 76-77.
Ninth-grade English teacher describes how a supermarket tabloid served as the impetus for class writing projects which brought together previous readings in mythology and sensational journalism techniques.

367   "Joining the 'People' Parade." *Business Week* (16 May 1977): 71, 74.
Details the financial success of *People* magazine and discusses the celebrity photo and gossip publications that have rushed to capitalize on the growing market for such journalism: *In the Know, Celebrity,* and the New York Times Company's *US*. Includes circulation and demographic statistics for publications discussed.

368   Jordan, Eileen Herbert. "Tuned In, Turned Off." *Modern Maturity* August/September 1992: 88.

Expresses a sense of alienation from the constant bombardment of bizarre talk show guests who confess all, ad nauseam, on daytime tabloid television.

369   Jossi, Frank. "Who Reads Supermarket Tabs?" *American Journalism Review* September 1993: 14-15.
Interviews Anthropology professor Elizabeth Bird who discusses findings reported in her book, *For Inquiring Minds: A Cultural Study of Supermarket Tabloids* (see entry #287). Included: the gullibility of tabloid readers; truthfulness of tabloid stories; tabloid tales as American folklore; and the tabloid's affect on mainstream media.

370   Kanfer, Stefan. "Book Publishing Kidnapped by Weird Aliens." *New York Times Book Review* (26 April 1992): 1, 29, 31.
Maintains that "tabloidism" has "trickled up" to the book publishing industry where paperbacks have come to predominate. Scandal stories find the quickest route to publication because publishers are trained in the newspaper and magazine business. Television's audience is also a major factor. Includes excerpts from recently-published, tabloid-influenced paperbacks.

371   Katz, Jeffrey L. "Why Did the L.A. Times Go with Troopergate?" *American Journalism Review* March, 1994: 11-12.
Examines why the same newspaper which criticized sensational news coverage of Bill Clinton during the 1992 presidential campaign decided to pursue Arkansas state trooper's charges of Clinton's sexual misconduct two years later. Competitive pressure and possible validity of the allegation are discussed.

372   Kelm, Rebecca Sturm. "The Lack of Access to Back Issues of the Weekly Tabloids: Does It Matter?" *Journal of Popular Culture* Spring 1990: 45-50.
Establishes the value of supermarket tabloid back issues to the researcher of popular culture (who wishes to read original stories which resulted in libel cases, or trace popular treatment of a story theme, e.g.). Because of high sales figures such publications can be said to represent broad public interests and attitudes. Believes it unlikely that academic libraries will begin subscribing to the tabloids because of widespread budget problems. Instead urges devotees of popular culture to find funding for subscriptions and indexing projects in order to sponsor scholarship in the field.

373   Kennedy, Dana. "Scandaling." *Entertainment Weekly* (4 March 1994): 18+.
Characterizes "Scandal, Inc." as Hollywood's greatest growth industry.

Describes essential elements in scandal construction: a lawyer who can sell (as well as defend) his/her client; ability to spot potential scandals early; make "victim referrals" to agency which specializes in scandals; avoid happy endings; and contact "instant book" specialists. Includes sections on principal scandal-building players and Hollywood scandal productions in their various media versions/incarnations.

374   Kiernan, Thomas. *Citizen Murdoch.* New York: Dodd, Mead & Company, 1986. 337 pgs.
Three-part biography which devotes roughly equal attention to Murdoch's sensational journalistic activities in Australia (pp. 1-85), England (pp. 89-179), and America (pp. 183-322). Appendix (pp. 323-325) lists Murdoch's media holdings.

375   Kurtz, Howard. *Media Circus: The Trouble With America's Newspapers.* New York: Times Books, 1993. 420 pgs.
Media reporter for *The Washington Post* argues for a return to the provocative, activist newspaper which features in-depth reporting on subjects of importance. The first five chapters (pp. 11-118) deal with important stories the press overlooked because of its obsession with sensationalism and celebrity as well as its unwillingness to challenge authority.

376   Lacayo, Richard. "Tarting Up The Gray Lady of 43rd Street." *Time* (6 May 1991); 44-45.
Attributes *New York Times* decision to name alleged rape victim in William Kennedy Smith case to the newspaper's attempt to attract younger readers. Executive editor Max Frankel has added more soft news with a bit of tabloid sensationalism.

377   Lamb, Dianne. "Joseph Pulitzer and the Large Mass Communication Class." *Journalism Educator* Winter 1994: 62-66.
Advocates adopting the sensational techniques employed by Joseph Pulitzer and the yellow press in order to educate large groups of mass communication students. The type of undercover exposées of volatile issues published by Pulitzer were rich in personal drama which spoke to mass audiences. Sees educational benefit in speaking to students at the level of their own interests. Included: social benefits derived from penny press, yellow press and Benjamin Harris's *Publick Occurrences* (colonial newspaper banned after one issue for reporting on the illicit affairs of the French King).

378   La Rocque, Paula. "The Excesses of Tabloid Journalism Can Be Contagious: Readers Have Rights to Opinions Without News Being Filtered." *Quill* January/February 1994: 58.

Warns journalists against use of subjective, unresponsive, flippant language commonly employed in the tabloid press. Several examples of both original and edited copy are provided.

379   Leapman, Michael. *Arrogant Aussie: The Rupert Murdoch Story.* Seacaucus: Lyle Stuart, Inc. 1985. 288 pgs.
Biography which contrasts Murdoch's great success and adverse reputation. Chapter 1, "Puff the Magic Founder" (pp. 17-44) describes Murdoch's sensational style in Australia. Chapter 2, "Go North, Young Man" (pp. 45-68) chronicles his move to Fleet Street. Chapter 4, "Rupert in Wonderland" (pp. 81-114), discusses Murdoch's move to America.

380   Lehnert, Eileen and Mary J. Perpich. "An Attitude Segmentation Study of Supermarket Tabloid Readers." *Journalism Quarterly* 59 (1982): 104-111.
Reports on study which identified three different types of supermarket tabloid readers: "Intent Diversion Seekers" who are serious about their entertainment; "Distracted Information Collectors" who read to learn and report new facts; and "Selfish Believers" who find all the stories credible and relate them to their own lives. Includes survey instrument and statistical tables.

381   Levin, Jack and Arnold Arluke. *Gossip: The Inside Scoop.* New York: Plenum Press, 1987. 250 pgs.
Views gossip, perhaps the most common subject matter of tabloid journalism, as a socially useful phenomenon. Gossip, as opposed to rumor—its distorted, exaggerated relation—is rarely nasty or vicious. Nor is it restricted to the tabloids. Rather, it is a cultural positive, offering escapism and hope for a better life to its participants. Merit is even found in the creation of "invisible neighborhoods" where the star-struck enjoy imaginary friendships with celebrities. Hero-building, a by-product of gossip, creates our cultural icons. The authors believe that gossip serves to remind the community of its values by ridiculing those who violate folkways. (Mores are rarely treated by gossip.) Gossip is democratizing, ensuring that celebrity and common citizen are judged by the same standard, not permitting the politician to hide from his/her constituency. The tabloid journalist is seen as a watchdog or anthropologist, getting the "inside scoop" on subjects by examining the manner in which they conduct their lives. When gossip is negative it performs a cathartic function permitting the reader to better appreciate his/her life in comparison to that of the individual whom gossip has disgraced.

382   Levin, Jack, Amita Mody-Desbareau, and Arnold Arluke. "The Gossip Tabloid as Agent of Social Control." *Journalism Quarterly* 65

(1988): 514-517.
Reports on findings of a study which attempted to determine whether
the gossip tabloids (*National Enquirer, Star, National Examiner* and
Globe) communicate a message to readers through praise and condemnation. Concludes that gossip tabloids reinforce the status quo by send-
ing the message that happiness is just around the corner. Such a message discourages protest and supports prevailing values. Criticism of
celebrities serves to demonstrate that wealth and power cannot guarantee contentment.

383   Liberman, Si. " 'Fiction': The Lifeblood of One Supermarket Tab." *The
          Editor and Publisher* (19 September 1992): 15.
       Reports on "fiction defense" employed by the tabloid *Sun* in an inva-
       sion of privacy trial earlier this year. (The contention that the ficti-
       tious nature of tabloid tale is a given failed to convince the jury which
       awarded the 96-year-old Nellie Mitchell $1.5 million in damages af-
       ter the *Sun* identified her as pregnant. See entries #454 and 655.) In-
       cludes interviews with competing supermarket tabloid editors who
       maintain that their stories are authentic.

384   Logan, Andy. "Around City Hall: Seesaw." *New Yorker* (6 April 1992):
          84-89.
       Discusses the fact that an informal study indicated only eight individu-
       als/celebrities dominated the headlines of New York City's establish-
       ment tabloid newspapers (*Daily News, Post,* and *Newsday*): Donald
       Trump, John Gotti, George Steinbrenner, Ivan Boesky, Mike Tyson,
       Rev. Al Sharpton, and John Cardinal O'Connor. The two women who
       were covered most often were accused lawbreakers Leona Helmsley
       and Imelda Marcos.

385   Lotz, Roy Edward. *Crime and the American Press.* New York: Praeger,
          1991. 170 pgs.
       Examines the scope and impact of crime coverage in the American
       press, arguing that such coverage has improved over the years. Chapter
       7, "Crimes and Criminals" (pp 103-119) includes a defense of the use
       of sensationalism, equating such a style with the use of greater detail
       which enhances the telling of a story. (Book is part of Praeger series in
       Political Communication.)

386   "The Magnate from Down Under: An Interview with Rupert Murdoch."
          Gannett Center Journal. Winter, 1989: 33-41.
       Briefly recounts Murdoch's career. Murdoch responds to questions
       regarding sensationalism and what constitutes important news.

387   Maittlen-Harris, John P. "Rupert Murdoch: Emergence of a Multina-
       tional Media Magnate." Paper presented at the Annual Meeting of
       the Association for Education in Journalism. Lansing, Michigan,
       (8-11 August, 1981).
       Describes Rupert Murdoch's use of tabloid journalism techniques to
       revive failing newspapers he has acquired, thereby generating profits.
       Such income allows Murdoch to repay the loans which made possible
       his newspaper purchases.

388   Mallette, Mal. "Tarred By the 'Supermarket' Tabloids." *The Editor and
       Publisher* (27 June 1992): 48.
       Relates lecture experience which led author to conclude that the younger
       generation associates all journalism with the supermarket press. Such
       association leads to erosion of one's belief in the First Amendment as
       freedom of the press comes to be associated with gross invasion of
       privacy.

389   Manley, Will. "Lowlife Info in a High Tech Age." *American Libraries*
       25 (1994): 355.
       Evaluates the scope and specialization of each of the six supermarket
       tabloids. Recommends the *National Enquirer* to libraries that can af-
       ford only one, because it is the master of America's favorite recreation—
       scandal-mongering.

390   Manley, Will. "What John Bobbitt's Penis Means to Librarians."
       American Libraries 25 (1994): 237.
       America's obsession with sleaze has resulted in a new "information-
       delivery food chain": supermarket tabloids —> trash TV —> newspa-
       pers report it —> journals tell us what it means —> Internet users joke
       about it. Libraries can no longer avoid the tabloids.

391   Manning, Fiona. *Inside Hollywood: Adventures of an Australian
       Tabloid Journalist.* Sydney: Allen & Unwin, 1989. 189 pgs.
       An account of the author's 2½ years as an employee of the tabloid *Star*
       where she created stories from celebrity gossip and scandal.

392   Mano, D. Keith. "Enquiring." *National Review* 29 (1977): 209-210.
       Evaluates the *National Enquirer* as a shrewd, lowbrow, socially conser-
       vative and very popular publication which has adopted broadcast tech-
       niques for a readership with a short attention span.

393   McCabe, Casey. "Our Need to Know: Gossip Takes Over the News."
       Utne Reader March/April 1992: 128.

Reprint of an article originally appearing in *The Nose* (Nov. 1991), a San Francisco publication. Juxtaposes the public's "Need to Know" with the current practice of journalists devoting column space and air time to trivial or nonexistent news issues. Discusses Noam Chomsky's observation that the public cannot absorb social information unless there is a face attached suggesting a rationale for much of tabloid TV's subject matter.

394   McDonald, Daniel. "*Enquirer* Stories Worth Thinking About." *ETC.* 44 (1987): 392-394.
Examines humorous questions raised by seventeen news items which appeared in the *National Enquirer* during the year 1986.

395   McDonald, Daniel. "God's Favorite Number." *The Christian Century* 107 (1990): 1158-1159.
Relates a compilation of fantastic religious stories gleaned from the tabloid press and gospel radio. Included: the precise location, appearance, and administration of heaven and hell.

396   McGauley, John. "Did Media Sensationalize Student AIDS Case?" *The Editor and Publisher* (8 November 1986): 19.
Reports on remarks made at Indiana Associated Press Broadcasters seminar held at DePauw University. Ron Colby, principal of Western Middle School in the Kokomo area, charged that reporters sensationalized coverage of AIDS patient Ryan White's attempt to attend his school, overemphasizing minority opposition and ignoring the non-confrontational majority. Remarks of Ryan White's mother and David McCarty, spokesman for the Indiana State Board of Health, are included.

397   Meuse, Mariane K. "Space Explodes in the Tabloids." *Ad Astra* January/February 1992: 42-46.
Examines some of the more absurd scientific stories in the supermarket tabloids ("Photos Confirm Moon Landing Hoax!" e.g.), explaining that NASA does take time to answer the questions of the more gullible tabloid readers. Attributes popularity of the tabloids in part, to Americans' lack of faith in government. In addition, poor coverage of science by the mainstream press grants the tabloids a monopoly on exciting, science-based stories.

398   "Michael Jackson Scandal." *Nieman Reports* Spring 1994: 34-38.
Edited excerpts of PBS's 3-part "Frontline" television report telecast on 15 February 1994. Assesses the questionable nature of "tabloid truth" which emerged from coverage of the Michael Jackson child molestation charges. Describes the carnival atmosphere surrounding the story and the roles played by its principal characters.

399   Mirotznik, Jerrold and Bernadette M. Mosellie. "Genital Herpes and
       the Mass Media." *Journal of Popular Culture* Winter 1986: 1-11.
       Examines popular newspaper and magazine treatment of the genital
       herpes "epidemic" in the early 1980's in order to determine if sensa-
       tionalism dominated the reporting. Concludes that popular media cov-
       erage of the ailment probably contributed, at least in part, to unwar-
       ranted public fear of the condition.

400   Montefiore, Simon Sebas. "Royal Scandal." *Psychology Today*
       July/August 1992: 32-37.
       Blames the tabloid press for, in large part, contributing to the disrup-
       tive behavior about which it so avidly reports. The press fails to prop-
       erly analyze whether their morality exposés have legitimate bearing on
       a leader's ability to perform his/her duties. Also traces the historical
       division of mystique and administration of our rulers in order to ex-
       plain the factors determining whether their personal behavior will be
       scrutinized.

401   Morrison, Donald. "The Battle of New York." *Time* (17 January 1977):
       52-54, 56, 59-61.
       Recounts Rupert Murdoch's takeover of the *New York Post, New West,*
       and *Village Voice* publications. Recaps Murdoch's career to date and
       describes his management style.

402   Nemeth, Mary. "Hot Off the Presses: Sensational Stories Fuel America's
       Tabloid-Inspired Media Machine." *Maclean's* (24 January 1994):
       66-67.
       Comments that the U.S. has become a "tabloid heaven," outdistancing
       any other country in their volume and variety of sensational news sto-
       ries. Even traditional journalistic sources such as the *New York Times*
       have concentrated on the Lorena Bobbitt and Nancy Kerrigan dramas.
       Breaking all tabloid television records, producers rushed the Branch
       Davidian TV movie to the screen even before the cultists stood trial.
       Disagrees with the notion that tabloid stories have redeeming social
       value because they initiate discussion of important issues. Such pos-
       sible benefits are lost in a rush to publicize sensationalism which is so
       great that longtime tabloids like the *National Enquirer* are being pre-
       empted by the media establishment. In Canada, stricter laws regarding
       pretrial publicity serve to curb tabloid excesses.

403   "New Boy." *The New Yorker* (25 February 1974): 30-31.
       Reviews Rupert Murdoch's *National Star* characterized as an attempt
       to introduce the tabloid style of the publisher's *London Sun* to America.
       Includes information on Murdoch's editor Larry Lamb, and an analysis
       of the *Star's* rhetorical style.

404   Nixon, Will. "The O.J. Environmental Story." *E: The Environmental
       Magazine* April 1995: 22-24.
       Claims that environmental news receives scant attention because jour-
       nalists have fallen in love with the "new sensationalism." Discusses
       whether the industry is losing credibility and sales as a result.

405   "Now It Can Be Told! How Tabloids Survived the Recession." *Business
       Week* (7 November 1983): 145, 148.
       Explains how supermarket tabloids prospered during recession while
       the rest of the publishing industry slumped: readers of the "tabs" are
       impulse buyers attracted by sensational headlines at the checkout stand;
       because most tab revenue comes from circulation, they need not tone
       down sensationalism to attract advertisers; and celebrity deaths (Prin-
       cess Grace) occurred at opportune times.

406   O'Hanlon, Tom. "What Does This Man Want?" *Forbes.* (30 January
       1984): 78-83, 86.
       Depicts Rupert Murdoch as a legitimate heir to publishing giants of the
       past such as Hearst, Luce, and Pulitzer. Accepts sensationalism as
       shrewd, market-oriented, popular journalism. Discusses Murdoch's move
       to acquire Warner Communications. Provides biographical background.

407   O'Neill, Michael J. "Who Cares About the Truth." *Nieman Reports*
       Spring 1994: 11-18.
       Edited transcript of a lecture delivered by the former editor of the *New
       York Daily News* at Long Island University, 5 October 1993. Addresses
       ethical problem of entertainment's conception of journalism. Mourns
       the absence of moral discourse and the increase of public apathy. Calls
       for a moral consensus in the media which will acknowledge the exist-
       ence of some ethical standards, maintaining that "the mores of the
       entertainment world are poor guides for a democracy."

408   Oring, Elliott. "Legend, Truth, and News." *Southern Folklore* 47 (1990):
       163-177.
       Argues for folklorists to study the news and the sensational stories re-
       ported by newspapers as folklore. Discusses the untenability of the
       newsman's standard of objectivity. Included: the relationship between
       news/folklore/legend; sensationalist stories as an ideological field; ev-
       eryday news as a symbolic construction (akin to legends or novels);
       and problems presented by news which should be investigated by the
       folklorist.

409   Ornstein, Norman J. "Foreign Policy and the 1992 Election." *Foreign
       Affairs* Summer 1992: 1-16.

The author, Resident Scholar at the American Enterprise Institute, calls for vigorous debate concerning America's rightful role in world affairs rather than the continued, erratic vacillation between isolationism and internationalism articulated by presidential candidates who have one eye on public opinion polls. Journalists must forsake their preoccupation with scandal in order to intelligently question the candidates about their vision of government. The media is deserving of severe criticism if they persevere in behaving like the supermarket tabloids.

410   Ornstein, Norman J. "Sexpress: Too Much Political News These Days is Not Fit to Print." *The Atlantic* October 1991: 24, 26.
Observes that a combination of sales competition and new candor have created an "upscale yellow press" which lives by the same standards as the supermarket tabloids. Criticizes publication of rumors, and opposes detailed coverage of officials' private lives when actions do not affect job performance.

411   Padgett, George E. "Let Grief Be a Private Affair." *The Quill* February 1988: 13, 27.
Argues against grief exploitation by national media in their coverage of personal tragedies. The Pulitzer Prize Committee should not continue to reward photographs which invade the privacy of grieving victims. Refutes arguments which defend such coverage (graphic coverage of grief helps prevent future tragedies; public's need to know/right to know). Favors stricter adherence to Society of Journalists Code of Ethics as alternative to privacy legislation.

412   Painter Jr., John. "Tonya Harding Orgy." *Nieman Reports* Spring 1994: 29-33, 52.
Criticizes tabloid tactics of print and television journalists who bought interviews, relied on unnamed sources, chased rumors, hyped the insignificant, and leaped to judgement.

413   Parrot, Andrea and John Omondroyd. "Can a Woman Really Be Pregnant For Twelve Years or is Scholarly Learning Possible From Reading the Tabloids?" *Teaching Sociology* 20 (1992): 158-164.
A reference librarian and a professor teaching sociology-related courses at Cornell University describe an instructional unit which they developed, utilizing supermarket tabloid headlines to develop critical thinking skills. Appendix (pp. 162-163) presents detailed instructional plan containing sources employed and procedures followed.

414   Pasadeos, Yorgo. "Application of Measures of Sensationalism to a Murdoch-Owned Daily in the San Antonio Market." *Newspaper Research Journal* Summer 1984: 9-17.

Reports that both content analysis and "Sendex" (semantic differential) studies found that the *San Antonio News* was significantly sensationalized after its acquisition by Ruppert Murdoch. Discusses the definition of the term "sensationalism" as well as the development of the methods to measure it. Includes statistical tables.

415   Paty, James Cameron. "A Content Analysis of Three Murdoch Newspapers." Ph.D. dissertation, Florida State University, 1988. 486 pgs.
Studies the extent to which Rupert Murdoch employs a formula for sensationalism in his American tabloid newspapers. Finds that although no precise formula is evident, a consistent pattern of sensationalism is discernible in the coverage of government and light news. The *New York Post, Boston Herald,* and *Chicago Sun-Times* were subjects of the study. Statistical tables included.

416   Pauly, John J. "Rupert Murdoch and the Demonology of Professional Journalism." In *Media, Myths, and Narratives,* edited by James W. Carey. 246-261. Newbury Park: Sage Publications, 1988.
Explores Rupert Murdoch's reputation as invidious outsider. Argues Murdoch is often misperceived and that his detractors are hypocrites. Regards the information/entertainment distinction as an "intellectually feeble" construct employed by the establishment in order to denigrate mavericks like Murdoch. Included: charges that Murdoch is driving out "good" journalism; attempts to stereotype all Murdoch publications; and Murdoch's stance vs. the concept of "professionalism."

417   Peer, Elizabeth and William Schmidt. "The Enquirer: Up from Smut." *Newsweek* (21 April 1975): 62.
Notes the *National Enquirer's* shift from a "sex-and -sadism" sheet to a more mainstream popular culture publication. Characterizes the change as a business decision resulting from increased competition in the smut market and the passing of neighborhood newsstands. Supermarket sales mandated the toning down of sensationalism.

418   Pesmen, Sandra. "Basking/Baking in Tabloid Glow." *Advertising Age* (19 February 1990): 56.
Discusses the impact which negative supermarket tabloid publicity has on celebrities' careers, and the propriety of responding to sensational charges levelled by such publications.

419   Peterson, Mark Allen. "Aliens, Ape Men, and Whacky Savages: The Anthropologist in the Tabloids." *Anthropology Today* October 1991: 5-7.
Examines the manner in which American supermarket tabloids con-

sider anthropology and anthropologists. Views the tabloids as a parody of mainstream journalism, taking the extraordinary and treating it as ordinary. Finds that the tabloid anthropology stories fall into four categories; aliens and ape men; whacky savages; whacky anthropologists, and silly studies. Concludes that anthropologists are overrepresented in the tabloid press and under-represented in the mainstream for the same reason—they study and interpret alien cultures.

420   Pfaff, Fred. "Headway for the Headlines." *Marketing and Media Decisions* May 1987: 66-68, 72-73.
Reports that the *National Enquirer* and the *Star* tabloids have had some success attracting advertisers like Proctor & Gamble by shunning bizarre and lurid stories in favor of more mainstream topics ("celebrity journalism," e.g.).

421   Phalon, Richard. "A Game of Poker." *Forbes* (4 July 1994): 45-56.
Reports that Enquirer Star Group has offered to buy out stockholders at $17.50 per share. Shareholders balked at what they considered the low bid, but would like to sell due to falling circulation and advertising rates of the supermarket tabloids. Included: discussion of Enquirer Star's moves to return their publications to profitability.

422   Pollitt, Katha. "Tabloid Women." *The Nation* 254 (1992): 880.
Excoriates misogynistic depiction of women by the tabloid media. Cites the double standard applied to Amy Fisher and Joey Buttafuoco in the so-called "Long Island Lolita case (a term the author attributes to "A Current Affair" tabloid television show). Male transgressions are treated cavalierly while women are seen as "cold, calculating, sex-crazed, and asking for trouble."

423   Porter, Bruce. "The Lucasville Follies." *Columbia Journalism Review* May/June 1994: 38-45.
Condemns sensational television news coverage of the Lucasville, Ohio prison riot (April, 1994) for reporting speculation, hearsay, and rumor as fact, and failing to correct blatant falsehoods (many murders, mutilated bodies, e.g.). Concludes that such reporting prevented an earlier resolution of the crisis.

424   Potterton, Reginald. "I Cut Out Her Heart and Stomped On It." *Playboy* April 1969: 117, 118, 120, 204, 206, 208, 211-212.
The author recounts his experiences as articles editor at the *National Enquirer*. Also discusses *Justice Weekly*, a Toronto tabloid featuring articles on sexual deviance; *Midnight*, a Montreal scandal sheet; the *National Informer*, a Chicago-based publication; and *Continental Flash*, a Toronto tabloid which occasionally covered the Vietnam War.

425   Rappleye, Charles. "A Star Reporter's Fall From Grace." *Columbia Journalism Review* July/August 1993: 41-45.
Chronicles journalist Tony Castro's fraudulent behavior as a tabloid reporter: inventing stories and sources, and pocketing checks intended as payment for tips—which later proved fictional. Castro's defense (such behavior was common in the supermarket tabloid industry) was apparently accepted by the court, at least in part. (The industry, rather than the individual, shouldered the blame.) Includes coverage of Castro's earlier, more respectable, journalistic career.

426   Reid, Jeff. "Supermarket Tabloids: *Utne Reader* March/April 1987: 57-60.
Views supermarket tabloids as post-modern journalism created for the fertile imagination of middle America. Divides readership into faithful believers and the incredulous condescending camps. Included: a survey of the five top publications.

427   Reilly, Patrick. "Deflated *Enquirer* $400M. Sale Price is More Like $200M." *Advertising Age* 3 April 1989: 2, 61.
Reports that sources knowledgeable about the bidding process involved in the sale of the *National Enquirer* expect the tabloid to sell for between 200 and 250 million dollars, rather than the $400-500 million originally anticipated. Comments upon founder and former owner Generoso Pope's proclivities for sparing little expense in search of sensational stories. Any new owner is expected to work to cut costs. Discusses relative interest and financial situation of prospective buyers.

428   Ressner, Jeffrey. "Enquiring Minds." *Rolling Stone* 30 June 1988: 53-54, 56, 64.
Profiles several young tabloid newspaper reporters and a "paparazzo" photographer. Also visits *National Enquirer* headquarters in Lantana, Fla. where the work environment is observed. Techniques for obtaining stories are discussed, including threatening to initiate a scandal in order to obtain "leverage." Cultivation of friendly working relationship with some celebrities is also described.

429   Riggenbach, Jeff. "Rupert Murdoch: That's Entertainment." *Inquiry: A Libertarian Review* July 1984: 24-27.
Answers critic's two principal complaints against Rupert Murdoch, namely that he can't distinguish between news and entertainment (witness his collection of lurid scandal sheets reporting "the news") and that he refuses to allow his editors any independence in supervising his newspapers. Demonstrates that Murdoch's newspaper holdings are varied and diverse, not merely sensational tabloids, and maintains that all readers of the news regard their papers as entertaining in the broadest sense of the term.

430   Rosenbaum, Ron. "Why Alexander Hamilton Would Have Liked Rupert
        Murdoch's *New York Post.*" *Harper's* January 1983: 19-21, 24.
        Defends tabloid sensationalism by tracing its origins to intellectual clas-
        sics such as Homer's *Iliad* and *Odyssey*, Milton's *Paradise Lost* and
        Alexander Hamilton's *Federalist Papers*.

431   Rudnitsky, Howard. "How Gene Pope Made Millions in the Newspaper
        Business." *Forbes* (16 October 1978): 77-78.
        Details how Generoso Pope created a new type of tabloid journalism—
        "soft core sensationalism"—incorporating *Readers Digest*-type inspi-
        ration in order to market his *National Enquirer* to America's middle
        class. Discusses relative markups on newspapers and magazines. Also
        includes lessons learned by Rupert Murdoch and his tabloid *Star*.

432   Sabato, Larry J. *Feeding Frenzy: How Attack Journalism Has Transformed
        American Politics.* New York: Free Press, 1991. 306 pgs.
        Criticizes journalists' obsession with gossip and scandal which has trans-
        formed political life into an endless lurid melodrama. Analyzes thirty-
        six case studies or "feeding frenzies" where journalists feasted on the
        embarrassment of political figures. Calls for rational standards which
        properly separate the public from the personal, and specifies instances
        in which public coverage of personal matters are warranted.

433   Salwen, Michael B. and Ronald B. Anderson, "The Uses and Gratifica-
        tions of Supermarket Tabloid Reading by Different Demographic
        Groups." Paper presented at the Annual Meeting of the Associa-
        tion for Education in Journalism and Mass Communication,
        Gainsville, Florida, 5-8 August 1984.
        Describes a survey conducted of supermarket tabloid readership which
        found that older readers with low income and education levels read the
        tabloids more for surveillance of society, utility, escape, anticipated
        interpersonal communication, and diversion than do other respondents.
        Entertainment was the main reason respondents in all age groups read
        the tabloids. Results also contradicted stereotypes which depict tabloid
        readers as blue-collar workers and housewives. Includes statistical tables.

434   Sandler, Norman D. "Panic Gluttons." *Technology Review* October
        1993: 72-73.
        Blames tabloid television reporting for the recent cellular telephone
        health scare. Unsubstantiated claims were treated as scientific fact, re-
        sulting in panic. Industry spokesmen were understandably hesitant to
        appear on talk shows with angry guests who blamed them for the deaths
        of family and friends. Scientists need to realize the importance of com-
        municating to the public. Calls on the media as well to become more

scientifically knowledgeable and willing to explain such knowledge to their audiences.

435   Savan, Leslie. "I Wrote Trash for a Living (and Lived!): True Stories From a Tabloid Reporter." *Mademoiselle* (June 1988) 184–185+.
Describes the author's six years of employment by the tabloid *Star*.

436   Scaffer, Deborah. "Shocking Secrets Revealed!: The Language of Tabloid Headlines." *ETC* Spring, 1995: 27-46.
Analyzes the manner in which supermarket tabloids sell themselves through the use of physical presentation (front-page layout) and linguistic devices ("connotation-rich vocabulary" and "pseudo-quotes"). Concludes that tabloids construct their headlines as businesses prepare advertising copy—in order to sell a product. Includes appendix listing samples of tabloid headlines (pp. 36-46).

437   Scherrill, Robert. "Newsdom's Number-One Dirtbag." *The Nation* 256 (1993): 613, 642-644.
Unflattering portrait of Rupert Murdoch, Australian-born tabloid newspaper mogul. Sees Murdoch as the personification of Thatcher-Reagan business ethics (which the author apparently considers oxymoronic). Yet, the author pessimistically muses that "Murdochism" may well represent the journalism of the future.

438   Schjeldahl, Peter. "Welcome to Helgaland." *Art in America* October 1986: 11, 13.
Ridicules media hype surrounding "discovery" of a number of Andrew Wyeth paintings whose subject is a "mysterious woman" named Helga. Sensational treatment of the story by newspapers and magazines concentrated on reports that the paintings were hidden, the subject unknown, and likely a romantic partner of Wyeth—all apparently untrue.

439   Schreiner, Tim. "You Can't Ignore News." *Washington Journalism Review* April 1992: 33-35.
Maintains that "the sleaze-prestige spectrum" between the supermarket tabloids and the mainstream press has narrowed due to the lowering of standards by the establishment publications. Increasingly, the tabloids break scandal stories which the mainstream press pursue. Discusses famous tabloid scoops: the Gary Hart/Donna Rice photo, and Gennifer Flower's interviews regarding Bill Clinton.

440   "Sensationalized Disasters." *Society* March/April 1988: 2.
Contends that the news media's emphasis on sensational aspects of disasters—such as Chernobyl—makes it difficult for the public to accurately gauge actual risk. Cites research presented at a symposium en-

titled "Communicating Risk: the Media and the Public."

441   Shaw, David. "Surrender the Gatekeepers." *Nieman Reports* Spring 1994:
3-5.
Laments the surrender of former ethical standard-setters in journalism
(the *New York Times,* television network news, e.g.) to tabloid sensibili-
ties. Cites marketplace pressures as undermining editorial authority.
Pleads for editors who will value being right rather than being first.

442   Shaw, Peter. "Reliable Sources." *National Review* (21 June 1993): 63-64.
This article, part of a special section, "The Decline of American Journalism," maintains that the tabloid press, with its tales of murder and
mayhem, more accurately reflects reality than the establishment newspapers which place their stories within a politically-correct context.
Not only was the *New York Post's* headline of 15 April 1983, "Headless
Body in Topless Bar," an accurate representation of a violent event, but
it communicated the information in appropriate trochaic meter(!)

443   Shawcross, William. *Murdoch.* New York: Simon & Schuster,
1993. 492 pgs.
Unauthorized biography of the newspaper magnate from his beginnings
in Australia to Fleet Street and America. Chapter 4 (pp. 81-100), deals
with Murdoch's practice of sensational journalism in Australia. Chapter 5 (pp. 103-131), covers Murdoch's migration to Fleet Street with his
purchase of *News of the World.* Chapter 6 (pp. 132-160) details purchase and transformation of the *New York Post* by Murdoch.

444   Shoemaker, Pamela J. "All The News That's Fit to Print: Newsworthiness
and Social Change." Paper presented at the Annual Meeting of the
Association for Education in Journalism and Mass Communication. Memphis, Tennessee; 3-6 August 1985.
Argues that much of the news which is reported is selected for coverage because of its deviance from social norms. Such publication of
deviance facilitates social change. Provides statistical, pathological,
normative, and self-conceptual definitions of deviance. Sensationalism, a common indicator of newsworthiness, is seen as most important
feature of violent and criminal deviance.

445   Sibbison, Jim. "Covering Medical 'Breakthroughs'." *Columbia Journalism Review* July/August 1988: 36-39.
Demonstrates that reports touted as medical breakthroughs frequently
tell less than the complete story. Balanced medical reporting which is
appropriately qualified has little commercial value. Calls on news editors to seek second scientific opinions whenever encountering sensational claims.

446   Singer, Eleanor and Phyllis Endrenry. "Reporting Hazards: Their Benefits
            and Costs." *Journal of Communication* Summer 1987: 10-26.
         Reports results of study which found that the media stresses harms
         rather than risks when covering disasters. In addition, media stories
         regarding potential hazards rarely mention possible benefits. Includes
         statistical tables.

447   Sissman, L. E. "Innocent Bystander: Pabulum to the General." *The
            Atlantic* June 1974: 28-29.
         Reviews two new publications: Rupert Murdoch's *National Star* and
         Time, Inc.'s *People* magazine, finding similarities in their focus on ce-
         lebrity gossip and scandal, and absence of any real news. Traces the
         Star's tabloid forbearers including discussion of Murdoch's *Sun*, Hearst's
         American Weekly, and Macfadden's *Graphic*. *People* is described as
         Time magazine's "People" section, expanded and rendered banal.

448   Slattery, Karen L. "Sensationalism Versus News of the Moral Life:
            Making the Distinction." *Journal of Mass Media Ethics* 9 (1994):
            5-15.
         Argues that some sensational news stories are worthy of newspaper
         coverage, because they speak to the moral standards of the community.
         Discusses the importance for the journalist of balancing sensational
         and responsible public affairs news coverage. Describes application of
         the Bok Test of Publicity for assistance in deciding whether or not to
         cover a sensational story.

449   Smilgis, Martha. "In Florida: The Rogues of Tabloid Valley." *Time* 15
            August 1988: 13-14.
         Reports on the activities of expatriate Fleet Streeters who work for
         American supermarket tabloids (*National Enquirer, Sun,* and *Weekly
         World News*) based in Lantana, Fla. Favorite headlines and stories are
         recounted.

450   Stein, M. L. "Has Journalism Run Amok in Sensationalism?" *The
            Editor and Publisher* (17 December 1994): 9-10.
         Reports on remarks of *Los Angeles Times* Washington bureau chief Jack
         Nelson and NBC Nightly News anchor Tom Brokaw at University of
         Southern California journalism awards ceremony. Both decry the
         profession's obsession with scandal and sensationalism at the expense
         of more serious news.

451   Stone, Emerson. " 'Simpsons' Gone Hellish: Case Offers Textbook
            Challenge for Media." *The Quill* November/December 1994: 24-25.
         Discusses the ethics of covering the trial of a celebrity (in this case, O.

J. Simpson) charged with murder. Included: reporting unsubstantiated rumors and speculation by paid consultants.

452   Streitmatter, Rodger. "The Bad-News Bearers: Lowlights of AIDS Summer '83." *The Quill* May 1984: 25, 27.
Cites Geraldo Rivera, Pat Buchanan, and the *New York Post*—among others—for irresponsible sensationalism and/or deplorable judgement in covering the AIDS story.

453   Swan, Jon. "The New Ballyhoo." *Columbia Journal Review* September October 1976: 39-44.
Comments on the revival of the 1920's-type "jazz journalism" by journalism magnates such as Rupert Murdoch in the 1970's. Notes divergent characterizations of the recent phenomenon (democracy or trivia). Offers four pages sampling sensational news stories of the past and present from Charles Lindbergh to the Loch Ness Monster.

454   "Tabloid Journalism 101." *Harper's* December 1992: 23-27.
Excerpt of courtroom testimony given by Manny Silver, a reporter for the tabloid *Sun*, during a 1991 trial in Arkansas. (Nellie Mitchell, a 97-year-old woman, sued for libel when she was falsely identified as pregnant by the *Sun*. See entries #383 and 655 for judicial ruling.) Mitchell's attorney elicits testimony which is indicative of how far the reporter has strayed from traditional journalistic ethics in his work, while Silver's attorney prompts his client to characterize tabloid stories as pure fiction, (and, therefore, not subject to ethical considerations).

455   "Tabloid Truth." *U.S. News & World Report* (16 December 1991): 39.
Notes decision in case which awarded $1.5 million to elderly newsdealer whose picture was used by the tabloid *Sun* in a story alleging the pregnancy of the "world's oldest newspaper carrier." (See entries #383 and 655.)

456   "The Tabloids That Time Forgot." *ISC Newsletter* Summer 1987: 9-10.
Reversing its previous stance (see entry #349), the International Society of Cryptozoology takes time to refute tabloid newspaper claims of dinosaur citings. States telltale signs of story fabrication: failure to specifically identify principal persons involved in story; failure to identify academic institutions with which "Doctors and Professors" are affiliated; conclusions and follow-up to fantastic stories are never provided.

457   Taubes, Gary. "Death Threats and Trial by Tabloid." *Science* 265 (1994): 732.
Relates the manner in which tabloid TV shows, "A Current Affair" and "Unsolved Mysteries" as well as New York's tabloid newspapers, sensationalized the story of a series of threatening incidents aimed at a team of Rockefeller University's molecular biologists.

458   Taylor, S. J. *Shock! Horror! The Tabloids in Action.* London: Bantam
        Press, 1991. 354 pgs.
        An inside look at the operations of the sensational tabloids in Britain
        and America. Chapters address aspects of celebrity worship, sex and
        violence obsession, and tabloid ethics. One part profiles tabloid indus-
        try personnel. Regards America's supermarket tabloid irreverence as
        having rescued the nation's journalism industry from apathy and elit-
        ism. Sees a pattern in Britain's cycles of journalistic boldness followed
        by government suppression. Celebrates the genre where "profit, not
        ethics, is the prevailing motivation."

459   Teinowitz, Ira. "Distrust of Media Pervasive." *Advertising Age* (29 May
        1995): 37.
        Reports the result of a survey conducted by the Times Mirror Center
        for the Press and Public which reveals that media's tabloid mentality is
        meeting with public disapproval. Specifically, respondents objected to
        the press's adversarial nature and its emphasis on scandal and sensa-
        tionalism. Survey also compares the views of journalists with those of
        the general public.

460   Toobin, Jeffrey. "Buying Headlines: Journalism and Justice Clash Over
        the Checkbook." *The Quill* November/December 1994: 21-23.
        Discusses checkbook journalism as practiced by the print and televi-
        sion tabloids including possible implications for the O. J. Simpson trial.

461   Tuccille, Jerome. *Rupert Murdoch.* New York: Donald I. Fine, 1989.
        288 pgs.
        Biography which portrays Murdoch as key figure in the modern com-
        munications revolution. Part One, "Press Baron" (pp. 1-105), covers
        Murdoch's practice of sensational journalism in Australia, England, and
        America. Subsequent parts discuss establishment of the Murdoch me-
        dia empire. Appendices detail Murdoch holdings.

462   "2-headed Tots, Nazi Astronauts & Gennifer." *U.S. News & World
        Report* (10 February 1992): 16.
        Distinguishes between the six most popular supermarket tabloids by
        commenting upon the types of stories in which they appear to specialize.

463   Updike, John. "Addressing the Scandal Glut." *The New Yorker.* 17
        January 1994: 92.
        Satirical attempt to handle celebrity scandal overload by either stem-
        ming the sleaze flow or training the consuming public to "guzzle."

464   Upshaw, Jim and John Russial. "See No Evil?" *Columbian Journalism
        Review* January/February 1994: 9-11.

Reports on public reaction to graphic sensational coverage of a mur-
der/suicide by both a Eugene, Oregon newspaper and television station. While the television station received few complaints, the newspaper was bombarded by letters from outraged readers.

465　Vaughan, Donald. "Elvis Reveals: Writers Make Millions Selling to
　　　　Tabloids." *Writer's Digest.* January 1993: 28-30.
　　　Former senior editor for the *National Examiner* advises free-lance writers
　　　on how to get stories published in the tabloids. Covers local newspa-
　　　pers as sources of story ideas; typical pay scale for stories; mastering
　　　"tabloidspeak"; "top-of-head" vs. factual stories; and the overseas tab-
　　　loid market.

466　Waters, John. *Crackpot: The Obsessions of John Waters.* New York:
　　　　Macmillan, 1986. 144 pgs.
　　　Alternative filmmaker comments on American popular culture in a se-
　　　ries of essays featuring his own peculiar preferences and aversions.
　　　Chapter 8, "Why I Love the *National Enquirer*" (pp. 80-87) expresses
　　　admiration for the publication's perversity but finds occasional fault
　　　with its tactics and treatment of subjects. Also discusses the *Weekly
　　　World News.*

467　Weisberg, Jacob. "Rough Trade: The Sad Decline of American
　　　　Publishing." *The New Republic* (17 June 1991): 16-18, 27.
　　　Laments that little real editing (done by "working editors") takes place
　　　anymore in the American publishing business. Instead, high-paid "ac-
　　　quiring editors" scout out the latest blockbuster project which is rushed
　　　into print, oversized and replete with errors. Cites Simon & Schuster's
　　　publication of Kitty Kelly's *Nancy Reagan: The Unauthorized Biogra-
　　　phy* as the outstanding example of declining industry standards. Tab-
　　　loid sensationalism was given priority over accuracy in order to guar-
　　　antee big profits.

468　Welles, Chris. "The Americanization of Rupert Murdoch." *Esquire*
　　　　(22 May 1979): 51-54, 56-59.
　　　Contends that Murdoch's tried-and-true formula for success—out-sen-
　　　sationalizing competitors in Australia and Britain—is failing in America,
　　　where success depends upon appealing to a more sophisticated upscale
　　　audience. Chronicles Murdoch's inability to overtake New York's *Daily
　　　News* despite acquiring the *New York Post,* and converting it to a copy
　　　of his sex-and-sleaze British tabloids. Includes an overview of
　　　Murdoch's earlier career.

469　"Wishing on a *Star*." *Time* (11 February 1974): 83-84.
　　　Reports on the arrival of Rupert Murdoch's supermarket tabloid *Star* at

American newsracks. At first glance, the paper appears to be a toned down version of Murdoch's sleazy Australian and British publications.

470   Wolkimir, Richard. "With Tabloids, 'Zip!' You're in Another World." *Smithsonian* October 1987: 240.
Facetious look at the style and content of "Tabloid World" where the sensational is commonplace.

471   Wyatt, Edward A. "Tabloid Account." *Barron's* (13 June 1994): 17-19.
Reports that Macfadden Holding's and Boston Ventures, the partnership which purchased the *National Enquirer* in 1989, is offering to purchase the 17.9 million Enquirer/Star shares they do not own for $17.50 each. Surveys circulation and advertising problems at the *Enquirer* and *Star* as well as improved net income and cash flow. Stockholders criticize offer as insufficient.

472   Zuckerman, Mortimer B. "Behind the Paula Jones Story." *U.S. News & World Report* (23 May 1994): 82.
Editorializes that the establishment media has reached a new low in its rush to report Paula Jones's improbable sexual harassment charges vs. Bill Clinton. Urges public stand vs. tabloid values.

473   Zuckerman, Mortimer B. "Money for Mischief." *U.S. News & World Report* (10 February 1992): 82.
Editorial by the magazine's editor-in-chief which calls for a zone of privacy beyond which the press should not intrude. Prompted by the journalistic feeding frenzy (led by the tabloid *Star*) which followed Gennifer Flowers's revelations about Bill Clinton.

3

U.S. TELEVISION

GENERAL WORKS

474   Epstein, Edward Jay. *News From Nowhere: Television and the News*.
       New York: Random House, 1973. 321 pgs.
       Seeks to explain how television networks create news. Chapter 3, "The
       Economic Logic" (pp. 78-130), discusses the necessity of capturing
       and maintaining an audience for advertisers. Chapter 5, "The Resur-
       rection of Reality" (pp. 152-180), covers the editorial decisions made
       in the manufacture of news. The importance of sensationalism to ac-
       tion stories (riots, demonstrations, wars) is indicated.

475   Fiske, John. *Reading the Popular*. Boston: Unwin Hyman, 1989. 228 pgs.
       Published simultaneously with *Understanding Popular Culture* (see
       entry #007), this volume is primarily analytical, rather than theoretical
       or political. Analyzed in terms of Fiske's concept of popular culture as
       a creation of a subordinate population in resistance to, or evasion of,
       the dominant are: shopping malls, the beach, video games, rock music,
       and quiz shows. Chapters 7 and 8 "News, History, and Videotaped
       Events" and "Popular News," (pp. 149-197) calls for popularization/
       sensationalization of television news to facilitate communication with
       the mass audience.

476   Fiske, John. *Television Culture*. London: Methuen, 1987. 353 pgs.
       Applies recent Marxist ideology to a cultural analysis of television.
       Viewers exhibit semiotic power by creating their own meanings and
       identities in resistance to the dominant culture conveyed through tele-
       vision. Chapter 13 "Carnival and Style," (pp. 240-264), examines the
       empowering aspects of carnivalesque television such as rock videos,
       wrestling, and commercials. Chapter 15, "News Readings, News Read-

ers," (pp. 281-308), views television news as "masculine soap opera," incapable of imposing a consistent, controlled version of reality upon the audience.

477   Himmelstein, Hal. *Television Myth and the American Mind.* New York: Praeger, 1984. 336 pgs.
Attempts an interpretation of the myths which frame America's television images in order to better understand the society which produces them. Sees Huxley's *Brave New World* as equivalent to "Television Land." Chapter 10, "The TV Talk show," (pp. 279-304), deals with the power of the medium to validate our existence. Offers ideas for an "oppositional television" to effectively counteract the tyranny of television's dominant values.

478   Postman, Neal. *Amusing Ourselves to Death.* New York: Viking, 1985. 163 pgs.
Asserts that Aldous Huxley's *Brave New World* has arrived embodied in our television culture, a passive, amusement-based framework which is not only inferior to a print-based society, but also dangerous to serious thought and discourse. Sees the answer in education which would address the true nature of television and its possible benevolent uses. Anticipates tabloid television and its implications/abuses.

479   Twitchell, James B. *Carnival Culture: The Trashing of Taste in America.* New York: Columbia University Press, 1992. 306 pgs.
Concentrates on the image created by the publishing, motion picture, and television industries. Success depends upon the ability of these industries to produce popular "vulgar" entertainment. The author argues the such "vulgar" or "carnival" culture is deserving of attention because it is so popular. It is also powerful in its simplicity, genuinely democratic and necessary (especially in adolescence). Describes the tabloid television scene indicating how Morton Downey Jr. overstepped current boundaries of taste in his self-destruction.

HISTORICAL OVERVIEW

480   "Anatomy of a TV Bully." *Look* 4 October 1966: M8-M11.
Profile of Joe Pyne, forerunner of tabloid TV talk show hosts, who featured a sensational confrontational style similar to Morton Downey Jr.'s. Includes on-the-air photographs.

481   "Killer Joe." *Time* 29 July 1966: 30.
Profiles Joe Pyne, prototypical tabloid TV talk show host of the 1960's. Describes the host's confrontational interview style which presaged Morton Downey Jr.

MODERN PRACTICE

482   Ailes, Roger. "The Truth About Tabloid TV." *TV Guide* (7 August 1993): 5.
       The author, a tabloid TV consultant, maintains there is no difference
       between tabloid TV and the network news magazine shows: they are
       doing the same stories (reported first by the tabloids), and both pay for
       them (in one way or another). The networks, however, better under-
       stand the importance of employing strong, star personalities on screen.

483   Altheide, David L. *Creating Reality: How TV News Distorts Events.*
          Beverly Hills: Sage Publications, 1974.
       Examines how events become news when reported (and altered) by the
       TV news industry. Chapter 2, "The News Environment" (pp. 29-59),
       discusses the impact of commercialism on news reporting beginning
       with the penny press. Argues that practical considerations dictate adop-
       tion of a news perspective which misrepresents news events. Urges view-
       ers to watch TV newscasts defensively in order to detect distortion.
       Includes a "methodological appendix" which describes the character
       of the author's research.

484   Anderson, Robin. " 'Reality' TV and Criminal Injustice." *The
          Humanist* September/October 1994: 8-13.
       Criticizes "reality TV" as, in fact, debasing reality through employment
       of limited perspective, lack of background, and condensed action. Real-
       ity programs misrepresent and glamorize "the war on drugs" while pre-
       senting urban crime as an incomprehensible phenomenon. Concludes
       that reality TV increases misunderstanding of criminal justice issues.

485   Bishop, Ed. "The Heather Sims Case: Overkill?" *The St. Louis
          Journalism Review* June 1989: 1, 6-7.
       Examines the "pack journalism" phenomena which ensued when an
       Alton, Illinois woman reported the kidnapping of her six-year-old daugh-
       ter by a masked man. Both print and electronic media devoted exten-
       sive amounts of time to the developing story during a two-week period.
       Discusses reasons for such protracted coverage including possible me-
       dia manipulation by the police. A statistical table detailing television
       coverage of the story is provided.

486   Blum, David. "Loud Mouth." *New York* (18 January 1988): 36-41.
       Profiles tabloid TV talk show host Morton Downey Jr. Describes the
       show as neither talk nor debate, but rather a "black-hat, white-hat enter-
       tainment" with Downey as hero. Documents the programs ratings suc-
       cess. Includes a list of claims Downey has made, their relative veracity
       (or lack thereof), and discusses several antagonistic scenarios which
       have taken place in front of the camera with Downey as bully/hero.

487   Bradford, Krista. "The Big Sleaze." *Rolling Stone* (18 February 1993): 39-43, 69.
Relates experiences gathered during five years employment in tabloid television (with *A Current Affair, The Reporters,* and *Now It Can Be Told*). Complains of tabloid TV's essential meanness—people matter little when it comes to getting the story. Charges the genre with racism, homophobia, and misogyny, exacerbated by the pervasiveness of Australians and Fleet Streeters who possess a distorted view of American life which is reflected in their work. Testifies to the corrupting influence of checkbook journalism.

488   Brock, Pope. "Steve Dunleavy." *People Weekly* (7 June 1993): 119-124.
Profile of the senior correspondent for Fox's *A Current Affair*. Details criticism of Dunleavy's professional ethics and penchant for practicing "checkbook journalism."

489   Brown, Merrill and Peter Ainslie. "The Brass at Cap Cities/ABC: Rethinking TV." *Channels* February 1989: 93-95.
Interview with Thomas S. Murphy, (Chairman and CEO of Capital Cities/ABC, Inc.) and Daniel B. Burke and John B. Sias, both of ABC Television Network Group. Murphy believes there is a place for tabloid television, and is satisfied in allowing advertising support to indicate whether the network should air such programs. The network's Standards & Practices Division will continue to operate.

490   Brown, Merrill and J. Max Robbins. "Breaking the Big Three's Stranglehold." *Channels* January 1990: 78-79.
Interview with Av Westin, former executive producer of *20/20*, who left to join King World in order to revamp *Inside Edition*. Backlash vs. oversensationalism was costing the show sponsorship. Also comments on disintegration of network-local relationships.

491   Brown, Rich. "Telemundo Adds Tabloid TV." *Broadcasting & Cable* (20 June 1994): 20, 22.
Reports that Hispanic television network *Telemundo* is adding to its lineup "Alta Tension," a tabloid TV program with comic overtones, and "Occurio Asi de Noche," modeled after "A Current Affair," in an attempt to boost ratings in its competition with Univision and other Hispanic cable networks.

492   Carpignano, Paolo et al. "Chatter in the Age of Electronic Reproduction: Talk Television and the 'Public Mind'" *Social Text* Issue 25/26 (1990): 33-55.
Argues that television talk shows have effectively undermined the news

as a social institution by breaking down the boundaries between producer of cultural products and consumer; authority and audience; expert and layperson. Discusses the changes wrought by television in news reporting, specifically a tendency toward media self-analysis and the process of reporting as conventional group discussion. Views the purpose of the talk show as therapeutic rather than cognitive. Analyzes the "Morton Downey Jr." show in order to illustrate contentions.

493   Chunovic, Louis. "Shake-Up in the Newsroom." *American Film* May 1991: 64.
       Describes and comments upon the manner in which "tabloid sensitivity" changed television news in the 1980's. Blames competition and deregulation for the rise of "infotainment."

494   Coe, Steve. "Networks Serve Up Heavy Dose of Reality." *Broadcasting & Cable* (12 April 1993): 26, 30.
       Observes that despite predictions to the contrary, reality programming's popularity continues. Discusses the ratings of specific programs with various age groups. Includes new shows being developed.

495   Collins, Monica. "Extra! Extra! Tabloid Clones Invade TV." *TV Guide* (18 November 1989): 14-16.
       Describes profusion of tabloid-style newsmagazine shows on television, and their effect on the more established, respectable representatives of the genre.

496   Collum, Danny Duncan. "Davenport Tonight—The Couch, Not the Town." *Sojourners* December 1992: 40.
       Nominates "Entertainment Tonight" as the ultimate infotainment program because "it presents information about entertainment as entertainment." Maintains that "Entertainment Tonight" more accurately reflects American life today than do the more conventional news programs, because its celebrity focus portrays life as most Americans would live it if they could. Its voyeuristic perspective also agrees with viewers "couch-potato" existence. Includes discussion of popular culture defining the language of politics.

497   Collum, Danny Duncan. "The Slippery Road from Edward R. Murrow to Tabloid TV." *National Catholic Reporter* (14 February 1992): 22.
       Bemoans the decline of television journalism as evidenced in the news division of CBS: the broadcasting giant that pioneered news with Edward R. Murrow now features segments on Bill Clinton's sex life (carried by "60 Minutes" on Super Bowl Sunday). A survey of other networks' offerings uncovers occasional gems among the slag.

498   Corelli, Rae and William Lowther. "Packaging the News." *Maclean's*
        (30 October 1989): 82-83.
        Expresses concern over television newscasts adopting questionable tech-
        niques to attract viewers: sensational subject matter; emphasis on star
        value of host rather than news content; and careless use of reenactments.

499   Corso, P. J. "Fact or Fiction?: Only Your TV Network Knows." *USA
        Today* November 1992: 82-84.
        Complains that tabloid-type reality shows blur the line between fact
        and fiction to the point where it is impossible for the viewer to distin-
        guish between the two. Dramatic reenactments or simulations should
        be clearly labelled as such. This type format is inexpensive to produce
        and popular with viewers, but should not be employed in order to pro-
        mote deception.

500   Douglas, Susan. "The Erasure of Revolt." *The Progressive* May 1995: 17.
        Views the O.J.-ification of television news as not merely the triumph of
        sensationalism over substance, but also as a deliberate attempt to ig-
        nore the increasing number of diverse protests occurring in response to
        the Republican "Contract With America."

501   Ehrlich, Mathew C. "The Ethical Dilemma of Television News Sweeps."
        Journal of Mass Media Ethics 10 (1995): 37-38.
        Discusses study which compared the manner in which two local news-
        rooms handled news reporting during sweeps week. The larger news-
        room, under heavy competitive pressure, produced a "sleaze series"
        aimed at attracting viewers with its sensationalism, while the smaller
        newsroom, not seriously challenged by competitors, featured an in-depth
        look at a substantive social issue (single-parent households). Concludes
        that socially responsible, ethical news reporting is difficult in an indus-
        try which is strongly driven by profit.

502   Elm, Joanna. "What Shows Featured These 10 Topics? Geraldo? Oprah?"
        TV Guide (3 February 1990): 24-25.
        Local news programs across the nation telecast scurrilous news fea-
        tures worthy of tabloid talk TV in order to capture audiences during
        ratings "sweeps week."

503   "Farewell Trash, Goodbye, Neilsens." *U.S. News & World Report* (15
        May 1989): 14, 16.
        Reports that the networks are moderating their programs' sensational
        content in order to prevent loss of sponsorship. Predicts that, should
        ratings remain high for tabloid-type TV, both networks and sponsors
        will continue to offer such programming.

504   Fox, Thomas C. "Inside NCR." *National Catholic Reporter* 19 April 1991: 2.
Editorial which criticizes television's preoccupation with the sensational
aspects of sin at the expense of humane and spiritual issues. (The ratings bonanza reaped by ABC's televised exorcism on "20/20" prompted
these comments.)

505   Freeman, Mike. "The Economics of First-Run Reality." *Broadcasting
& Cable* (12 April 1993): 34-37.
Reports that tabloid-type news magazine television programs are beginning to decline in popularity. Reality-based cops and robber shows
appear to be capturing the news magazine audience. Discusses the con-
tinuing success of "Entertainment Tonight" due to its "advertiser-
friendly" appeal. Includes projected reality programming aimed at daytime viewers, and preview of "Crusaders," a new, weekly, syndicated
reality show.

506   Freeman, Mike. "Ratings Are Reality for Off-Net." *Broadcasting &
Cable* (12 April 1993): 30, 32.
Reports on success of reality television programs such as "Cops" and
"Rescue 911" in syndication. Such shows are being inserted in time
slots that challenge traditional prime time access rules, which may
prompt the FCC to act.

507   Freeman, Mike. "Tabloid Tip Sheet Has the Fax." *Broadcasting & Cable*
(12 April 1993): 40.
Reports on establishment of Industry Research & Development, a new
business which serves as a clearinghouse for hard-to-find tabloid-type
stories of the violent and bizarre. Subscribers pay $500 monthly for the
company's faxed "tip sheet." The company was started by Tom Colbert,
former story director on "Hard Copy."

508   Freeman, Mike. "Time Warner Leaps Into Reality." *Broadcasting* (20
July 1992): 16-17.
Reports that Time Warner has hired King World Production's Av Westin
to help transform Time Inc.'s magazine properties into reality-based
television programming.

509   Gay, Verne. "The TV Magazine Glut." *Mediaweek* (8 March 1993): 14.
Reports that primetime newsmagazine programs are proliferating on
television, spelling trouble for advertisers who prefer well-defined entertainment shows. Increasingly, the newsmagazines go in for "reality"
format and tabloid-type topics with which advertisers do not like to be
associated. It is also believed that viewers are less relaxed watching
newsmagazines and, therefore, less receptive to commercials.

510   Glynn, Kevin. "Tabloid Television's Transgressive Aesthetic: 'A Current Affair' and the 'Shows That Taste Forgot.'" *Wide Angle: A Film Quarterly of Theory, Criticism, and Practice.* April 1990: 22-44. Rejects analysis depicting tabloid TV as either a degenerate form of high culture or the capitalist's method of controlling the masses. Prefers instead Mikhail Bakhtin's and John Fiske's views of carnival/tabloid culture as offering escape from the officially-sanctioned societal norms. Includes discussion of the ambiguity, subjectivity, and contradictions of tabloid television news.

511   Goode, Erica and Katia Hetter. "The Selling of Reality." *U.S. News & World Report* (25 July 1994): 49-56. Asserts that tabloid television has helped turn reality into a commodity. News becomes entertainment in "reality television." The process is described as: real news—>talk shows—>tabloid shows and news-magazines—>movie of the week. Also discusses how television technicians create their own version of reality for viewers.

512   Gorney, Carole. "Numbers Versus Pictures: Did Network Television Sensationalize Chernobyl Coverage?" *Journalism Quarterly* 69 (1992): 455-465. Reports results of study examining television news coverage of the Chernobyl Nuclear accident. Concludes that some sensationalism was present in the verbal reports, although visuals were largely innocuous. Includes statistical tables.

513   Graham, Fred. *Happy Talk: Confessions of a TV Newsman.* New York: W.W. Norton & Company, 1990. 352 pgs. Discusses the position occupied by the news division in television from respectable loss leader on CBS in Eric Sevareid's day, to profitable entertainment today. Chapter 10, "Infotainment," (pp. 206-237), describes the impact of the phenomenon at CBS, 1981-'86.

514   Haley, Kathy. "Boston Faces Reality." *Channels* February 1989: 86-87. Surveys the 7:30 pm TV competition in Boston as newsmagazines adopt sensationalism in order to boost ratings.

515   Harmon, Mark D. "Mr. Gates Goes Electronic: The What and Why Questions in Local TV News." *Journalism Quarterly* 66 (1989): 857-863. Asserts that charges of sensationalism levelled at local TV news are overstated. Sensational stories comprise a distinct minority of local news reported and much of it is limited to sweeps weeks.

516   Hickey, Neil, Ileane Rudolph, and Ty Holland. "Simpson Saga Continues; Media Coverage Takes Knocks." *TV Guide* 9 July 1994: 33.

Surveys criticism of media circus surrounding the O.J. Simpson case. Included: paying potential witnesses for stories; reporting rumors; airing 911 tapes.

517 Hofstetter, C. Richard and David M. Dozier. "Useful News, Sensational News: Quality, Sensationalism, and Local TV News." *Journalism Quarterly* 63 (1986): 815-820, 853.
Reports on study which reveals that local television newscasts in Houston, though rather sensational, contain important information on events, issues, and problems. In addition, it is maintained that political fringe groups are better informed by sensational—rather than non-sensational—newscasts.

518 Hynes, James. "That's Infotainment!" *Mother Jones* November 1986: 59.
Defends tabloid TV program, "Entertainment Tonight," as a benign celebrity newsmagazine that does a respectable job of reporting, and refuses to trade in gossip. Compares the show to *Life* or *Look* magazines of the 1950's as opposed to today's *People*. Cites Walter Cronkite's praise of the program.

519 Jacobs, Jerry. *Changing Channels: Issues and Realities in Television News.* Mountain View, California: Mayfield Publishing, 1990. 165 pgs.
A portrait of the broadcast news industry aimed at the college journalism student. Chapter 5, "The Buck Starts Here" (pp. 62-79), discusses the commercialization of TV news which has caused some stations to operate by the formula "sensationalism = viewers = ratings = profits." Chapter 6, "The News Meddlers" (pp. 80-88), addresses the implications of commercialization run rampant resulting in "ersatz news," or tabloid TV.

520 Jenish, D'Arcy. "Cashing in on Tragedy." *Maclean's* (8 November 1993): 48.
"A Current Affair" tabloid television show has aired a segment on the murder of two teenagers in Ontario. Some Canadian homes received the show via satellite dish despite a publication ban imposed by a Canadian judge in order to insure a fair trial for the defendant.

521 Kanner, Bernice. "Testing, 1-2-3." *New York* (21 September 1992): 22-24.
Warner-Lambert's early pregnancy test television ads are characterized as "tabloid" advertising because they employ real people in dramatic real-life events, turning the audience into voyeurs. The J. Walter Thompson ad agency feels it has captured genuine "drama and humanity." Critics claim the ads are exploitative and embarrassing.

522 Katz, Jon. "Rock, Rap, and Movies Bring You the News." *Rolling Stone* 5 March 1992: 33, 36, 37, 40, 78.

Charges that "Old News," as produced by the establishment journalists is archaic and dying. The "New News," which accurately reflects our current culture, is a combination of youth-oriented music, film, and tabloid media. Hails tabloid news telecasts for employing dramatic re-enactments which interpret compelling social issues in a manner which speaks realistically to viewers.

523   Katz, Richard. "Turmoil Touting Tabloid TV." *Channels* July/August 1989: 66-67.
Discusses ethical problems raised by decisions concerning when and where to run on-air promotions for tabloid television shows, whose sensational topics are offensive to some viewers. Several television station executives are interviewed.

524   Keillor, Garrison. "The Chuck Show." *The New Yorker* (24 July 1989): 26-29.
Humorous piece about a serious local talk show host trying to hold out against the network's sensational competition.

525   Keller, Teresa. "Trash TV." *Journal of Popular Culture* Spring 1993 195-205.
Defines and surveys the world of "trash TV," arguing in the end against censorship. Identifies the characteristics of the genre as: sexual and/or violent content; confusion of news and entertainment; sensational language; melodramatic music; and recreations.

526   Klein, Joe. "Tabloid Government." *New York* 28 October 1991: 28-31.
Finds the Clarence Thomas confirmation hearings to be a disgraceful proceeding, the product of political cynicism and tabloid sensationalism. Only public outrage would put an end to the type of political spectacle which developed surrounding Anita Hill's charge of sexual harassment, but the American public appears too much influenced by tabloid television to demand such a change.

527   Knight, Graham. "Reality Effects: Tabloid Television News." *Queen's Quarterly* 96 (1989): 94-107.
Addresses the changes wrought by tabloid television news in the distinction between reality and representation, with the latter overwhelming the former in a barrage of images and words. Traces the emergence of TV tabloid news from the 1970's with the accompanying technological advances (i.e. videotape). Discusses factors which identify the genre: condensation of the perceived essential characteristics of the subject; hyperactivity; hyperrealism; and populism.

528   Konner, Joan. "The Press is AWOL." *Columbia Journalism Review*
         March/April 1995: 4.
         Excerpts the remarks of Bernard Kalb who addressed an awards ban-
         quet at Columbia University's Graduate School of Journalism, 26 Janu-
         ary 1995. Condemns "the dance with trash" with which television news
         is engaged. Sees dire consequences for our democracy if the public con-
         tinues to be ill-informed. Expresses pessimism concerning the future.

529   Kurtz, Howard. "The Tabloid Style." *American Journalism Review*
         September 1993: 26-27.
         Criticizes tabloid television newscasts as inflammatory and fear-pro-
         voking, lacking any attempt at understanding the nature of our violent
         culture.

530   Kurtz, Paul. "Media Messiahs, Psychic Saviors, and Space Gurus." *The
         Humanist* January/February 1978: 4-5.
         The Editor-in Chief of *The Humorist* repeats complaints his publica-
         tion has voiced concerning unsubstantiated, sensational television pro-
         grams which treat "paranormal" encounters as facts (see entry #563).
         The article concludes with a transcript of an official complaint lodged
         with the Federal Communication Commission calling for balanced treat-
         ment of the "psychic phenomena" issue.

531   Lane, Randall. "The Dean of Tabloid TV." *Forbes* 28 February 1994:
         100-101.
         Details the career of Edmund Ansin, owner of WSVN in Miami, Fla.,
         an affiliate of Rupert Murdoch's Fox network. The TV station provides
         seven hours of tabloid-type local news per day and reaps high profits.

532   Leerhsen, Charles. "Sex, Death, Drugs, and Geraldo." *Newsweek* 14
         November 1989: 76.
         Profile of "reality television" practitioner, Geraldo Rivera.

533   Leo, John. "All The News Fit to Script." *U.S. News & World Report*
         (4 May 1992): 26.
         Takes issue with *Rolling Stone* media critic Jon Katz who proclaimed
         "Old News"—balanced, objective, fact-oriented—dead, replaced by
         "New News"—a combination of Hollywood, music, pop art, and tab-
         loid telecasts (see entry #522). Maintains that Katz accurately identi-
         fies the entertainment-oriented trend in current news reporting, but ig-
         nores the fact that some important concepts (the budget deficit or in-
         flation rate) must be understood even though they don't lend them-
         selves to an entertaining portrayal.

534   Lesher, Stephen. *Media Unbound: The Impact of Television Journalism on the Public.* Boston: Houghton Mifflin, 1982. 285 pgs.
Argues that the often erroneous reports of television journalists are afforded too much respect and credibility. Chapter 3, "A Sensational Story" (pp. 22-39), discusses why television journalism rewards the sensational. Chapter 10, "Reality Competitive With Make-Believe" (pp. 140-164), examines the docudrama and anticipates reality TV of the 1990's.

535   Lewis, Robert. "Tabloid Journalism?" *Maclean's* (24 January 1994): 2.
Philosophizes about the wisdom of giving the viewing public what they want, an issue raised by recent television coverage of the Harding/Kerrigan conflict and the trial of Lorena Bobbit. Included: the media's motives, and differences in tabloid availability in the U.S. and Canada.

536   Maio, Kathi. "Hooked on Hate?" *Ms.* September/October 1990: 42-44.
Maintains that tabloid television programs contribute to our culture's misogynist exploitation of women by focusing on rapes and murders in a salacious manner, and labelling such coverage "victim advocacy."

537   Marchiano, Sam. "My Life in Tabloid TV." *Cosmopolitan* February 1994: 74+.
Concentrates on the education of a young journalist who worked behind the scenes for the tabloid television show "Inside Edition." Several "war stories" are recounted.

538   Marin, Rick. "Miami's Crime Time Live." *Newsweek* (20 June 1994): 71-72.
Reports on lurid, all-news TV station in Miami, Fla., WSVN. Characterized as "CNN Meets 'Hard Copy,'" nine Florida hotels have screened out the station's signal because of its tabloid sensationalism. Includes chart highlighting typical WSVN news day.

539   McClellan, Steve. "Local TV News Directors Grapple With Smaller Budgets, Changes in Compensation, Tabloid TV." *Broadcasting* 21 September 1992: 50, 54-55.
Reports concern among affiliates that Rupert Murdoch will force Fox television news to adopt a totally tabloid format. In addition, the big three network affiliates in New York have been accused of trying to out-sensationalize each other. Down-sizing of news divisions results in greater sensationalized reporting because such coverage is quick and cheap.

540   McClellan, Steve. "Tabloids Pull Out the Checkbook Proudly." *Broadcasting & Cable* (9 May 1994): 42.
Tabloid television shows maintain that use of checkbook journalism is

a competitive necessity and cite standards dictating when it should be used. Discusses use of similar tactics by network news shows. Disclosure of such practices enables viewers to properly evaluate the information they receive.

541   McClellan, Steve. "What is Reality? The Thin and Blurring Line." *Broadcasting & Cable* 12 April 1993: 37-38.
Discusses the difficulty in defining the nature of reality programming. Complains that reality shows see themselves as news programs but prefer to be governed by entertainment guidelines thereby avoiding any responsibility to serve the public. Remarks on the pervasiveness of made-for-television-movie personnel at the scene of breaking news stories.

542   McDonell, Rafael Charles. "A Survey on Student Uses and Attitudes Toward Broadcast Television News and 'Tabloid' Television." Master's Thesis, University of North Texas, 1990, 81 pgs.
Reports the results of a survey of three hundred students at the University of North Texas which concluded that tabloid television programs were not major informational sources for college students in the spring of 1989, despite the popularity of such shows with the general viewing public during the 1988-89 season. Includes statistical tables and appendices.

543   Meeks, Fleming. "The Price of Cheap Eyeballs." *Forbes* 20 March 1989: 188-189.
Claims that advertisers who avoid supermarket tabloids are less reluctant to associate themselves with tabloid television programs. Several of the larger corporations (Campbell Soup, McDonald's, Proctor & Gamble, and Kellogg's, e.g.), however, have demurred, citing their desire to maintain a family-oriented image. There are not enough available advertisers to support all the shows planned for the upcoming season.

544   Menglekoch, Louise. "When Checkbook Journalism Does God's Work." *Columbia Journalism Review* November/December 1994: 35-38.
Defends tabloid television—specifically the Sally Jesse Raphael, Phil Donahue, and Hard Copy programs—for publicizing a Minnesota rape/murder incident which was mishandled by the local authorities and journalists. Tabloid TV allowed all sides to be heard and provided payments ("checkbook journalism") which enabled one defendant to obtain competent legal representation. Demonstrates that the tabloids can play a positive role in championing the oppressed and comforting the afflicted if such victims are in possession of a sensational story which the shows can use.

545   Miller, Annetta. "The Odd Couple of Sensationalism." *Newsweek* (14
        November 1988): 74-75.
        Describes popular new tabloid TV programs hosted by Maury Povitch
        and Morton Downey Jr.

546   "Movie of the Week." *Entertainment Weekly* (28 January 1994): 7.
        Humorous *TV Guide*-type entry satirizes the rush to turn sensational
        news stories into television movies, in this case "Tragedy on Ice: The
        Nancy Kerrigan Story."

547   Mundy, Alicia. "Victim of 'Exposé'—Chuck Robb or NBC News?"
        Washington Journalism Review July/August 1991: 28-33.
        Claims that "tabloid journalism is a two-edged sword" which injured
        the reporter, NBC News, as well as the subject, Virginia senator Chuck
        Robb. Traces the history of the Robb scandal story, and the ethical
        decisions involved.

548   Nelson, Scott A. "Crime-Time Television." *FBI Law Enforcement
        Bulletin* August 1989: 1-9.
        Assesses pros and cons of law enforcement involvement with reality-
        based crime shows. Advantages of such involvement include apprehen-
        sion of fugitives, encouraging citizen involvement with police, and
        building a partnership between law enforcement and media. Disadvan-
        tages: pretrial publicity jeopardizes court cases; sensationalist TV crime
        depictions detract from public credibility; vigilantism, and copycat
        crimes are encouraged.

549   Paternostro, Silvana. "News Caliente: Tabloid TV With a Latin
        Accent." *Columbia Journalism Review* May/June 1993: 11, 14.
        Reports on the popularity of Latin tabloid television newsmagazine
        programs, Univisión's "Noticias y Más" and Telemundo's "Ocurrió Asi"
        which reach 24 million U.S. Hispanics. Includes criticism received re-
        garding taped coverage of violent episodes.

550   Postman, Neil and Steve Powers. *How to Watch TV News.* New York:
        Penguin Books, 1992. 178 pgs.
        Seeks to explain the sensationalization of television news in terms of
        advertising's interest in the medium. Chapter 2, "What is the News?"
        (pp. 11-25), raises questions and proposes possible answers regarding
        why sensational tragedies dominate the news at the expense of creative
        events. Chapter 10, "Television in the Courtroom" (pp. 129-143), voices
        reservations concerning televising trials, because by focusing on the
        sensational our legal system is trivialized.

551   Prato, Lou. "Don't Bash Consultants for Tabloid TV News." *American Journalism Review* November 1993: 44.
Contends that consultants often blamed for converting local TV newscasts to tabloid format, are not responsible for such a change. Consultants claim: while many local newscasts are tabloid in style, few contain real tabloid content; viewers confuse tabloid-style local news with real tabloid newsmagazines; and there isn't great audience potential for hardcore tabloid news programming. Includes discussion of WSVN's tabloid news programming in Miami.

552   Randall, Stephen. "Understanding the TV Newsmagazine Without a TV Set." *Playboy* June 1993: 35.
Asks and answers sixteen questions regarding TV newsmagazines. Issues addressed: the correct newsmagazine for each demographic group; the relationship between newsmagazines and made-for-TV movies; the use of "experts"; "newsmag" power; and the difference between newsmagazines and the more conventional variety.

553   Range, Peter Ross. "Walter Cronkite is Mad as Hell." *TV Guide* (11 July 1992): 15-18.
Interview with pioneer television news anchorman. Cronkite condemns tabloid television shows as serving no public function. He regrets that political campaigns are now run by Madison Avenue and the spin doctors. Revelations concerning a politician's personal life are appropriate but should not be belabored. Calls for more formal debates and lengthier, more sober analysis of politicians' stands on the issues.

554   Raphael, Chad. "The Political Economy of Reali-TV." Paper presented to Radio-TV Journalism Division of the Association for Education in Journalism and Mass Communication, Montreal, 1992.
Argues that "Reali-TV" (reality-based television which includes tabloid TV programming) emerged as a direct response to rising production costs and fragmented audience shares faced by television networks in the 1980's. Suggests that the genre itself is not innovative, but rather a format shared by global media corporations who have produced similar programs in Europe and Japan. Discusses finance and syndication rule changes enacted by the FCC in 1970 and their implications.

555   Rapping, Elayne. "Tabloid TV and Social Reality." *The Progressive* August 1992: 35-37.
Sees both "reality" and tabloid type news programs as promulgating elements of fascist ideology. Both present the world as degenerate, corrupt, and out-of-control, crying for law and order. Interspersing stories

of scandals involving society's leaders (the Kennedy's e.g.) among tales of the outright sociopathic and bizarre, tabloid programs (such as "Hard Copy" and "Inside Edition") effectively undermine whatever idealism citizens may retain in our society. Believes that such corrosive influences may be responsible for the type of decision we witnessed in the Rodney King trials.

556   Reddicliffe, Steven. "Shock Therapy." *American Film* June 1988: 17-19. Reviews Morton Downey Jr.'s confrontational talk show, drawing parallels with Joe Pyne's program of the 1960's. Discusses how the program was conceived, provides examples of guest abuse, and hypothesizes about the nature of G. Gordon Liddy's upcoming talk show. Concludes that the show's high decibel level precludes the transmission of much information.

557   Relin, David Oliver. "Trash TV: News or Noise?" *Scholastic Update* (8 September 1989): 23-24.
Surveys the world of "infotainment" television, focusing on how sensationalism hooks viewers; the pressure on intelligent talk shows (like Donahue) to compete with the outrageous (like Morton Downey Jr.); and the debate over whether tabloid TV performs any public service.

558   Robins, J. Max. "Here Come the News Punks." *Channels* September 1988: 39.
Emphasizes the positive aspects of tabloid "confrontainment" TV news programs—they break new stories, inform viewers, and increase awareness of political and social issues. Discusses reasons for the genre's success, particularly its appeal to viewers' sense of righteous indignation and taste for salaciousness. Explains that the shows are produced as if they were reporting events. Includes comments from producers, directors, network executives and media critics.

559   Robinson, Kathryn. "Trash is Good For You." *Glamour* May 1989: 133. Extols the value of junk food and tabloid TV as a temporary release from an overorganized life in the fast lane.

560   Rose, Frank. "Celebrity Victims: Crime Casualties Are Turning Into Stars on Tabloid TV." *New York* (31 July 1989): 38-44.
Chronicles the transformation of the manner in which society perceives crime victims: from loser to celebrity. Theorizes that higher crime rates in recent years enable the public to more strongly identify with the victim. Tabloid TV, thriving on viewers voyeuristic identification with the victims of sensational crimes, has both benefitted from and helped publicize the victims' rights movement.

561   Ryu, Jung S. "Public Affairs and Sensationalism in Local TV News
           Programs." *Journalism Quarterly* 59 (1982); 74-78, 137.
       Reports on a study which analyzed local television newscasts in 1976,
       '78, and '80 in order to determine the extent of sensational content.
       Concludes that sensational stories serve to maintain high ratings; are
       easy to obtain; appeal to immediate concerns of the audience; and do
       not offend any political powers. Includes statistical tables.

562   Sanders, Ernest. "A TV Tabloid Vows to Clean Up Its Act." *American
           Journalism Review* May 1994: 15.
       Reports that "Hard Copy" has broadened its coverage to include more
       mainstream news stories (earthquakes and wildfires, e.g.) along with
       celebrity scandals which usually dominate their programming schedule.

563   Scheaffer, Robert. "In Search of Media Fairness." *The Humanist*
           September/October 1977: 45-48.
       Charges that television coverage of the "paranormal" ranks with the
       supermarket tabloids in its catering to sensationalism. Fantastic claims
       are given credibility while scientific rebuttal is virtually absent. NBC-
       TV coverage is considered particularly offensive. Strategies for deal-
       ing with the problem: speak out; enlist responsible, sympathetic me-
       dia; and embarrass sensational media with the facts.

564   Sholle, David. "Buy Our News: Tabloid Television and Commodificat-
           ion." *Journal of Communication Inquiry* Winter 1993: 56-72.
       Examines tabloid TV "reality" shows (i.e. "A Current Affair,"
       "Hard Copy," and "Inside Edition") as examples of the complete
       commodification of television. Tabloid techniques serve to position the
       viewer as a consumer who is seduced into new methods of gratification.
       In the process, attachment to reality is damaged. Observes also that na-
       tional television news is evolving in a similar, if less extreme, manner.

565   Stein, Harry. "Does TV Sensationalize Debate on Homosexuality?" *TV
           Guide* (6-12 February 1993): 45.
       Asserts that TV sensationalizes extreme positions while ignoring the
       broad middle ground when covering debates on controversial issues.
       Even this policy, however, represents progress when compared to past
       practice which refused to acknowledge controversy.

566   Stein, M. L. "O.J. Media Circus Threatens Trial Access." *The Editor
           and Publisher* (27 May 1995): 16, 36.
       Reports the comments of Gerald F. Uelmen, former dean of Santa Clara
       University Law School, in a speech before a combined Conference of
       the California Society of Newspaper Editors and the Associated Press

News Executives council. Uelmen complains the "tabloidization" of the Simpson trial argues against future television coverage of such courtroom dramas.

567   "Tabloid Reality." *The Nation* 248 (1989): 3-4.
Editorializes that television is bringing us a series of trials (Jean Harris, John Hinckley, Bernhard Goetz, Joel Steinberg/Hedda Nussbaum) which reduces social issues to personal tragedy. Such representations do not encourage explanation or understanding of social behaviors which, in milder form, may be common to many citizens. Instead, transgressors are depicted as inexplicably evil pariahs, worthy only of condemnation. There is little to distinguish between tabloid fiction and televised trials.

568   "Tabloid TV." *Rolling Stone* (15-29 December 1988): 68.
Reports on the popularity of the new sensational "TV vérité"—tabloid talk and news programs. Producers claim they are merely satisfying viewer demand, but the fact that such shows are significantly cheaper to produce than ones with scripts and actors, also makes them attractive.

569   Tharp, Mike and Betsy Streisand. "Tabloid TV's Blood Lust." *U.S. News & World Report* (25 July 1994): 47-48.
Reports on the excesses of tabloid television and their effect on mainstream news coverage: the tabloid's checkbook journalism monopolizes key sources, leaving the networks to report unsubstantiated rumors; the use of dramatizations convey a distorted picture of news events; and the sleaze is driving out serious news. Some evidence of anti-tabloid backlash is cited.

570   "This Is What You Thought: 80% Think TV Has Become Too Trashy." *Glamour* May 1989: 179.
Results of reader poll reported.

571   Toepfer, Susan. "Critics Say His Mouth Needs Washing, But Morton Downey's Talk Show is a Screaming Hit." *People Weekly* (11 April 1988): 33-34, 39.
Profiles Morton Downey, Jr., host of his own popular tabloid TV talk show. Describes Downey's abusively confrontational attitude toward his guests, but focuses on his difficult childhood, especially the strained relationship with his father.

572   Trow, George W. S. "Eyes On." *The New Yorker* 8 June 1992: 32-33.
Satirical look at a scandal-hungry tabloid TV newsmagazine.

573   Viles, Peter. "News Execs Grumble About Tabloid TV." *Broadcasting*

& *Cable* 27 September 1993: 42-43.
Reports that broadcast news executives find fault with tabloid news-magazine programs' sensationalism which blurs the information/entertainment line and damages the credibility of journalists. They praise, however, tabloid TV's technical innovations (bold graphics, increased use of music, e.g.) which render telecasts more visually compelling.

574   Waters, Harry F. "Trash TV." *Newsweek* (14 November 1988): 72-78.
Sees tabloid TV as a desperate survival tactic by an industry which has lost viewers to cable and home video. Notes that the "tabloid virus" has spread from syndicated programming to the networks as ratings have risen. Concern is voiced over the lowering of journalistic standards in television news. Explanations for the tabloid trend: new breed of ratings-chasing managers, and local affiliates abandoning network standards.

575   Weiss, Philip. "Bad Rap For TV Tabs." *Columbia Journalism Review* May/June 1989: 38-42.
Finds virtue in tabloid television: features the "democracy of video;" the segments are daring, taking chances; and they don't take themselves too seriously. Considers the information vs. entertainment debate artificial and tiresome. Detects class bias in some of the criticism of tabloid TV (whose subjects tend to be middle or lower-middle class).

576   "What Is Truth?" *The Economist* (14 October 1989): 106-107.
Reports on American television's recent trends in news programming: simulations, anchors who are media stars, and sensationalism. Complains about the decline in hard news, blurred distinction between news and entertainment, and control of the news industry by conglomerates interested too much "in the bottom line"—cost.

577   Wilson, Mike. "Rock'em, Sock'em: Punchy, Action-Packed News With a Miami Beat." *The Quill* March 1994: 33-35.
Discusses WSVN-TV in Miami which offers viewers all-day, sensational news coverage in "Entertainment Tonight", tabloid TV fashion.

578   Zoglin, Richard. "The Fact-To-Film Frenzy." *Time* (29 March 1993): 56-57.
Describes and comments upon the rush to transform sensational news stories into television movies. An executive involved in the production of such movies attributes their profusion to the success of features which have appeared on the tabloid television news shows "Hard Copy" and "Inside Edition."

579   Zoglin, Richard. "TV News Goes Hollywood." *Time* (9 October 1989): 98.

Maintains that news suffers when reenactments blur the line between information and entertainment. Viewers become disoriented and confused when journalists depart from their duty—conveying reality.

580   Zoglin, Richard. "Easing The Sleaze." *Time* (6 December 1993): 72-74. Discusses how tabloid TV and mainstream television shows are beginning to resemble each other. Tabloid shows are down-playing sensationalism in order to attract advertisers (who are, ordinarily, reluctant to be associated with less than respectable news coverage), while mainstream news telecasts increasingly cover the sensational. The practice of paying informants for news stories is also explored.

581   Zoglin, Richard. "Fact vs. Fiction on 'Reality TV'." *Time* (16 May 1988): 97. Observes that fact and fiction are becoming increasingly difficult to distinguish on "reality TV" which employs reenactments and uses actual witnesses and victims in its recreations.

582   Zoglin, Richard. "The Pit Bull of Talk-Show Hosts." *Time* (4 January 1988): 76.
Discusses the success of "The Morton Downey Jr. Show" and the bullying tactics of its host. Includes anecdotes of irate guests, (one of whom is suing the host for assault) vigilante studio audiences, and Downey's eclectic career history.

583   Zoglin, Richard. "A Walk on the Seamy Side." *Time* (31 October 1988): 78. Considers tabloid television a natural alternative to traditional newscasts, yet fears that increased ratings may plunge television too deeply into such fare. Traditional newsmagazines support stories with evidence, while the tabloids depend primarily on sensational innuendo.

4

LEGAL IMPLICATIONS

HISTORICAL OVERVIEW

584   Barron, James H. "Warren and Brandeis, 'The Right to Privacy', 4 Harv. L. Rev. 193 (1890): Demystifying a Landmark Citation." *Suffolk University Law Review* 13 (1979): 875-922.

Contends that Warren and Brandeis possessed narrow views of what was newsworthy due to their elitist positions in society as well as their affiliation with the moralistic Mugwump movement. As a result, their subsequent creation of the privacy tort (see entry #606) stands on a weak foundation and is of little use in dealing with privacy problems. Sees Warren, Brandeis and fellow Mugwump, journalist E. L. Godkin as oversensitive and hostile to the new, yellow journalism.

585   "Cat-O'-Nine-Tale." *Time* (8 August 1955): 66.

Reports that *Confidential* magazine has sued United Feature Syndicate columnist Inez Robb for her printed attack on the publication's scandalous exposées and the people who read such stories. Includes excerpts from Robb's article.

586   "*Confidential* Clean-Up?" *Newsweek* (25 November 1957): 81.

Reports that *Confidential* magazine has published its intention to eliminate exposé stories from its publication, satisfying requirements of a compromise negotiated with the California attorney general's office. In return, libel charges were dropped.

587   "*Confidential* vs. the U.S." *Newsweek* (19 September 1955): 96.

Reports that *Confidential* publisher Robert Harrison has sued to prevent the Postmaster General from barring the January 1956 issue of the exposé publication from the mail.

588   *"Confidential* Revisited." *Time* (18 March 1957): 74.
Reports that *Confidential* magazine was named in a six-count indictment for publishing an article which specified how abortions may be induced.

589   *"Confidential* Wins a Round." Time (17 October 1955): 91.
Reports that federal court lifted a post office ban against *Confidential* magazine, explaining that the Postmaster must bring evidence of obscenity to court in order to obtain a temporary injunction. *Confidential* was instructed to turn over next issue to postal authorities for inspection.

590   Ernst, Morris L. "Don't Write That." In Ernst, Morris L. *The Best is Yet...* 229-233. New York: Harper & Brothers, 1945.
Advocates retraction, rather than libel suits, as the proper method for redressing journalistic excesses.

591   Ernst, Morris L. "Don't Write That." In Ernst, Morris L. *The Best is Yet...* pp. 226-229. New York: Harper & Brothers, 1945.
Takes issue with the Warren and Brandeis strict protection of privacy doctrine enunciated in their Harvard Law Review article (see entry # 606). Such handcuffing of journalism would prevent the proper recording of an era's social history. Let tradition, not government, set limits on what may be written.

592   "The 'Exhausting' Juror." *Newsweek* (14 October 1957): 74.
Reports that the libel trial of *Confidential* magazine ended in a hung jury (8-4 in favor of conviction). Includes information on one reportedly obstreperous juror.

593   Glancy, Dorothy J. "The Invention of the Right to Privacy." *Arizona Law Review* 21 (1979): 1-39.
Interprets the Warren and Brandeis doctrine of right to privacy (see entry #606) as a practical formula for the individual achievement of natural respect. Credits E. L. Godkin's article concerning "newspaperization," or aggressive "yellow press" reporting, in *Scribner's Magazine* (see entry #073) with influencing Warren and Brandeis who argued for legal intervention only when private facts about a person were publicized against the individual's will, and when such publication was extraordinarily indecent. Also discusses limitations to right of privacy as envisioned by Warren and Brandeis.

594   "Gutterdammerung?" *Time* (11 March 1957): 67.
Reports on hearings held by a California state senate investigating committee aimed at preventing individuals from obtaining and selling scandalous information to exposé magazines such as *Confidential*.

595   Jordan, Louis F. "Court's Views Vary on a 'Person's Right to Be Let
            Alone.'" *The Editor and Publisher* (29 May 1926): 24.
        Traces the legal course of the right-to-privacy concept beginning with
        the Brandeis/Warren *Harvard Law Review* essay in 1890 (see entry
        #606). Concentrates on the propriety of publishing photographs with-
        out the permission of the subject. Reveals that a right of privacy is not
        well established, and that unless a photograph is used for commercial
        purposes, redress by the subject is not likely to be available. Refers to
        cases in New York, Louisiana, Rhode Island, Missouri, and Kentucky.

596   "Judge and a Witness." *Newsweek* (19 August 1957): 83.
        Reports on the testimony of the first major prosecution witness in the
        libel trial against *Confidential* magazine being held in California.

597   "Lid on the Sewer." *Time* (19 September 1955): 74.
        Reports on Postmaster's barring *Confidential* magazine from the mail.
        Discusses reasons for such a ban and likely implications for the exposé
        publication.

598   Manning, George H. "Commission Attacks 'Trial By Newspaper.'"
            The Editor and Publisher, The Fourth Estate (18 July 1931): 8.
        Discusses condemnation of the "trial by newspaper" contained in the
        Wickersham Commission's report on criminal procedure. The Com-
        mission report alluded to the practice of some newspapers setting forth
        prosecution and defense arguments in advance of the trial.

599   "Minneapolis Journal Sees Continued Need For Scandal Sheet Gag."
            The Editor and Publisher, The Fourth Estate (13 June 1931): 30.
        Samples editorial opinion of several newspapers to Supreme Court de-
        cision which overturns a Minnesota law aimed at silencing scandal
        sheets. Ten editorials are reprinted, nine of which support the decision,
        citing free press principles, and the fact that libel law provides suffi-
        cient remedy for journalistic excesses.

600   Prosser, William L. "Privacy." *California Law Review* 48 (1960):
            383-423.
        A major revision of the Warren/Brandeis legal characterization of the
        right to privacy, this article discusses four different torts which have
        come to constitute invasion of one's privacy: intrusion upon one's pri-
        vate affairs, public disclosure of embarrassing private facts, publicity
        placing one in a false light before the public, and appropriation of one's
        name or likeness for personal advantage. Calls attention to the fact that
        since the Warren and Brandeis article, "The Right to Privacy" in 1890
        (see entry #606), privacy law has expanded haphazardly to encroach on

many other aspects of legal jurisprudence without any clearly defined limits in sight. Too often established defendant safeguards recognized in other areas of the law, are disregarded in privacy cases. Calls for recognition of reasonable legal boundaries within which privacy law may be contained. (Attributes impetus for the Warren and Brandeis article to Warren's anger over invasion of his daughter's wedding by overly-aggressive representatives of the yellow press.)

601   "Putting the Papers to Bed." *Time* (26 August 1957): 61.
Reports on progress of the libel trial of *Confidential* magazine, highlighting testimony concerning methods employed in order to obtain scandalous information. Includes discussion on how newspapers chose to report on the trial, given the opportunity to feature salaciousness which would ordinarily prove too controversial for their publications.

602   "Sewer Trouble." *Time* (1 August 1955): 48.
Reports on a series of libel suits brought by celebrities against scandal publications *Confidential*, *Hush-Hush*, and *Rave*.

603   Spiegel, Irwin O. "Public Celebrity vs. Scandal Magazine—The Celebrities' Right to Privacy." *Southern California Law Review* 30 (1957): 280-312.
Argues that the intrusive revelations of the 1950's scandal magazines (i.e. *Confidential*, *Exposed*, *Inside Story*, *Lowdown*, *QT*, *Suppressed*, *Top Secret*, *Uncensored*, *Whisper*) violate celebrities' right to privacy and inflict emotional distress. Characterizes the typical scandal magazine story as a combination of fact and salacious fiction resulting in offensive and outrageous falsehoods.

604   "Ssh!" *Time* (2 April 1956): 86.
Reports on the status of libel suits pending and settled against exposé magazine *Confidential*.

605   *Varnish vs. Best Medium Publishing Co.* 405 F. 2d 608 (1968).
Appeals Court affirms district court's verdict that publication (the *National Enquirer*) invaded defendant's privacy by publishing a false and reckless story concerning his wife's murder of their children and her suicide. Portions of the wife's suicide note expressing despondency were omitted in order to support a sensational story of a happy home destroyed by an inexplicable act. Award of $5,000 compensatory and $15,000 punitive damages is upheld. In a dissenting opinion it is argued that had the omitted section of the suicide note been included in the story, the plaintiff would not have been portrayed in a better light. In addition, the false or reckless statements present are not offensive enough to justify the verdict.

606   Warren, Samuel D. and Louis D. Brandeis. "The Right to Privacy."
        Harvard Law Review 4 (1890): 193-220.
        Landmark article which attempts to draw the legal line separating in-
        formation of legitimate public concern from purely private matters and
        to indicate proper penalties for violations. The authors cite the techno-
        logical innovations of "instantaneous photographs" and "numerous
        mechanical devices" employed by the newspapers which necessitate
        enunciating "the right to be let alone." Previously developed law deal-
        ing with libel, slander and artistic property rights form the basis of the
        authors' suggested resolutions (which do not recognize truthfulness or
        absence of malice as a defense for publication.)

607   Westin, Allen F. *Privacy and Freedom.* New York: Atheneum, 1970. 487 pgs.
        Traces the concept of privacy in civilized society and the threats posed
        by advancing technology. Chapter 13, "Privacy and American Law"
        (pp. 330-364), discusses the attempt to protect individual privacy from
        the yellow press by establishing a legal "right to be let alone." In-
        cluded: discussion of classic articles by E. L. Godkin (see entry #073)
        and Samuel Warren/Louis Brandeis (see entry #606) championing the
        protection of one's privacy and reputation from a prying press.

608   "The Woes of *Confidential.*" *Time* (22 July 1957): 76-77.
        Reports on the failure of a countersuit by *Confidential* magazine charg-
        ing California's attorney general with censorship. Incudes description
        of a rare *Confidential* editorial claiming persecution.

MODERN PRACTICE

609   Ackerman, Robert M. "Bringing Coherence to Defamation Law Through
        Uniform Legislation: The Search For an Elegant Solution." *North
        Carolina Law Review* 72 (1994): 291-349.
        Proposes instituting a tripartite verdict procedure—in which the
        plaintiff must demonstrate defamation, falsity, and actual malice—
        to resolve defamation cases. Damages would be limited to economic
        losses, attorney fees, and vindication (appropriately publicizing
        plaintiff's victory). Punitive damages are disallowed. If plaintiff
        demonstrates defamation and falsity, but not malice, vindication is
        obtained by declaratory judgement alone—no damages are awarded.
        The author cites the Carol Burnett case (*Burnett v. National Enquirer*
        193 Cal. Reptr. 206 [1983], see entry #616) to illustrate uneven ap-
        plication of the malice standard as well as the primary importance
        of vindication.

610   Ashdown, Gerald G. "Of Public Figures and Public Interest—The Libel Law Conundrum." *William and Mary Law Review* 25 (1984): 937-956.

Argues that only stories/articles which involve public policy should be protected by the actual malice defamation standard. Whether or not the persons involved are public figures should be irrelevant. Under this "subject matter standard" much of what tabloids print about celebrities would not enjoy strict free press protection. The Carol Burnett case (see entry #616) is employed to illustrate principles involved.

611   Barret, David A. "Declaratory Judgements for Libel: A Better Alternative." *California Law Review* 74 (1986): 847-882.

Defends Representative Charles Shumer's bill for declaratory judgement in libel cases against the criticism of Prof. Marc Franklin (see entry #631). Author points out that only public figures would be affected by the Shumer bill. Such figures openly court and crave publicity, and must countenance greater public scrutiny of their private lives. Publicity entails greater risk of defamation. Allowing the defendants in libel cases to opt for declaratory judgement (admittedly a reversal of the common law tradition that the plaintiff is master of the claim) would still permit the plaintiff quick vindication while eliminating vindictiveness. Author minimizes the deterrent value of large damage settlements, citing low conviction rates and the incorrigible attitude of irresponsible publishers such as the *National Enquirer*. Imposition of a strict liability standard for false statements, which the Shumer bill mandates, would result in a much higher rate of defamation convictions.

612   Benedict, Helen. "Symposium: The Privacy Rights of Rape Victims in the Media and the Law: Panel Discussion." *Fordham Law Review* 61 (1993): 1141-1145.

Assistant Professor of the Graduate School of Journalism at Columbia University, urges the media to stop concentrating on the private lives of rape victims rather than the actual reasons that rape occurs. The media plays detective in rape stories, but unlike the justice system, assumes guilt until innocence is proven. Cites headline in tabloid *Globe* to prove the point—"Kennedy Rape Gal Exposed." Media reform should be voluntary because freedom of the press is crucial to democracy.

613   Bienen, Leigh B. " 'A Good Murder'." *Fordham Urban Law Journal* 20 (1993): 585-607.

Contends that America's criminal justice system is strongly influenced by the manner in which the media portrays murder. An examination of homicide cases in the state of New Jersey revealed that the death penalty is more likely to be sought and imposed for murders which conform to the Hollywood-like story lines dramatized in the media. Tabloid murder coverage is compared to comic book storytelling in both content and style. Concludes that our methods for prosecuting murder must be reformed, and the death penalty abolished.

614   Bloom, Lackland H. "Proof of Fault in Media Defamation Litigation." *Vanderbilt Law Review* 38 (1985): 247-394.
       Maintains that existing standards for proving media fault in defamation cases work well: the actual malice requirement protects the press adequately, while the plaintiff can prevail by demonstrating reckless disregard. Cites *Carson v. Allied News Co.* 529 F.2d 206 (1976) (see entry #617) as well as cases in which wire services found themselves in court because they relied on allegations and quotes taken from sensational tabloids for their stories (*Ammerman v. Hubbard Broadcasting Inc.*, 91 N.M. 250, 572 P.2d 1258, [1977]; *Mehau v. Gannet Pac. Corp.* 66 Hawaii 134, 658 P.2d. 312).

615   Brown, Lisa. "Dead But Not Forgotten: Proposals for Imposing Liability for Defamation of the Dead." *Texas Law Review* 67 (1989): 1525-1567.
       It is not merely reputation of the deceased that should be considered in cases concerning defamation of the dead, but rather the real impact of defamatory statements upon the family and society; the interest of the state in encouraging responsible press; and the need for compensation when injury has occurred (which will probably require legislative action). Cites tabloid article announcing the posthumous nuptials of Natalie Wood and Elvis Presley as illustrative of the totally unrestrained manner in which the media treats dead celebrities.

616   *Burnett v. National Enquirer* 144 Cal. App. 3d 991, 193 Cal Reptr 206 (July 1983).
       Court of Appeals affirms judgement of $50,000 compensatory damages, reduces punitive award of $750,000 to $150,000 to entertainer who sued weekly tabloid publication for falsely reporting her behavior at restaurant in 1976 as drunken and argumentative. The paper had printed a retraction with which the entertainer was not satisfied. Libel protection afforded newspapers by civil code does not apply to weekly tabloid because the publication does not fit the normal definition of a newspaper: it covers little politics, sports or crime, and its stories are one to three weeks old. Punitive damages were reduced because the original award represented thirty-five percent of the tabloids net worth. (Landmark case which demonstrated the possibility of successfully limiting the freedom with which the tabloid press traditionally operated.)

617   *Carson vs. Allied News Co.* 482 F. Supp. 406 (1979).
       Court grants motion for summary judgement by entertainer who was

subject of tabloid article which claimed he moved his television show to California in order to be with the woman who eventually became his second wife. The article also maintained that Joanna Holland, the woman in question, was responsible for the breakup of Carson's first marriage. Judge rules that the tabloid, *National Insider*, committed libel by demonstrating a reckless disregard for the truth in its adaptation of an article from a Chicago newspaper for its own purposes. By distorting and magnifying speculative comments in the Chicago article and adding blatant fabrications of its own design, the defendant demonstrated malice.

618   *Cher vs. Forum International, Ltd.* 692 F.2d 634 (1982).
Court of Appeals modifies ruling which found entertainer had been damaged by free-lance writer who interviewed her, and publications which eventually printed the interview. The magazine, for which the interview was originally intended, decided not to publish it at the entertainer's request. The interviewer subsequently sold the interview to two other publishers, one of which (*News Group Publications, Inc.*) produced the tabloid *Star*. The judge reverses the trial court's decision against publishers of *Star*, finding the entertainer was not damaged by the publication of the interview. *Star*'s claim that the interview was exclusive is true, and did not constitute an endorsement by the entertainer of the tabloid. Purchase and publication of the interview by the tabloid is protected by the first and the fourteenth amendments. It is noted that similar interviews with the entertainer had previously appeared in the publication. However, trial court's finding against *Forum International, Ltd.*, second publisher of the interview, is upheld because they knowingly published false ads claiming the entertainer endorsed their publication.

619   Collins, Ronald K. and David M. Skover. "The First Amendment in the Age of Paratroopers." *Texas Law Review* 68 (1990): 1087-1126.
Maintains that our current entertainment-centered culture undermines the traditional first amendment values of "civic restraint and serious dialogue." Yet, the first amendment protects this very destructive process. Poses the question: should anything be done to thwart such a culture? Cites broadcast journalist Bill Moyers' condemnation of tabloid television which repackages news as entertainment hosted by an anchorperson with "star" status. Such "news" is bereft of discourse. (The title of the article derives from a Marshall McLuhan quote which expresses the need to discover a new way to "Cross the Rubicon".)

620   Collins, Ronald K. and David M. Skover. "Pissing in the Snow: A Cultural Approach to the First Amendment." *Stanford Law Review* 45 (1993): 783-806.
Uses James Twitchell's *Carnival Culture: The Trashing of Taste in America* (see entry #479) in order to introduce a cultural approach to

the first amendment, based on the assumption that entertainment—rather than enlightenment—forms the rationale for protecting the established freedoms of speech and press. Consequently, it is the commercial mass media whose free expression rights must be addressed in light of the constitution. Tabloid entertainment is transforming American society: associative, rather than logical thought predominates; Perot's "electronic town hall" recognizes the new nature of democracy; all forms of dissent are validated, promoted and sold. (The article's title derives from both a quote describing the sacrifices of Machiavelli, in demonstration of his patriotism, and Andres Serrano's "Piss Christ" artwork which tests the limits of the first amendment.)

621   Cox, Gail Diane. "Privacy's Frontiers At Issue: Unwilling Subjects of Tabloid TV Are Suing." *The National Law Journal* (27 December 1993): 1+.
Discussion of news reporters' first amendment rights in reporting catastrophes vs. accident victims' rights to suffer in privacy. Due to the proliferation of cable outlets and tabloid news programs, there is a great demand for live accident footage which can be recorded in greater detail with ever-improving electronic technology. Several impending law suits are discussed.

622   *Dempsey v. National Inquirer, Inc.* 687 F. Supp 692 (D.Me. 1988).
District Court judge grants tabloid publisher's motion to dismiss case brought by airplane pilot who sued for invasion of privacy after newspaper published an account of a plane accident. Pilot fell through door hatch of a small commercial plane but survived with only minor injuries by clinging to door rails under plane's body while co-pilot executed an emergency landing. Articles in both the *Enquirer* and *Star* were mentioned in the complaint which accused defendant of placing him in a false light and appropriating his likeness and words for commercial profit. While *Enquirer* acknowledged use of "fictionalized dialogue" which constituted 21 of the 33 short paragraphs in the story, the court ruled that such misrepresentations would not be highly objectionable to a reasonable person. In addition, newspapers, under Maine law, may engage in incidental publication of a subject's name or likeness. Such action does not constitute commercial use, especially when such use is not for the purpose of commercial endorsement.

623   *Dempsey v. National Inquirer, Inc.* 702 F. Supp 934 (D.Me. 1988).
News America Publishing, Inc. publishers of the *Star* and codefendant with the *National Enquirer* moves to dismiss complaint by pilot who was also the subject of a story in its tabloid publication. While the court again dismisses the pilot's commercial appropriation of name and likeness claim, judge finds that the *Star's* version of the airplane acci-

dent, by falsely contributing authorship to the pilot, achieves a higher degree of offensiveness than the *Enquirer's*. As a result, a jury should decide whether the account would be highly offensive to a reasonable person. Judge also finds portions of the *Star's* story more intrusive of plaintiff's privacy than the *Enquirer's*. In addition, the court rules that the First Amendment does not allow publication of a false account even when the event in question actually occurred.

624   Denno, Deborah W. "The Privacy Rights of Rape Victims in the Media and the Law: Perspectives on Disclosing Rape Victims Names." *Fordham Law Review* 61 (1993): 1113-1131.
Discusses arguments for and against revealing rape victims' identities which include the issues of stigmatizing the victim, male chauvinism, editorial prerogative, public (nonprofit) disclosure, accuser's rights, and reporting of rape. The Supreme Court has generally upheld freedom of the press in its rulings on the question of disclosure. In referring to the William Kennedy Smith case, the article identifies two tabloids—the British *Sunday Mirror* and the *Globe*—as the first publications to publish the alleged rape victim's name and photograph.

625   *Eastwood v. Superior Court* 149 Cal. App. 3d 409 (Dec 1983).
Appeals Court reverses decision of trial court regarding entertainer's charge that the *National Enquirer* appropriated his name and likeness for commercial gain without authorization. Lower court dismissed appropriation claim because entertainer's name and likeness were used as part of a news account in a manner permitted by state law, and were not used to imply an endorsement of the publication. Court of Appeals rules that California civil law does not protect news accounts from liability when they are knowingly or recklessly false. Similarly, the first amendment does not protect the publisher of an entirely false article. Deliberate publication of a false account may constitute the basis of a commercial appropriation charge as well as one for false light invasion of privacy. Plaintiff needs to state by amendment, however, that the publisher acted knowingly or with reckless disregard of the truth.

626   Elwood, John P. "Outing, Privacy and the First Amendment." *Yale Law Journal* 102 (1992): 747-776.
Argues that only when a public figure's homosexuality is of legitimate public concern should such information be protected under the first amendment. Tabloids and the establishment press have violated the privacy of persons by participating in the "outing" frenzy, and should be held legally responsible under the privacy tort.

627   Fairstein, Linda. "Symposium: The Privacy Rights of Rape Victims in the Media and the Law: Panel Discussion." *Fordham Law Review* 61 (1993): 1137-1140.

Chief of Sex Crimes Prosecution Unit, New York County District Attorney's Office argues against requiring public identification of rape victims, though victims should be encouraged to voluntarily identify themselves. Rebuts media arguments in favor of disclosure: supports long-standing gentlemen's agreement forbidding such revelations. Contends that disclosure does not lend story more credibility; naming accuser does not rectify prejudice directed against the accused, nor does it destigmatize the victim. Only the victim knows when the time is right to publicly come forward.

628   Feigelson, Jeremy. "Fabricated Quotations as Cause for Libel Recovery by a Public Figure." *University of Chicago Law Review* 57 (1990): 1353-1386.
Liability for fabricated quotations should be based on two factors: the fabrications should create an injury that an accurate quotation would not have caused; the journalist should have demonstrated knowledge of the quotation's defamatory or reckless disregard for its ability to injure. Cites *Carson v. Allied News Co.* 482 F. Supp. 406 (1979) (see entry #617) and *Varnish v. Best Medium Publishing Co.* 405 F2d 608 (1968) (see entry #605) as providing examples of fabricated quotes, the creation of which were motivated by sensationalism or ill will, resulting in injury.

629   *Fellows v. National Enquirer, Inc.* 42 Cal. 3d 234 (July 1986).
Supreme Court of California reverses Court of Appeals decision which permitted suit for false light invasion of privacy to go forth even though proof of special damages was not present. Plaintiff is movie producer who was named by the defendant as romantically involved with actress Angie Dickenson. The trial court dismissed the case for lack of proof regarding special damages, but Court of Appeals ruled that the damage requirement should not apply in false light invasion of privacy cases, but rather should be limited to defamatory actions. The Supreme Court, in review, finds that California law requiring proof of damages applies equally to both types of cases. If it did not, proof of damages could never be required in either instance, because virtually every defamation could be presented as a false light invasion of privacy case. A concurring opinion stresses the importance of a free press unfettered by restrictive legal codes.

630   Ferris, Charles D. and Terrence J. Leaky. "Red Lions, Tigers, and Bears: Broadcast Content Regulation and the First Amendment." *Catholic University Law Review* 38 (1989): 299-327.
Addresses the question of whether television broadcasters should enjoy the same first amendment protection as print publishers, or whether they are public trustees subject to greater government regulation. Author points out that the Supreme Court recognizes the necessity for varying degrees of regulation over different types of media. The lim-

ited number of broadcast frequencies available has traditionally resulted in substantial regulation of the airways by the Federal Communications Commission. Marketplace forces are a poor substitute for government regulation. Regulation is necessary to curb obscenity and protect the quality of children's television. The recent rise of tabloid television demonstrates the undesirable effects of uncontrolled market pressures as programming stoops to satisfy the least common denominator, thereby attracting the largest possible audience. The author concludes that a limited amount of government oversight is required in order to protect the public interest.

631   Franklin, Marc A. "A Declaratory Judgement Alternative to Current Libel Law." *California Law Review* 74 (1986): 809-845.
Proposes an alternative to traditional libel law by which plaintiffs seek redress for defamation. Author's proposal would allow for declaratory judgement that a given statement is false and defamatory. No damages may be awarded under this judgement. Author's proposal, however, differs significantly from that brought before Congress by Representative Charles Shumer in 1985 in that the Shumer proposal would permit the defendant to transform an action for damages into a declaratory judgement case. Such a provision, states the author, would fail to adequately deter irresponsible publishers, such as those in the tabloid press, from defaming at will. Franklin cites *Burnett v. National Enquirer* (1983) (see entry #616), *Fellows v. National Enquirer* (1986) (see entry #629), and *Selleck v. Globe International* (1985) (see entry #667), in asserting that reckless publishers are being held increasingly accountable for their actions and, therefore, should not be allowed to escape judgement for damages.

632   Gallagher, John. "Actor's Libel Lawsuit Leaves Media Asking How to Cover Outing." *The Advocate* (13 August 1991): 21.
Reports that actor Tom Selleck has filed a $20 million defamation lawsuit against the tabloid *Globe* for repeating allegations that he is gay. Discusses relative merits of such legal action as well as the practice of outing. Includes information on the group Outpost whose outing campaign involves posters which parody Absolut vodka ads.

633   Gartner, Michael. "Symposium: The Privacy Rights of Rape Victims in the Media and the Law: Panel Discussion." *Fordham Law Review* 61 (1993): 1133-1135.
The President of NBC News explains why the name of the victim in the William Kennedy Smith rape case was revealed: journalists must report the news—not conceal it; news personnel—not lawyers—should make the editorial decisions; "conspiracy of silence" stigmatizes rape victims; in the interests of fairness both the accuser and accused should be named.

634   Gilles, Susan M. "All Truths Are Equal, But Are Some Truths More
       Equal Than Others?" *Case Western Reserve Law Review* 41 (1991):
       725-743.
       Argues against the idea that the judiciary should decide which truths
       have value, and therefore, may be published. The author considers such
       judgement a violation of the first amendment, and consequently, sees
       little merit in the section of the privacy tort dealing with the publica-
       tion of true private facts. The truths exposed in tabloid newspaper ar-
       ticles have value, because they educate many about the nature of the
       community in which they live. Such stories are representative of
       journalism's oldest traditions. To denigrate such communication is to
       unnecessarily restrict the manner in which people learn. In addition,
       the author believes it is impossible to isolate one "valueless" item of
       knowledge from the larger valuable context in which it is found. Dis-
       tinguishing between the torts of libel and privacy would enable the
       courts to avoid addressing the issue of a statement's truth, but the torts
       are so similar that such distinction appears impossible.

635   Gilmore, Robert S. "Attacking the Negligence Rule in Defamation of
       Private Plaintiffs: *Embers Supper Club* v. *Scripps Howard Broad-
       casting Co.*" *Ohio State Law Journal* (1986): 503-520.
       Disagrees with Ohio Supreme court ruling which ordered a jury trial,
       because a broadcast station may have acted negligently in failing to
       ascertain the truthfulness of information it publicized which likely
       proved defamatory. Such a simple negligence standard of liability should
       not be used in cases involving first amendment rights. Freedom of speech
       and press must be upheld even at the expense of suffering the irrespon-
       sible journalism of the sensational tabloids.

636   Graubard, Stephen R. "The Anthony Perkins Saga." *The Journal of
       Contemporary Health Law and Policy* 9 (1993): 177-181.
       Calls for an end to the kind of social fear which caused HIV-infected
       actor Anthony Perkins to seclude himself during the last two years of
       his life. Society must live up to its humane ideals in its treatment of
       AIDS patients. This applies especially to the press which, led by the
       National Enquirer, hounded the Perkins household incessantly for a
       story. The *Enquirer* first revealed Perkins' illness when apparently, re-
       sults of a blood test were leaked to the paper. Discretion is necessary to
       a civil society even at the expense of a totally free press.

637   Halpern, Sheldon W. "The Right of Publicity: Maturation of an Inde-
       pendent Right Protecting the Associative Value of Personality."
       Hastings Law Journal 46 (1995): 853-873.
       Argues that the right of publicity has rightfully achieved status inde-
       pendent of privacy considerations. Common sense prevails when the
       celebrity, whose image has become famous, profits commercially

through such fame, rather than a stranger whose interest is purely exploitative. Acknowledges the distastefulness of personality commodification but rejects such repugnance as an excuse to ignore the realities of the marketplace. Discusses media's role in the creation of marketable celebrity, and the effort of celebrities such as Clint Eastwood to restrict the tabloids' use of their image.

638   Harvey, G. Michael. "Confidentiality: A Measured Response to the Failure of Privacy." *University of Pennsylvania Law Review* (1992): 2385-2470.
Argues that privacy can be better guaranteed by focusing legally on sources, rather then on publishers, of information. Recommends an adoption of a breach of confidence doctrine, similar to one recognized in England, as the basis for privacy protection in this country. Attempting to regulate publication of private information does not work, because such regulation runs counter to the spirit of the first amendment. Documents the flood of recent media-publicized, scandalous revelations in establishing the enormity of the problem.

639   Hemphill, James A. "Libel-Proof Plaintiffs and the Question of Injury." *Texas Law Review* 71 (1992): 401-431.
Advocates application of the libel-proof plaintiff doctrine in appropriate situations. The doctrine maintains that, in certain circumstances, a plaintiff whose reputation is already sullied may not be further damaged by a specific instance of libel. It might appear that this doctrine would encourage the tabloids to become even more aggressive in their rumor-mongering. The author argues, however, that past history indicates courts will find such publications guilty of reputational harm on occasion; many readers do not believe the assertions made in tabloid stories, therefore, reputational harm cannot occur; and the tabloids could still be held liable for intentional infliction of emotional distress.

640   Hutt, Sarah Henderson. "In Praise of Public Access: Why the Government Should Disclose the Identities of Alleged Crime Victims." *Duke Law Journal* 41 (1991): 368-414.
Maintains that recent state laws prohibiting public access to information which identifies crime victims violate the public's right of access under the first amendment. The victim's right to privacy is outweighed by the public's interest in a fair and open criminal justice system. The article notes that the supermarket tabloid *Globe* was one of the few publications to ignore the taboo against publishing victim information when it revealed the name of the woman who charged William Kennedy Smith with rape in 1991.

641   Ingber, Stanley. "Rethinking Intangible Injuries: A Focus on Remedy."
        California Law Review 73 (1985): 772-856.
        Challenges the traditional remedy of applying tort law to cases of in-
        tangible injury. Damage to one's reputation, invasion of privacy or in-
        fliction of emotional distress are not adequately treated in a system
        which relies on the awarding of money damages. Freedom of speech
        and press are jeopardized by large awards. Criticizes the all or nothing
        approach usually adopted in cases of intangible injury which results in
        awarding either full compensation or no compensation. Instead pro-
        poses a new damages model which limits damages for pain and suffer-
        ing, and emotional distress. Damages for defamation should be limited
        to actual loss (income or therapy expenses, e.g.). Punitive damages
        should not be allowed . Declaratory judgements are inadequate because
        they are insufficiently publicized. In addition, calls for institution of a
        privacy statute which would protect the individual while minimizing
        intimidation of the media. Rejecting the notion that the legal system is
        most capable of judging what is in the public's interest to view or hear,
        the author supports the rights of those who believe the tabloid press's
        articles on the personal lives of celebrities speak more meaningfully to
        them than the president's budget report.

642   Inman, Lucy Noble. "*Hall v. Post*: North Carolina Rejects Claim of
        Invasion of Privacy by Truthful Publication of Embarrassing Facts."
        North Carolina Law Review (1989): 1474-1494.
        Agrees with North Carolina Supreme Court decision which rejected claim
        of invasion of privacy by publication of private facts. The state similarly
        rejected the tort of false light invasion of privacy in *Renwick v. News &
        Observer Publishing Co.*, 310 N.C. 312. These decisions appear to grant
        greater protection to truthful speech than the U.S. Supreme Court or
        any other state courts provide. Victim of private fact publication may
        seek relief by claiming intentional infliction of emotional distress, but
        even in such instances free press doctrine may prevail. Asserts the right
        of tabloids, such as the *National Enquirer*, to publish any true informa-
        tion that is not obtained by illegal or dishonest means, in the name of free
        expression and free access to a variety of publications.

643   "It's Star Wars on the Tabs." *People Weekly* (15 October 1990): 34-37.
        Reports that Elizabeth Taylor has filed a $20 million libel suit against the
        National Enquirer. Also covered: the tabloid's penchant for indulging in
        checkbook journalism, and charges that the *Enquirer* pays pseudo-infor-
        mants, creating the impression that real information has been leaked.

644   Kaufman, Joseph H. "Beyond *Cole v. Cowles Media Co.*: Confidenti-
        ality Agreements and Efficiency Within the Marketplace of

Ideas." *University of Chicago Legal Forum* (1993): 255-273.
Author investigates the question of whether an informant should be permitted to collect damages from a reporter who violates a confidentiality agreement. An economic model is developed for analyzing the impact of such agreements on the amount of information made available to the public in the long run (assumed to be the goal of the first amendment). The author concludes that confidentiality agreements are cost efficient. In discussing the effect of a newspaper's reputation upon the marketplace, the author theorizes that papers which pay their informants, such as the tabloids, do not highly value their reputation.

645   Kozinski, Alex and Stuart Banner. "Whose Afraid of Commercial Speech?" *Virginia Law Review* 76 (1990): 627-653.
Argues in favor of extending the same constitutional protection to commercial speech as is offered to noncommercial. In demonstrating that such protection already exists in some instances, the authors cite the supermarket tabloids which publish "nothing but the most absurd falsehoods" with impunity.

646   Lerner, Max. "Some Reflections on 'The First Amendment in an Age of Paratroopers.'" *Texas Law Review* 68 (1990): 1127-1136.
There is no need to deny first amendment protection to electronic media because America, as in the past, has the power to transform technology for the betterment of society. (Response to Collins and Skover article; see entry #619).

647   Line, Julie A. "Fourth Amendment—Further Erosion of the Warrant Requirement for Unreasonable Searches and Seizures: The Warrantless Trash Search Exception." *The Journal of Criminal Law and Criminology* 79 (1978); 623-646.
Discusses the legality of searching and seizing material contained in an individual's trash, without a warrant, for use in criminal cases. The author contends that the searches are prohibited under the fourth amendment, because application of principles established in *Katz v. United States* 389 U.S. 347 (1967) dictate such a conclusion in instances when society reasonably expects privacy to be honored. Supreme Court Justice Brennan, dissenting in *California v. Greenwood* 108 S. Ct. 1625 (1988), also expressed this opinion. In support of his contention, Brennan cited the flood of social criticism in response to the revelation that a reporter for a tabloid newspaper had published a story based on his examination of Henry Kissinger's trash (see entries #323, 345, 661). Such criticism, reasoned Brennan, was indicative of society's expectations.

648   Madow, Michael. "Private Ownership of Public Image: Popular

Culture and Publicity Rights." *California Law Review* 81 (1993): 125-240.

Argues against the practice of legally recognizing a celebrity's name or likeness as private property. Believes that such publicity rights erroneously characterize social goods, such as fame, as purely individual achievements. Favors a more democratic management of popular culture in which cultural images are regarded as common property to be used in the evolution of new social values. Traces the history of tabloid journalism in order to chronicle emergence of America's image-based society. States that the sensationalism of the late nineteenth century tabloids was largely limited to their format rather than their content. Uses the experience of modern tabloids to illustrate the boundaries of publicity rights—stories may focus on celebrities' "life stories", but appropriation of a celebrity's name or likeness for commercial gain is forbidden. Stops short of advocating abolition of publicity rights, maintaining that further investigation needs to determine the consequences of such a step. Suggests that compulsory licensing scheme or "fair use" privilege might represent acceptable reforms.

649   *Maples v. National Enquirer* 763 F. Supp. 1137 (N.D. Ga. 1990).

District Court denies publisher's motion to dismiss suit brought by father whose daughter was the subject of tabloid's article. Suit alleged libel: commercial appropriation of name, likeness and story; false light invasion of privacy. *Enquirer* published story about Marla Maples, Donald Trump's reputed mistress, based on a fabricated "exclusive interview" with Stan Maples, Marla's father. The newspaper tested the sufficiency of plaintiff's complaint by filing a motion to dismiss for failure to state a claim. Judge rules that the complaint states a claim for libel by attribution, because the article gives the impression that plaintiff would sell intimate information regarding his daughter for publication. In addition, plaintiff's claim for false light invasion of privacy is warranted because story's false statements may be highly offensive to a reasonable person. Finally, defendant may well have appropriated plaintiff's name and likeness for commercial advantage by publicizing or advertising the Maples story on its cover. While news is protected by the first amendment, factually inaccurate accounts, such as the one in question, are not so protected.

650   McClurg, Andrew Jay. "Bringing Privacy Law Out of the Closet: A Tort Theory of Liability for Intrusions in Public Places." *North Carolina Law Review* 13 (1995): 989-1088.

Argues for establishment of a tort of "public intrusion" to protect against highly offensive use videotaping, photography, or surveillance of individuals in public places. Includes discussion of the current state of privacy law, excesses of the tabloid media (particularly those facilitated by advanced technology); a proposed theory of "public privacy"; some courts' instinctive recognition of the need for a public intrusion tort; and a proposed test which would identify instances of actionable pub-lic intrusion. Also comments upon an apparent decline in social civil-ity which serves to sanction increased invasion of other's privacy.

651   Moretti, Barbara. "Outing: Justifiable or Unwarranted Invasion of Privacy? The Private Facts Tort as a Remedy for Disclosure of Sexual Orientation." *Cardozo Arts & Entertainment Law Journal* 11 (1993): 857-903.
Contends that "outing" of homosexuals constitutes invasion of privacy which should be remedied by application of the private-facts tort, pro-tecting persons against unjustified infliction of mental distress. The author agrees with Prosser's revision of the Warren/Brandeis privacy agreement (see entry #600) in that there should be legal protection against public disclosure of embarrassing private facts. Names the su-permarket tabloids as the prime offenders in publicizing the outing of Malcolm Forbes and other personalities.

652   Moshayedi, Megan. "Defamation by Docudrama: Protecting Reputa-tions from Derogatory Speculation." *University of Chicago Legal Forum* (1993): 331-345.
Author proposes that speakers who willfully present derogatory specu-lation as fact should be held legally liable even though the injured party is incapable of proving the falsity of such speculation. Defamation law provides no remedy for those whose reputation suffers due to the de-rogatory speculation, yet when such speculation concerns significant rather than minor issues, reputational damage is great. Because specu-lation is almost always false, defamatory plaintiffs should be exempted from proving the falsity of such statements. The author supports requir-ing speakers to notify audiences regarding their level of certainty be-fore speculating (via a disclaimer, e.g.). Derogatory speculation has become a particular problem recently due to the television networks' increasing reliance on sensational, tabloid docudramas.

653   O'Brien, David M. "Between the Nightmares of Orwell and Huxley: A Note on the Noble Dream of the First Amendment." *Texas Law Review* 68 (1990): 1137-1145.
Television's negative influence on participatory democracy might be overstated, but there is cause for concern that the first amendment may need protection from our thoroughly commercialized technology. (Re-sponse to Collins & Skover, "First Amendment in an Age of Paratroop-ers," see entry #619.)

654   "$1.1 Million Libel Judgement Against National Tabloid." *The Editor and Publisher* (7 May 1994): 5.

Reports on successful lawsuit against the *Globe* brought by a former free lance photographer who the newspaper implied was the actual assassin of Robert F. Kennedy.

655   *Peoples Bank & Trust Co. v. Globe International Inc.* 786 F. Supp. 791 (W.D. Ark. 1992).

U.S. District Court denies motion of tabloid publication *Sun* for judgement, new trial, or reduction of jury award in case in which the paper falsely identified Nellie Mitchell, a 96 year-old newspaper carrier as pregnant. (Earlier proceedings found in 773 F. Supp. 1235). The judge finds the publication's actions outrageous and likely to cause extreme emotional distress. Privacy was invaded by placing the subject in a false light. In addition, the tabloid's behavior constituted malice. The decision responds to the publication's contention that its stories were purely fictional (and, therefore, incapable of defaming the subject) by indicating that the authors of the tabloid's stories appeared incapable of distinguishing fact from fantasy. Trial testimony had indicated that the publication's story writers created stories from headlines and photographs supplied to them by management. Evidence had indicated that the headlines were creations of the editor. The judge characterized the *Sun's* stories as "muck, mire and slime."

656   *Pierson v. News Group Publications, Inc.* 549 F. Supp. 635 (1982).

Soldier brought suit against publisher of tabloid *Star* for invasion of privacy and intentionally inflicting emotional distress by publishing story about prisoner of war training program. District Court grants summary judgement for publisher on the privacy question, because the army granted permission for coverage of the training and no private facts were disclosed. Summary judgement was denied on the question of emotional distress, because the nature of the publishers conduct and its consequences is a question for the jury to decide. Decision will be based on conflicting accounts regarding the nature of the training program. (Publication reported that soldier was dragged for three miles by a pickup truck and hosed down for three hours in 40°F temperatures as a part of training, resulting in his near-death. Soldier contends that dragging never occurred, hosing down lasted fifteen minutes, and he was quickly treated and released by local hospital.)

657   Pollack, David H. "Forced Out of the Closet: Sexual Orientation and the Legal Dilemma of 'Outing.' " *University of Miami Law Review* 46 (1992): 711-750.

Notes the role played by tabloid publications in publicizing the homosexuality of public figures, while arguing that one's sexual orientation is a purely private manner only for individuals who live their lives out of the public spotlight. Prominent public figures cannot legitimately claim right to such privacy.

658   Redish, Martin H. "Killing the First Amendment With Kindness: A Troubled Reaction to Collins and Skover." *Texas Law Review* 68 (1990); 1147-1153.
In response to Collins and Skover's article concerning applicability of the first amendment in our entertainment-centered culture (see entry #619), the author contends there is no need to treat the electronic media any differently than the print. There are many thought-provoking radio and television programs which encourage discourse counterbalancing the tabloid-type offerings.

659   Rheinhardt, Christine. "Stars v. Tabs: Who's Winning?" *McCall's* (January 1992): 64.
Briefly summarizes positions taken by plaintiffs and defendants in celebrity lawsuits vs. tabloid newspapers. Includes scorecard detailing basic facts of recent cases.

660   Ruben, Edward. "Television and the Experience of Citizenship." *Texas Law Review* 68 (1990): 1155-1167.
No need to consider reworking the first amendment in light of electronic media's influence, because television's affect on the audience's thoughts and values has not been demonstrated. Moreover, the possibilities posed by interactive television might be conducive to discourse. (Response to Collins and Skover, "The First Amendment in an Age of Paratroopers;" see entry #619.)

661   Rue, Nancy Burke. "Warrantless Search and Seizure of Curbside Garbage." *University of Cincinnati Law Review* 58 (1989): 361-377.
In arguing for allowing warrantless search and seizure of an individual's refuse only if authorities can demonstrate reasonable suspicion of unlawful activity, the author includes the dissent of Supreme court Justice Brennan in *California v. Greenwood*, 108 S.Ct. 1625 (1988). Brennan refers to the public outcry which accompanied revelation that a tabloid reporter had searched Henry Kissinger's trash in order to obtain information for a story, in holding that such behavior is an invasion of privacy. (See entries #322, 345, and 645.)

662   Sanders, Karl J. "Kids and Condoms: Constitutional Challenges to the Distribution of Condoms in Public Schools." *Cincinnati Law Review* 61 (1993): 1479-1513.
In arguing the legality of condom distribution programs in public schools, the author notes an instance where the program curriculum was leaked to the tabloid press, which proceeded to sensationalize the

use of zucchini and cucumbers to demonstrate proper condom use. Such publicity helped mobilize opposition to the program.

663 Schardt, Arlee. "Hollywood's Stars v. The *Enquirer.*" *Newsweek* (8 December 1980): 86.
Reports that Carol Burnett's law suit against the *National Enquirer* (see entry #616) has triggered nine more, all brought by Hollywood personalities charging defamation. Mentions the *Enquirer's* legal "war chest," claims of accuracy, and practice of paying sources for scandalous tips.

664 Schauer, Frederick. The Role of the People in First Amendment Theory." *California Law Review* 74 (1986): 761-788.
Observes that, unlike the time of John Peter Zenger, today juries are seen as a threat to the press's first amendment freedom. Recent defamation cases including *Burnett v. National Enquirer* (see entry #616), are cited to support contention. Surveys conflicting theories regarding the extent to which majority rule should govern free speech. Favors more popular involvement in free speech decisions in order to foster greater modern interest and respect for the issue, acknowledging that such an approach would likely result in further restrictions on speech. Criticizes free speech theories that look to the past, paternalistically preventing the current populace from interfering at all with constitutional guarantees. While people need to be prevented from giving away their own political liberties, perhaps they should be involved in establishing limits on the tabloid press's activities, sexually-explicit speech, and religious proselytizing. We must acknowledge that the paternalism implicit in the first amendment is antidemocratic though, in some cases, necessary.

665 Schiller, Herbert I. "Television is a Social—Not a Biological or Technical—Problem." *Texas Law Review* 68 (1990): 1169-1178.
No need to deny first amendment protection to electronic media because television is not the problem. Rather, corporate manipulation of the media and its audience, pose the real danger. Collins and Skover are in error when they blame the audience for emergence of our amusement-centered culture. (Response to Collins and Skover. "The First Amendment in the Age of Paratroopers," see entry #619.)

666 Schwartz, Gary T. "Explaining and Justifying a Limited Tort of False Light Invasion of Privacy." *Case Western Reserve Law Review* 41 (1991): 885-919.
Proposes that the tort of false light invasion of privacy be further narrowed, because much of it overlaps the tort of defamation (California courts stated as much in *Selleck v. Globe International, Inc.* 166 Cal. App. 3d 1123). The tort should concentrate on situations in which the falsity of publication's statements render them highly offensive, de-

spite the fact that they are not disparaging. (If they are disparaging, they fall under the tort of defamation.) Many tabloid stories would still be legitimate targets of law suits under their newly-focused definition of false light invasion of privacy. Cites situations described in *Eastwood v. Superior Court* 149 Cal. App. 3d 409 (see entry #625); *Fellows v. National Enquirer* 42 Cal. 3d. 234 (see entry #629); and *Dempsey v. National Enquirer* 702 F.Supp. 934 (see entry #623) as examples. Also believes that courts should require proof of reckless or intentional falsification in the false light cases in order to bolster the claim that the falsity is highly offensive.

667   *Selleck v. Globe International, Inc.* 106 Col. App. 3d 1123 (April 1985). Appeals Court reverses in part trial court's dismissal of libel action brought by father of actor Tom Selleck against the *Globe*, a weekly tabloid. The article in question purported to reveal Tom Selleck's love secrets as related by his father. The trial court held that the article was not libelous and that special damages were not demonstrated. Appeals Court finds article libelous, because it asserts that plaintiff revealed information about his son in an interview which apparently never occurred. For this reason the trial court is directed to require the defendant to answer the charge. The Appeals Court, however, affirms trial court's dismissal of invasion of privacy charge because its specifications as well as relief sought are already contained in the libel action.

668   Smolla, Rodney A. "Let the Author Beware: The Rejuvenation of the American Law of Libel." *University of Pennsylvania Law Review* 132 (1985): 1-94.
       Blames the new narcissistic "me generation," in which public figures create their own personas, for the proliferation of libel suits deluging the courts. Cites Carol Burnett's suit against the *National Enquirer* (see entry #616) as adding impetus to the trend. Proposes simplification of libel law as a solution: actual malice needs to be demonstrated when public figures claim libel, and common law checks and balances on libel and slander need to be reintroduced.

669   Smolla, Rodney A. "Report of the Coalition for a New America: Platform Section on Communications Policy." *University of Chicago Legal Forum* (1993): 149-185.
       Presents a fictional construct set in 1996 which paints a picture of American society in crisis. The fictional "Coalition for a New America" is a new political party of non-politicians calling for a peaceful revolution which would restructure society and change the constitution, particularly the first amendment. Coalition resurrects 1947 Hutchins Commission Report, "A Free and Responsible Press" (University of Chicago Press) which redefined freedom to incorporate the concepts vir-

tue, quality, and obligation. The press, corrupted by market forces and cultural trends, has been unwilling to reform itself. Journalism should elevate, rather than be bound by the interests of the masses. As a result, the Coalition recommends: enforceable codes of journalistic ethics; required public debate and discussion provided by media; stricter laws protecting privacy and reputation, stressing retractions and right to reply rather than money damages (aimed at counteracting the "pernicious tendencies" of tabloid journalism); restrictions on hate speech and pornography; greater public funding for the arts and humanities; greater press access to public institutions; greater individual access to media; outlawing monopolistic control of mass media; restrictions of commercial advertising that promotes image or life-style; elimination of paid political advertisements; and greater limits on campaign spending.

670   Smolla, Rodney A. *Suing the Press.* New York: Oxford University Press, 1986. 277 pgs.

Examines the reasons for the recent marked increase in libel lawsuits against the media. Discusses cultural changes which have resulted in placing greater value on one's reputation and less trust in journalists. One chapter is devoted to Carol Burnett's landmark judgement against the *National Enquirer* (see entry #616). Suggestions for reform of the American libel law system include: requiring the losing side to pay for the winner's legal fees; greater emphasis on retraction (rather than damages) to correct injurious speech; elimination of punitive damages; elimination of libel suits arising from public officials' duties; and simplification of the law itself.

671   Stephen, Robert S. "Prejudicial Publicity Surrounding a Criminal Trial: What a Trial Court Can Do To Ensure a Fair Trial in the Face of a 'Media Circus'. " *Suffolk University Law Review* 26 (1992): 1063-106.

Calls upon courts to employ traditional and innovative methods (from "gag orders" and changes of venue to media committees and liaisons) for dealing with the excesses of modern media, which threaten both the defendant's right to a fair trial and the state's interest in achieving justice. Specifically criticizes tabloid television programs' penchant for paying witnesses in return for revealing sensitive information. ("A Current Affair" is mentioned as a particular offender.)

672   Sunstein, Cass R. "Emerging Media Technology and the First Amendment: The First Amendment in Cyberspace." *Yale Law Journal* 104 (1995): 1757-1804.

Argues for the continued relevance of the Madisonian free speech ideal even given the current profusion of technology-driven free speech marketplaces available to the consumer. Discusses the sensational/scandalous type of programming proliferating in commercial media which poses risks to our participatory democracy. Considers the Supreme Court's decision in *Turner Broadcasting System, Inc. v. FCC*, 114 S. Ct. 2445 (1994) for its discussion of free speech and modern technology.

673   Tushnet, Mark V. "Decoding Television (And Law Reviews)." *Texas Law Review* 68 (1990): 1179-1183.

No need to deny first amendment protection to electronic media because threat to rational discourse posed by television is not very different from similar dangers our culture faced in the past. (Yellow journalism, e.g.) If first amendment doctrine should need any adjustment, the legislature or Supreme Court can act. (Response to Collins and Skover. "The First Amendment in the Age of Paratroopers," see entry #619.)

674   Weaver, Russell L. and Geoffrey Bennett. "Is the *New York Times* 'Actual Malice' Standard Really Necessary? A Comparative Perspective." *Louisiana Law Review* 53 (1993) 1153-1190.

Based on interviews conducted with both American and British newspaper personnel and defamation lawyers, the authors conclude that America's "actual malice" requirement in defamation cases (established in *New York Times Co. v. Sullivan* 376 U.S. 254, 84 S.Ct. 710 [1964]) has had a beneficial affect on news reporting. While presenting a robust appearance, the British press is, in fact, significantly intimidated by continual, numerous law suits, facilitated by a relatively weak standard of proof required of plaintiffs. The notorious British tabloids concentrate on the royal family because they rarely sue, and cabinet ministers because by custom they cannot sue without governmental permission. By contrast, the American news media experiences no corresponding chilling effect.

675   "Woman Awarded $1.5 Million in Libel Verdict." *The Editor and Publisher* (4 January 1992): 70.

Reports on Nellie Mitchell's successful lawsuit v. the *Sun* after being identified in one of its stories as 101 years old and pregnant. (See entry #655). Comments on the newspaper's unusual "fiction defense" which, if accepted (it was not) would have established different journalistic standards for outlandish publications.

676   Zimmerman, Diane L. "Requiem For a Heavyweight: A Farewell to Warren and Brandeis's Privacy Tort." *Cornell Law Review* 68 (1983): 291-367.

Sees the Warren/Brandeis right of privacy argument (see entry #606) as unworkable within a legal framework, and calls for its demise. Attributes the Warren/Brandeis thesis to an overreaction by Victorian-mannered Bostonians to the behavior of the popular press.

5

INTERNATIONAL PERSPECTIVES

AUSTRALIA

Historical Overview

677   Coleman, Peter. *Obscenity, Blasphemy, Sedition: Censorship in Australia.* Brisbane: Jacaranda Press, 1963? 196 pgs.
Chronicles the history of Australian Censorship campaigns against sexual explicitness, blasphemy, revolutionary politics, and libel. Chapter 6, "The Scandal Mongers" (pp. 125-142) details the successful prosecution of nineteenth-century newspapers such as the *Satirist and Sporting Chronicle* (1843) for the common law crime of obscene libel. (The publication commented upon the fornication of the rich and powerful.) Includes a chapter on censorship of entertainment.

678   Ingleton, Geoffrey Chapman. *True Patriots All, or News from Early Australia as Told in a Collection of Broadsides, Garnered & Decorated by Geoffrey Chapman Ingleton.* Sidney: Angus & Robertson, 1952. 280 pgs.
A collection of early Australian broadsides relating in prose and verse, sensational tales of murder, mutiny, shipwreck, piracy, and cannibalism. Covers the period 1785-1855 when a heavy tax on newspapers prevented their wide circulation in the country. "Patterers" sold their broadsides, also displayed as posters, in Australia's towns and cities.

679   MacKaness, George. "Australian Broadsides and 'True Patriots All.'" *The Australian Quarterly* June 1953: 95-102.
Paying tribute to publication of Geoffrey Ingleton's collection of broadsides published by Angus and Robertson of Sidney (see entry #678),

this article discusses the genre in general and its sensational subject matter. Refers to the Samuel Pepys collection as well.

680   Mayer, Henry. *The Press in Australia*. Melbourne: Landsdowne Press, 1968. 281 pgs.
Comprehensive examination of journalism in Australia including history of the popular press (chapter 2, pp. 10-26). Traces Australia's yellow journalism back to *The Currency Lad* of 1833. Chapter 6, "The Press Indicted," deals with charges that the press is too biased and sensational. Includes a content analysis of Australia's newspapers.

681   Pearl, Cyril. *Wild Men of Sidney*. London: W. H. Allen, 1958. 255 pgs.
A view of New South Wales roguery in the late nineteenth/early 20th century. Focuses primarily on John Norton (1858-1916), English-born journalist, who rose to great influence in Australia as a sensational, scandal-mongering newspaper publisher, labor leader, politician, and demagogue. Provides vivid coverage of the lurid papers which proliferated in turn-of-the-century Australia, and through which John Norton wielded power. Included: the *Sidney Evening News*, *Truth* (Norton's successful muckraking sheet), *The Innocents in Sidney*, and *Dead Bird/ The Bird of Freedom* (name changed after conviction for obscenity, banned in 1891).

Modern Practice

682   Henningham, John. *Issues in Australian Journalism*. Melbourne: Longman Cheshire, 1990. 247 pgs.
Collection of essays, originally appearing in the *Australian Journalism Review*, focusing on problems in Australian journalism, chiefly strict limits placed on press freedom (libel laws, and monopolistic proprietorship), and unfair, irresponsible behavior of the press itself. Articles include Brian Hogben's "In Defense of Tabloids," John Lawrence's "The Defamation Industry," and "The Nine Myths of Murdochphobia" by John Wallace. Articles are grouped into five sections: "News Values," "Ethics," "Journalists," "Law," and "Ownership."

683   Trembath, Brendan. "All Over the Press Down Under." *Washington Journalism Review* December 1992: 11.
Reports on the government financed Australian television program "Media Watch: The Last Word," anchored by Stuart Littlemore, which critiques the ethical operations of other journalists. The sensationalism of television tabloid reporters is a favorite target. While Littlemore claims to "use the techniques of modern journalism to criticize modern

journalism," others argue that Media Watch" is guilty of the same sensationalism it finds reprehensible in others.

684   Wearing, Michael. "Professional Discourse and Sensational Journalism: Media Constructions of Violent Insanity." *Australian Journal of Communication* 20 (1993): 84-98.
Argues that the media misrepresents or exaggerates the personal history of violently insane criminals in order to maximize sensationalism in the news they report. Examines collusion between media and health professionals in Sidney, Australia during 1991 in order to illustrate such selective misrepresentation. Includes discussion of media stereotyping of socially differentiated groups in general and the ability of sensationalism to exclude more mundane considerations (such as poverty or unemployment) as reasons for violent crime.

685   Wicklein, John. "Fun and Profit with Libel." *Columbia Journalism Review* November/December 1991: 32, 34.
Reports on the successful use of libel suits against the press by Australian politicians to intimidate newspapers and win large settlements. In the absence of legislation guaranteeing freedom of expression, media defendants routinely lose in courts.

CANADA

Historical Overview

686   Osler, Andrew M. *News: The Evolution of Australian Journalism.* Toronto: Copp Clark Pitman Ltd., 1993. 242 pgs.
Broad, historical view of the development of journalism in Canada. Reviews the penny press/yellow journalism traditions (pp. 79-83), and addresses the issues of libel and obscenity (pp. 142-150), and journalism and celebrity (pp. 197-203). Includes John Milton's *Aeropagitica, The Canadian Charter of Rights and Freedoms,* the *Code of Ethics of the American Society of Newspaper Editors,* and *The Canadian Publishers' Code.*

687   "Prelate Discusses Crime News." *The Editor & Publisher* (6 February 1926): 45.
Reports that Archbishop Georges Gauthier of the Montreal Diocese has complained about sensationalized crime news in a letter to the city's newspapers. Gauthier believes that lurid details should be omitted from crime reports. Journalists should exercise leadership, not merely follow public opinion on the matter.

688   Rutherford, Paul. *The Making of the Canadian Media.* Toronto: McGraw-Hill Ryerson, 1978.
History of the media and the impact of communications in Canada. Documents the use of sensationalism in mid-nineteenth century colonial newspapers such as the *Toronto Patriot* and *Globe.* Discusses the yellow press which employed dubious tactics to obtain muckraking scoops at the end of the nineteenth century, and the 1930's tabloids (such as the *Montreal-Matin*) emphasizing crime and scandal.

Modern Practice

689   Morton, John. "Canada's Tabloid Success Formula." *Washington Journalism Review* July/August 1989: 39.
Attempts to explain the reasons for the success of Toronto Sun Corporation's tabloids (*Toronto Sun, Edmonton Sun,* and *Calgary Sun*). Argues such success rests upon nonunion production, appeal of tabloid style and sensationalism to recent European immigrants, and targeting sales to subway riders.

690   Russell, Nick. *Morals and the Media: Ethics in Canadian Journalism.* Vancouver: UBC Press, 1994. 249 pgs.
The first published book on journalism ethics in Canada, issues addressed include "Giving Audiences What They Want?" (pp. 7-8); "Sensationalism" (pp. 19-22); "Pack Journalism and Celebrity" (chapter 6, pp 63-71); "The Media and Violence" (chapter 10, pp 103-117); "Privacy" (chapter 11, pp. 118-130); and "The Media and Sex" (chapter 13, pp. 139-149). Favors further professionalization of journalism and "green light" ethics which stress what journalists should (rather than should not) do.

691   Slack, Lyle. "Alien Brainchild Lands in Supermarket. Libels Oprah, Dies." *Saturday Night.* November 1992: 17-18, 20, 71.
Examines how the Montreal tabloid, *News Extra,* decided to run a questionable scandal story concerning Oprah Winfrey's companion which resulted in a defamation lawsuit. Includes information on the Canadian origins of the U.S. supermarket tabloid, the *Globe.*

692   Sonmor, Jean. *The Little Paper That Grew Inside the Toronto Sun Publishing Corporation.* Toronto: Toronto Sun Publishing Corporation, 1993. 408 pgs.
Relates the first twenty years of *Toronto Sun* history, focusing primarily on the personalities of the tabloid's management and staff. Includes discussion of the paper's formula of sex and crime coverage. Index is limited to names of persons mentioned.

CHINA

693   "Tabloids Make a Splash in China." *Asian Mass Communication Bulletin* May/June 1993: 6.
        Reports on the success of the new tabloid newspapers in China. Employing color, new technology, and sensational content, they are now outselling the older publications.

694   Zha, Jianying. *China Pop: How Soap Operas, Tabloids, and Best-sellers are Transforming a Culture.* New York: The New Press, 1995. 210 pgs.
        Discusses how China's rulers have allowed the development of commercialization and growth of popular culture in order to relieve government of financial burdens and ease social discontent after Tiananmen. Chapter 5, "The Whopper," (pp. 105-128) relates the transformation of the *China Cultural Gazette* (official organ of China's Ministry of Culture) "from red to yellow" with the appearance of its weekend edition, *Cultural Weekend*, featuring nudity, sex, and popular culture reports.

CZECH REPUBLIC

695   Kelly, Erin. "Tab Plagues Prague!" *Columbia Journalism Review* March/April 1993: 46-47.
        Reports on Swiss-owned tabloid *Blesk* ("lightning flash") which began publishing in 1992. Featuring stories on unscrupulous foreigners; the damaging effect of quick wealth on families; and philandering politicians, the publication reflects many of the post-communist societal adjustments being experienced in the Czech Republic. The sensational daily is now the nation's best selling paper.

ENGLAND

Historical Overview

696   Berridge, Virginia. "Popular Sunday Papers and Mid-Victorian Society." In *Newspaper History from the Seventeenth Century to the Present Day,* edited by George Boyce, James Curran and Pauline Wingate. 247-264. London: Constable, 1978.
        Analyzes popular British Sunday newspapers of the second half of the 19th century, *Lloyd's* and *Reynold's,* newspapers combining radicalism and sensationalism in a commercially successful formula which served to efficiently obscure the real causes of social and economic stress.

697   Brendon, Piers. *The Life and Death of the Press Barons.* New York: Atheneum, 1983. 288 pgs.
A biographical history of the personalities most important to the development of the English and American press. Practitioners of popular/sensational journalism included are Americans James Gordon Bennett, Charles Dana, Joseph Pulitzer, Randolph Hearst, Joseph M. Patterson; and English/Irish/Australian subjects W. T. Snead, T. P. O'Connor, Lord Northcliffe, Cecil King, and Rupert Murdoch.

698   "By Rags to Riches." *New Statesman* (11 October 1974): 500-502.
Profiles Rupert Murdoch as a new breed Australian capitalist who has risen to power by promoting "the tabloid school of sex, sport, and razzmatazz layout." Recounts Murdoch's victories over publishing rivals Robert Maxwell and Hugh Cudlipp for control of *News of the World.* Comments on the irony of Murdoch's closely-guarded private life which is marked by an opulence built on his newspaper's ability to expose the lives of so many others to public view. Predicts Murdoch's migration to America, and ultimately condemns him for "mindless trivialisation" of the popular press.

699   Carson, W. E. "Northcliffe—Genius of a Hundred Successes." *The Editor & Publisher* (19 August 1922): 5-7.
Recounts the career of Alfred Harmsworth (Lord Northcliffe), pioneer of mass-appeal journalism in England, from his early publication *Answers*, to the founding of the *Daily Mail,* and his rise to national power and influence. Analyzes Northcliffe's philosophy, working habits and many accomplishments. Offers reasons for his success.

700   "Checkbook Journalism." *Time* (23 March 1962): 76-77.
Describes the British journalistic practice of paying persons involved in a criminal trial to tell their stories to newspapers. Such a policy allows the papers to satisfy a sensation-seeking readership while obeying British law which mandates that the press limit its coverage to actual testimony. Includes discussion of fees paid and newspapers involved in the practice.

701   Chesterton, Gilbert K. "The Mildness of the Yellow Press." In *Modern Essays,* edited by John Milton Berdon, John Richie Schultz, and Hewette Elwell Joyce. 292-302. New York: Macmillan, 1915.
Complains that Great Britain's yellow press is feeble compared to the journalistic purveyors of sensationalism in other nations, because it has not the courage to attack persons of power nor challenge issues of substance. Its sensationalism appears to be restricted to form only (i.e. large headlines).

702   Collison, Robert. *The Story of Street Literature: Forerunner of the Popular Press.* Santa Barbara, California: ABC-CLIO, 1973. 182 pgs.
Relates the history of penny chapbooks and broadsheets sold on British streets in the eighteenth century. Chapter 3, "Crime" (pp. 31-51), surveys sensational stories, songs, and poems which anticipate penny press reporting in popular newspapers.

703   "The Crippen Story: How the London Papers Handled the Murder Sensation." *The Editor and Publisher* (6 August 1910): 1, 4.
Reprint of article from the *Newspaper Owner of London* analyzing the manner in which London's popular half-penny dailies introduced coverage of the story involving Dr. Hawley Harvey Crippen (charged with the murder of his wife). Indicates that the most effective introduction contained in the *Daily Express*, employed neither melodrama nor luridness, but rather skillfully created a suspenseful atmosphere through masterful use of language.

704   "*Daily Mail* Vigor is Its Success Secret." *The Editor and Publisher* (22 May 1919): 18, 36.
Recounts the story of Alfred Harmsworth's revolutionary half-penny daily founded in 1896—the first such newspaper in England. Discusses innovations: compact size, condensed news articles, writing style which appealed to a mass audience. Includes use of foreign correspondents, local editions, promotion of new modes of transportation, success in uncovering scandal.

705   Dawbarn, Charles. "The Public and the Press." *English Review* 21 (1915): 490-496.
Observes that the British press is servile and cowed, especially when compared to the American. What is labelled as "sensational" or "muckrake" is really only the rare instance when truth is being reported (such as the nation's less than thorough preparedness for war).

706   Dennett, Prescott. " 'Tay Pay' O'Connor Reviews His 50 Years in Journalism." *The Editor and Publisher, The Fourth Estate* (16 November 1929): 28.
Discusses the journalistic career of T. P. O'Connor, whose British newspaper the *Star* pioneered in the presentation of the news in an entertaining, dramatic manner. O'Connor reminisces about Fleet Street in the nineteenth century. Includes memories of "penny-a-liner" journalism, George Bernard Shaw (as leader writer and music critic), and the training of journalists.

707   "Early Yellow Paper." *The Editor and Publisher* (3 December 1910): 12.
Reports that England's *Pall Mall Gazette* has charged the *Illustrated London Times* with having practiced American-style yellow journalism in its coverage of several poisonings in the town of Rugeley in 1856. The *Times* issued a special issue devoted exclusively to the crime and appeared to try the case in the paper. Includes response of the *Times* to the charge.

708   "English Journalism." *The Editor and Publisher* (6 January 1906): 4.
Reports the views of H. R. Chamberlain, London correspondent of the *New York Sun*, comparing the general character of the American and English press. Chamberlain contends that the English need to incorporate more human interest stories in their new reporting.

709   Escott, T. H. S. *Master of English Journalism: A Study of Personal Forces*. London: T. Fisher Unwin, 1911. 368 pgs.
Chronicles the development of the modern English newspaper, focusing on the nation's prominent journalists. Chapter 8, "The Men Who Made the Penny Press" (pp. 186-215), recounts the story of the first popularly-priced newspapers in England. Chapter 11 "A Gladstonian Forecast Fulfilled" (pp. 266-282), covers T. P. O'Connor and Lord Northcliffe (Alfred Harmsworth) establishing the first half-penny, mass-appeal newspapers.

710   Esdaile, Arundell. "Autolycus' Pack: The Ballad Journalism of the Sixteenth Century." In *Highlights in the History of the American Press, e*dited by Edwin H. Ford and Edwin Emery. pp. 6-24. Minneapolis: University of Minnesota Press, 1954.
Recounts the history of the English news ballad of the 16th century which was frequently devoted to the subjects of monstrous births, executions, fires, and scandal. By comparison, the defeat of the Spanish Armada received meager coverage.

711   "Europe Imitating Our Journalism." *The Literary Digest* 46 (1913): 76.
Quotes A. Maurice Low, American correspondent of the *London Morning Post*, in reporting that sensational journalism is sweeping England due to U.S. influence. Muses that such influence is inevitable in a world grown smaller in the last quarter century.

712   "A Feature of the Evening Papers." *The Spectator* 71 (1893): 795-796.
Takes issue with constant reporting of shocking disasters, catastrophes, and crimes. Analyzes an issue of the *Pall Mall Gazette* to demonstrate the prevalence of such stories. Deplores the impression of a world in constant distress and upheaval thus conveyed.

713   Ferris, Paul. *The House of Northcliffe: The Harmsworths of Fleet Street*
          London: Weidenfield and Nicolson. 1971. 340 pgs.
          Biography of the Harmsworths contains the story of Lord Northcliffe's
          founding of the *London Daily Mail*, England's first popular/sensational
          newspaper targeted for the masses. Chapters 3 through 8 (pp. 18-86),
          recount Northcliffe's rise to success as a popular journalist. Relies heavily
          on the Northcliffe papers collected by Geoffey Harmsworth who used
          them to produce his 1959 Northcliffe biography with Reginald Pound
          (see entry #735). Includes Harmsworth family tree.

714   Fyfe, Hamilton. *Northcliffe: An Intimate Biography.* New York:
          Macmillan, 1930. 357 pgs.
          An affectionate biography of Lord Northcliffe (Alfred Harmsworth),
          founder of the half-penny *Daily Mail* (1896)—Fleet Street's first widely
          popular newspaper with mass appeal. Chapter 3, "The Young Man Makes
          Good" (pp. 32-48), discusses the inception of Harmsworth's popular/
          sensational publications, beginning with *Answers.*

715   Gardiner, A. G. "Scott and Northcliffe." *The Living Age* 342 (1932):
          155-162.
          Chronicles the impact upon English journalism registered by C. P. Scott
          (the *Manchester Guardian*) and Lord Northcliffe/Alfred Harmsworth
          (the *Daily Mail*). Emphasizes the revolutionary nature of Northcliffe's
          journalistic appeal to the masses and his business methods. Credits
          George Newnes (*Tit-Bits*) with demonstrating the potential of a popu-
          lar press to Northcliffe.

716   "Giant Northcliffe Institution Built on Boy's Bright Idea." *The Editor
          and Publisher* (22 May 1919): 24.
          Relates how Alfred Harmsworth achieved his first journalistic success
          with *Answers*, a small weekly paper which appealed to the masses with
          its brief articles, stories, jokes, and contests. Discusses Harmsworth's
          successful ventures with a series of cheap periodicals. Includes infor-
          mation on Harmsworth's educational publications for home instruction
          and his efforts on behalf of England during World War I.

717   "Harmsworth Views." *The Editor and Publisher* (14 October 1905): 3.
          Reports on Alfred Harmsworth's article contributed to the diamond ju-
          bilee issue of London's *Newspaper Press Directory* in which the En-
          glish journalist proclaims modern newspapers to be superior to their
          predecessors in virtually every way. Older sheets, claims Harmsworth,
          were more "personal," "scurrilous," and "indecent." Modern papers are
          efficient, news-gathering machines.

718   "He Made England Read Newspapers." *The Editor and Publisher*
       (19 August 1922): 7-10.
       Views Lord Northcliffe's career as a result of his innovative, influential
       ideas which revolutionized journalism. Discusses contests and crusades
       which dominated *Answers* and the *Daily Mail*, appealing to the popular
       readership. Includes the influence of George Newne's *Tit-Bits*, success with
       "penny dreadfuls," and the founding of the tabloid *Daily Mirror*. Accom-
       panying chart details all the publications in the Northcliffe Empire.

719   Herd, Harold. *The March of Journalism: The Story of the British Press
       From 1622 to the Present Day.* London: George Allen & Unwin
       Ltd., 1952. 352 pgs.
       Surveys the history of English journalism. Chapter 12, "The New Jour-
       nalism" (pp. 222-251), discusses the introduction of human interest and
       mass appeal to the English press. Lord Northcliffe (Alfred Harmsworth)
       and his immediate predecessors (W. T. Stead, George Newnes, and T. P.
       O'Connor) are covered. Appendices provide information on English news
       agencies and newspaper chains.

720   Hindley, Charles. *The History of the Catnach Press, at Berwick-Upon-
       Tyne, in Northumberland, and Seven Dials, London.* Detroit: Sing-
       ing Tree Press, 1969. 308 pgs.
       A reissue of the 1887 London edition which chronicles the history of
       John and James Catnach's popular nineteenth-century printing busi-
       ness in London. Contains a large selection of ballads, broadsides, and
       street papers featuring popular stories about sensational murders, tri-
       als, executions, and scandals—both in prose and verse.

721   Hindley, Charles. *The Life and Times of James Catnach (Late of Seven
       Dials) Ballad Monger.* London: Reeves and Turner, 1878. 432 pgs.
       Biography of "Jemmy" Catnach, son of John, printer and publisher of
       nineteenth-century street literature. Contains many of the ballads and
       broadsides, including the sensational, which Catnach produced.

722   Hindley, Charles, ed. *The Boxburghe Ballads.* London: Reeves and
       Turner, 1873.
       A two-volume collection which reproduces over 1,300 English broad-
       side ballads both mundane and sensational, between the years 1560-1700.

723   "Interest in *Daily Mirror* Wanes." *The Editor and Publisher* 19 Decem-
       ber 1903: 14.
       Characterizing Alfred Harmsworth's London *Daily Mirror* the "Daily
       Female," *Punch* claims that the tabloid is failing, holding appeal only
       for women. Notes W. T. Stead's plans to begin publication of the *Daily
       Paper*, a rival tabloid.

724   Lee, Alan J. *The Origins of the Popular Press in England*. London: Crown Helm, 1976. 310 pgs.
        Chronicles the death of the liberal ideal of the newspaper as an enduring civil and social institution in England. As in America and France, the process of commercialization produced a cheaper, more sensational press which replaced the more staid, venerable variety by appealing to the mass readership more effectively. Chapter 4, "The Old Journalism and the New" (pp. 73-130), covers the contributions of W. T. Stead, T. P. O'Connor, and Lord Northcliffe (Alfred Harmsworth) in the development of a cheap, popular press. Includes statistical tables illustrating the political distribution of many English dailies.

725   "London's Three New Dailies." *The Editor and Publisher* (19 December 1903): 7.
        Reports on the imminent debut of three new daily newspapers in London: W. T. Stead's *Daily Paper*, a new illustrated penny paper to be offered by owners of the *Graphic,* and a new half-penny paper to be published by T. P. O'Connor specializing in "light literature and gossip."

726   Low, A. Maurice. " 'Tabloid Journalism': Its Causes and Effects." *Forum* 31 (1901): 56-61.
        Relates how Mr. Alfred Harmsworth introduced tabloid journalism to England in the form of his publications: *Answers*, an entertainment sheet, and the *Daily Mail* newspaper. Predicts dire consequences: debasement of the nation's literary tastes and weakening of the power of thought. American newspapers are superior to the British tabloid because they still contain some substantial articles.

727   "*Mirror* History is Business Romance." *The Editor and Publisher* (22 May 1919): 28, 38.
        Recounts how London's sensational tabloid was rescued from a failing women's paper in 1904 by transformation into a photo newspaper which featured dramatic illustrations of sensational news events: espionage trials, mountain climbing, battles, sinking of the Titanic, volcanic craters. Includes information on correspondents' coverage of World War I and the first photographs of tanks.

728   Morison, Stanley. *The English Newspaper: Some Account of the Physical Development of Journals Printed in London Between 1622 and the Present Day*. Cambridge: University Press 1932. 335 pgs.
        Examines the format changes in London's newspapers from the seventeenth to the twentieth century, and analyzes the reasons for such changes. Chapter 15, "The 'New Journalism', 1883-1896" (pp 277-296), presents the birth of the first sensational newspapers with mass appeal operated by W. T. Stead, T. P. O'Connor, and Lord Northcliffe

(Alfred Harmsworth). Includes many full-page reproductions for the newspapers discussed.

729   " 'New Boy' on Fleet Street." *Newsweek* (10 May 1971): 97-98.
Comments on Rupert Murdoch's 3 year rise in British newspaper publishing through acquisition and reinvigoration of *News of the World* and the *Sun*, the latter of which he converted into a sensational tabloid regularly featuring nudity.

730   "A New Headliner Rocks Fleet Street." *Business Week* (12 September 1970): 32.
Discusses how Rupert Murdoch has successfully applied a "sex-and-scandal" formula in reviving Fleet Street journals *News of the World*, and the *Sun*. Anticipates a clash with the journalists' union which threatens to strike vs. Murdoch's publications. Discusses Murdoch's career, including his non-tabloid interests.

731   "New Journalism." *Cornhill Magazine* 49 (1920): 441-448.
Describes Britain's pioneering "New Journalism" newspapers which "cut things short"—both in content and in sheet size: Frederick Greenwood's *Pall Mall Gazette* and the *Daily News* of the 1870's. The author was an employee of such newspapers (identified only as "An Old Journalist") who enjoyed the freedom from convention and inventiveness of the new newspapers. Acknowledges the influence of American journalism on the English newspaper industry. Regrets the overemphasis of sensationalism, however, which results , at times, in fabrication of stories. Also dislikes the quick turnover of journalists which he attributes to the fast, high-pressure work environment.

732   "Pages of Sin." *Time* (2 December 1946): 63-64.
Reports that England's sensational *News of the World* weekly newspaper has a new editor, but will maintain the same style, emphasizing sex, sports, and contests. Relates the newspaper's history of crime and scandal coverage.

733   Pemberton, Max. *Lord Northcliffe: A Memoir*. London: Hodder and Stoughton, 1922. 250 pgs.
Affectionate, personal biography of Lord Northcliffe (Alfred Harmsworth), founder of the *London Daily Mail*, England's revolutionary half-penny daily aimed at the masses. Chapter 6, "The Daily Mail" (pp. 53-72) relates the story of the paper's inception.

734   Pierce, Robert N. *Lord Northcliffe: Trans-Atlantic Influences*.

Lexington, Kentucky: Association for Education in Journalism, 1975. 41 pgs.
Traces the influence of Bennett's *Herald* and Pulitzer's *World* upon Lord Northcliffe (Alfred Harmsworth) and his *London Daily Mail*. Includes discussion of the popular French daily, *Le Petit Journal*. Covers Northcliffe's adaptations of American models, his contact with Joseph Pulitzer, Adolph Ochs, and E. W. Scripps. (Number 40 in the series "Journalism Monographs.")

735   Pound, Reginald and Geoffrey Harmsworth. *Northcliffe.* London: Cassell, 1959. 933 pgs.
Comprehensive biography of Lord Northcliffe (Alfred Harmsworth) whose *Daily Mail* popularized the New Journalism in the late 19th century London. Chapter 8, "May 4, 1896" (pp. 193-215) details the founding of the half-penny newspaper. A reproduction of a "trial run" of the *Daily Mail* appears on p. 195.

736   Priestly, J. B. "The Popular Press." In *Thoughts in the Wilderness.* 188-193. New York: Harper & Brothers, 1957.
Believes the salaciousness of Britain's sensational press is harmless and probably much tamer than the country's Victorian newspapers. Curiosity is harmless and even luridness can be educational. The more serious problem with British tabloids is the triviality of their subject matter. New York's tabloids, in comparison, contain a greater amount of intelligent news and commentary.

737   "The Problem of Truth in Journalism." *Current Opinion* 67 (1919): 180-181.
Presents response of the *New Statesman* to Sir Charles Walston, who asserted in his book—*Truth: An Essay in Moral Reconstruction*—that the journalist has undermined the public's regard for the truth. The *New Statesman* responds that the press is influenced by the readership's love of sensation in at least equal measure.

738   "Progress of British Journalism." *The Editor and Publisher and Journalist* 13 (1913): 63, 75.
Discusses the popularization of British journalism which has incorporated American and French innovations, replacing the solemn and staid conservatism of the older British press. Includes contributions of W. T. Stead (whose series of articles in the *Pall Mall Gazette*, "The Maiden Tribute of Modern Babylon," dared debate the proper age of consent for English girls), and Alfred Harmsworth (founder of *Answers* and the *Daily Mail*, popular journals upon which he founded a journalistic empire and emerged as Lord Northcliffe).

739   "Racy News of the World." *Newsweek* (25 November 1946): 73.
Reports the Britain's sensational weekly *News of the World* leads the
nation in newspaper circulation. Includes brief history of the publication and discussion of crime/sex/astrology/sports formula. Comments
on British libel laws and methods of avoiding them (base stories strictly
on trial records, e.g.).

740   Ridout, Herbert C. "Lord Burnham Fights for Liberty to Print
'Crimson News.' " *The Editor and Publisher* (16 July 1921): 12.
Reports that Lord Burnham, owner of the *London Daily Telegraph*, successfully argued for the deletion of a section of England's Matrimonial
Causes Bill which declared it illegal to publish information concerning
divorces or photograph any of the parties involved, before the conclusion of the case. Details Burnham's arguments which included objections to the manner in which only certain kinds of news were being
selected for such discriminatory treatment.

741   Roche, John F. "British Press Becoming 'Sensational.' " *The Editor
and Publisher, The Fourth Estate* (22 November 1930): 7.
Discusses British newspapers' emphasis on entertainment and gossip
in order to successfully compete in continual circulation wars. Interviews Beckel Willson, *London Daily Express* editor, who notes that
British papers once regarded American yellow journals as sensational
and unstable, but now the situation is reversed. Includes information
on British reporting practices, interview techniques, and national vs.
local outlook.

742   Rollins, Hyder E. *Cavalier and Puritan: Ballads and Broadsides
Illustrating the Period of the Great Rebellion 1640-1660.* New
York: New York University Press, 1923. 531 pgs.
A collection of 75 ballads and broadsides in verse demonstrating that
puritanical rule during the Cromwell era did not eliminate the sensa-
tional street literature which preceded newspapers.

743   Scott, T. H. S. *Masters of English Journalism: A Study of Personal
Forces.* London: T. Fisher Unwin, 1911. 368 pgs.
English newspaper history with emphasis upon the individuals who
most influenced the nation's journalism. Included are the prophets of
the "New Journalism" with mass appeal: George Newnes, W. T. Stead,
T. P. O'Connor, and Lord Northcliffe (Alfred Harmsworth).

744   Scott-James, R. A. "The Crisis in London Journalism." *The English
Review* 11 (1912): 85-98.
Perceives a journalistic crisis in England precipitated by the success of

yellow journalism imported from America. Newspapers of this type are entirely commercial, appealing to most ignorant and gullible elements of society. Intelligent publications believe they must imitate the successful papers, at least in part. As a result, many such newspapers have sacrificed quality without really securing their economic survival.

745   Shaaber, M. A. *Some Forerunners of the Newspaper in England 1476-1622.* New York: Octagon Books, Inc. 1966. 368 pgs.
Reprint of 1929 edition which relates the history of printed news in England before the newspaper. Chapter 6, "Popular News" (pp. 137-167), covers the reporting of sensational murders, miracles and monsters in pamphlets/newsbooks, ballads, and broadsides. Chapter 8, "Ballad News" (pp. 189-203), is devoted to the sixteenth-century narrative which transmitted news of sensational events, and was often converted into a broadside. Separate chapters deal with news writers and publishers.

746   Simonis, H. *The Street of Ink: An Intimate History of Journalism.* London: Casell and Company, Ltd., 1917. 372 pgs.
A history of Fleet Street newspapers written by a journalist who witnessed the birth of the popular press in England. Chapter 2, "The Birth of the Popular Press. Old and New Journalism" (pp. 9-22), describes the transition, while chapter 7 (pp. 59-67), discusses Lord Northcliffe's *Daily Mail.* The phototabloid *Daily Mirror* is covered in chapter 10 (pp. 79-85).

747   Stephens, Mitchell. "Sensationalism and Moralizing in 16th and 17th Century Newsbooks and News Ballads." *Journalism History* 12 (1985): 92-95.
Comments upon the anomalous coupling of sex and violence with moral platitudes in medieval news broadsides. Discusses methods of moralizing and the need of sensationalists to preach in this manner.

748   "T. P. O'Connor Dies; His Life Spanned 62 Years of Journalism." *The Editor and Publisher, The Fourth Estate* (23 November 1929): 41.
Reports the death of T. P. O'Connor, English journalist whose human interest approach to the news paved the way for Lord Northcliffe's innovations. Recounts O'Connor's career, highlighting his work on the *Pall Mall Gazette,* and the publication of the *Star,* the *Sun,* and the *Weekly Sun, M.A.P.* ("Mainly About People").

749   "T. P. O'Connor Prints Widely Read Papers." *The Editor and Publisher* (30 June 1917): 23.
Reports on the visit of popular Irish journalist Thomas Power O'Connor to the United States. Discusses O'Connor's pioneering activities in mass-

appeal journalism as practiced in his *M.A.P.* (Mostly About People) *and T.P's Weekly*, which focuses on personalities in the news and enjoys wide circulation in the United Kingdom.

750   "Warns 'Sensational' Press." *The Editor and Publisher and Journalist* (11 November 1911): 1.
Reports that England's Secretary of Foreign Affairs Sir Edward Grey, warned the press that sensational news reports risk inciting international incidents by publicizing falsehoods.

751   Wilson, R. Macnair. *Lord Northcliffe: A Study.* Philadelphia: J. B. Lippincott, 1927. 304 pgs.
Concise biography of Lord Northcliffe (Alfred Harmsworth), whose *Daily Mail* reports the news to London's masses. Chapters 20 through 22 (pp. 121-233) cover the founding and formative stages of the half-penny newspaper.

Modern Practice

752   Brand, David. "Editor, Heal Thyself." *Time* (11 December 1989): 89.
Reports that 20 of England's leading newspapers, including the tabloids, signed a Newspaper Publishers Association code of ethics in order to prevent threatened government censorship. The code pledges to honor privacy, correct mistakes, and provide opportunity to reply. It also includes hiring of mediators to guarantee fairness. No penalties, however, are specified for violations.

753   Clarkson, Wensley. *Dog Eat Dog: Confessions of a Tabloid Journalist.* London: Fourth Estate, 1990. 206 pgs.
Anecdotal compilation of the author's 10 years as a tabloid journalist on Fleet Street in the 1980's.

754   Connell, Ian. "Tales of Tellyland: The Popular Press and Television in the UK." In *Communication and Citizenship: Journalism and the Public Sphere in the New Media Age,* edited by Peter Dahlgren and Colin Sparks. 236-253. London: Routledge, 1991.
Seeks an answer to why Britain's popular tabloid press concentrates so heavily on scandalous stories of entertainers. Recognizes a symbiotic relationship between the tabloid press and television stars: TV stars are lifted above the ordinary citizen to a higher caste, but are expected to conform to a higher moral standard, as a result. Finds tabloid takes of television stars attractive because the revelations reported have a populist aspect, forcing the star down from the pedestal.

755 Diamond, John. "Reading Between the Lines." *New Statesman & Society* (22 May 1992): 12-13.
Maintains that Britain's tabloids have successfully circumvented the nation's Press Complaints Commission by turning their attention to the royal family and politicians—subjects not protected by the PCC code. Differentiates between old-time tabloids which sensationalized legitimate news stories and their modern descendants whose stories contain little news of substance. Appears to favor legislation to deal with the tabloid problem.

756 Diamond, John. "A Right Royal Ragging." *New Statesman & Society* (19 July 1991): 14-15.
Contends that the tabloids' recent royal-bashing does not signal a basic political shift leftward. The tabloids regard the royal family as a valuable source of stories, and a tool with which to attack the left.

757 Dunning, Eric, Patrick Murphy and John Williams. "Spectator Violence at Football Matches: Towards a Sociological Explanation." *The British Journal of Sociology* 37 (1986): 221-244.
Faults the tabloid press for reporting violence at soccer matches in a sensational manner beginning in the 1960's, thereby publicizing football stadiums as places where fighting is likely to occur. Combative fans were attracted by such accounts. Does not charge the media with causing the violence but, rather, significantly contributing to it.

758 "Fourth Estate: A Regular Monitor of the Tory Press." *New Statesman & Society* (11 December 1992): 6.
Chronicles the spectacle of the usually pro-Tory tabloid press turning on its own with typical hyperbole and melodrama.

759 Fuhrman, Peter. "The Sage of Fleet Street." *Forbes* (17 February 1992): 50-54.
Reports that Lord Rothermere (Vere Harmsworth) turned the failing British newspaper *Daily Mail* into a profitable publication by transforming to a tabloid format in the 1970's, and tailoring its news coverage to appeal to middle-aged women.

760 "The Good in Tabloids." *The Economist* (5 December 1992): 20.
The tabloid newspapers in Britain offer the public their best opportunity to voice distaste for the establishment. Correctly discerning the mood of the times, the tabloids are incessant in their attacks on the establishment, and the public responds with their patronage. Tabloids perform "a necessary if wretched service."

761   Gray, Michael "Britain Puts Its Press on Probation." *Washington Jour-
         nalism Review* June 1989: 14.
         Reports on formation of press review commission in Britain in an
         attempt to curb the excesses of the tabloid press. Should this effort fail,
         it is likely that anti-press legislation will be enacted.

762   Jenkins, Jolyon. "The Green Sheep in 'Colonel Gadaffi Drive.' " *New
         Statesman* (9 January 1987): 8-10.
         Criticizes misinformation contained in the British tabloid *Sun'*s sensa-
         tional political attacks upon Labour-controlled councils. Maintains that
         for every example of "loony left" legislation, a Tory counterpart can
         be cited. (Examples of both are provided.)

763   Kirkpatrick, Curry. "Killer Tabs Strike Again." *Sports Illustrated* 6 July
         1992: 64-67.
         Relates how Britain's tabloid journalists feast on the personal lives (real
         and imagined) of the tennis players at Wimbledon. Divides British tab-
         loid reporters into Beasties (aggressive/gonzo sports journalists) and
         Rotters (specialists in the esoteric).

764   Lamb, Christina. "Tab Rags Face Gags." *Nieman Reports* Spring 1994: 9-10.
         Chronicles the tabloid-engineered departure of British government min-
         isters during the previous eighteen months, David Mellor, Norman
         Lamont, Michael Mates, and Tim Yeo. Surveys recent efforts at press
         regulation, stating there is little public support for a privacy law which
         would likely protect only the privileged.

765   Laver, Ross. "New Standards of Vulgarity." *Maclean's* (19 October 1987): 39.
         British tabloid *Star* has outdone its rivals recently in titillation and
         salaciousness. While circulation has risen, so have staff resignations
         and advertisers' cancellations.

766   Leapman, Michael. *Treacherous Estate: The Press After Fleet Street.*
         London: Hodder & Stoughton, 1992. 304 pgs.
         Optimistic look at the current British journalism scene where, the
         author states, there are "more and better writers producing more and
         better newspapers." The tabloids must be free to sensationalize. The
         public tells them when they have had enough by withdrawing patron-
         age. Chapter 10, "Shame and Scandal" (pp. 190-202), describes how
         tabloids invite failure when they verge on the pornographic.

767   Lumsden, Andrew. "Let's Hear it for AIDS to Circulation." *New
         Statesman* (8 February 1985): 17.
         Criticizes British tabloids' "queer-bashing subtexts" in coverage of the

AIDS epidemic. Also calls upon gay journalists to step forward in order to argue for fair coverage of gay issues.

768   McAlpine, Joan. "World of Extremes." *New Statesman & Society* (28 July 1989): 42.
Reports on the state of British television offerings between the hours of midnight and 5 am, which include tabloid talk shows such as Phil Donahue and his British equivalent, "The Time, The Place." Observes that such programs belabor the personal aspect of the subjects under discussion yet treat guests as if they possessed no individual worth.

769   Miller, Bill. "Am I What I Read." *New Statesman & Society* (24 April 1992): 17.
The author, head of Glascow University's politics department, credits sensational political coverage in the Tory tabloids with providing the party with victory at the polls. Charges the tabloids are untruthful in supporting their particular bias. Admits, however, that the tabloids do not intrude into people's private lives as much as they have in past elections.

770   O'Connor, Robert. "British Tabloids—Losing Touch With Readers?" *The Editor & Publisher* (7 September 1991): 12-13, 38.
Reports on decline in circulation of British tabloid newspapers. Explanations discussed: economic recession, self-censorship of tabloids to avoid government regulation, changing habits of the public, and recurring patterns of publishing excess/government crackdown. Relies heavily on interview with S. J. Taylor, author of *Shock! Horror! The Tabloids in Action* (see entry #458).

771   "Out of Order." *New Statesman & Society* (2 August 1991): 4.
Editorial which indicates the irony of British tabloids, which live by scandal, suddenly objecting to the "outing" of undeclared homosexuals.

772   Platt, Steve. "Fanning the Flames of Bigotry." *New Statesman & Society* (4 March 1994): 12-13.
Criticizes British tabloid sensationalism in its coverage of a fatal fire at a pornographic film club. By focusing on, and publicizing the sexual predilections of the club's clientele, the fire victims were dehumanized.

773   Platt, Steve. "A Zoom With a View." *New Statesman & Society* (12 November 1993): 16-17.
Ridicules the furor accompanying the tabloid *Mirror's* publication of photographs revealing Princess Diana exercising at local gym. Cries of outrage are out of proportion to the offense and hypocritical as well.

774   Post, Tom. "The Selling of the Royals." *Newsweek* (22 June 1992): 70-71.
       Historical overview of British royalty's relationship with the press.
       Describes Queen Elizabeth II's skillful use of publicity to further royal
       interests. Touches upon current obsession with the royals facilitated by
       the palace's refusal to sue.

775   "The Press: Naughty Vicars Can Relax." *The Economist* (15 February
          1992): 68-69.
       Reports that the threat of legislation further protecting people's privacy
       has restrained the tabloid press's usually obnoxious behavior, although
       politicians remain targets. There is also some evidence that readers are
       repelled by the tabloid's worst excesses.

776   "Privacy and Sensationalism: A British View." *Columbia Journalism
          Review* January/February 1978: 35-39.
       Excerpts from Britain's third Royal Commission on the Press report,
       completed in July 1977. Castigates sensational journalism as
       "unsavory" and "intolerable", but does not recommend censorship,
       acknowledging that irresponsibility is the price a free society pays for
       continued liberty.

777   Richardson, Kay. *The Mikhail and Maggie Show: The British Popular
          Press and the Anglo-Soviet Summit* Working paper #14, First
          Annual International Conference on Discourse, Peace, Security
          and International Society. 9-16 August 1987. San Diego: Univer-
          sity of California Institute on Global Conflict and Cooperation.
          1988. 16 pgs.
       Discusses the manner in which the British tabloids reported on Prime Min-
       ister Margaret Thatcher's visit to Moscow for arms control talks with the
       Soviet Premier Mikhail Gorbachev. Concentrates on the language used to
       communicate information and convey attitudes to their readership. While
       not defending the tabloids against charges of sensationalism, the author
       believes that the papers' ultimate political influence is questionable.

778   Richler, Mordechai. "Rue, Britannia." *Gentleman's Quarterly* January
          1990: 57-59.
       A traveller's impression of Britain's flourishing newspaper scene. Ex-
       cerpts of several tabloid tales are provided and commented upon.

779   Sanders, Claire. "Anatomy of a Sex Romp." *New Statesman & Society*
          (24 February 1989): 33-36.
       Chronicles how the British tabloid *News of the World* sensationalized
       the story of a woman who left her children with a baby-sitter to take a
       three-day vacation with a man. Argues for the need to protect the pri-
       vacy of ordinary people.

780   Soames, Emma. "Royal Scandals Have the Tabloids Thriving. But What
        Are They Doing to the Monarchy?" *Vogue* June 1991: 90-94.
        Maintains that both the scandal-hungry British tabloid press and the
        wildness of the new generation of royalty are responsible for the inces-
        sant stream of soap-opera type stories featured in England's five daily
        tabloids. Notes one instance of a publication apologizing for an
        especially deplorable piece of misinformation.

781   "Spanish Grill." *The New Leader* (5 October 1987): 9.
        Reports on the anti-Hispanic bias regularly displayed by Rupert
        Murdoch's tabloid, *Sun*, as evidenced in its derogatory references to
        Spaniards and King Juan Carlos which continually appear in its pages.

782   Sparks, Colin. "Good-bye, Hildy Johnson: The Vanishing Serious Press."
        In *Communication and Citizenship: Journalism and the Public
        Sphere in the New Media Age,* edited by Peter Dahlgren and Colin
        Sparks. 58-74. London: Routledge, 1991.
        Surveys the current state of British journalism, remarking upon the
        distinctly different social profile of each newspaper's readership. News-
        papers are produced for different social classes. Reports on the con-
        tinuing trend toward entertainment, and away from serious news, espe-
        cially in the tabloids. Identifies three trends of the modern media: in-
        ternationalization of news production; erosion of entertainment/news
        boundary; and audience fragmentation.

783   "Tabloid Tussle." *The Economist* (25 August 1990): 50.
        Reports on increased competition between British tabloids *Daily Mir-
        ror* (Robert Maxwell's) and *Sun* (Rupert Murdoch's). Discusses reasons
        for slumping sales in the 1980's, current technological
        advantages of the *Sun*, and plans by the *Mirror* to meet the challenge.

784   "Tabloids and the Tories." *The Economist* (24 October 1992): 66.
        Contends that the tabloids attack Prime Minister John Major in part
        because Margaret Thatcher made for better copy, but also cites high
        interest rates; the Mastricht treaty; and the recession which have hurt
        tabloid owners Rupert Murdoch and Conrad Black.

785   Underhill, William. "The Princess Beats a Retreat." *Newsweek* (13 Decem-
        ber 1993): 47.
        Reports that Princess Diana blames the tabloids for her decision to largely
        retire from public life. The more cynical members of the press believe
        she is being forced out of the limelight by the more established members
        of the royal family who are jealous of the attention she has garnered.

786   "A Week in Politics." *New Statesman & Society* (12 June 1992): 26.
Offers a day-by-day chronicle of the previous week's royal family melodrama as reported by the tabloids.

787   Wentz, Laurel. "Fleet Street Frenzy: Eddie Shah's *Today* Shakes Up
U.K." *Advertising Age* (3 March 1986): 40-41.
Reports that new nonunion tabloid, *Today*, utilizing the latest comput-
erized printing technology, will offer ad rates which are 75% less than
its competitors. This could mean a new profitable era for Fleet Street
newspapers which will be attractive to investors.

788   Williams, Paul and Julie Dickinson. "Fear of Crime: Read All About
It?: The Relationship Between Newspaper Crime Reporting and
Fear of Crime." *British Journal of Criminology* 33 (1993): 33-56.
Reports on findings of a study which measured the amount of space
and prominence given to crime by the British press; the correlation
between people's fear of crime and the crime stories they read; and the
qualitative aspects of reporting styles in different newspapers. While
not establishing a causal link between crime reporting and the fear of
crime, the study indicates that readers of papers that report the most
crime in the most sensational manner, (i.e. the tabloids) fear crime the
most. The author argues for more dispassionate reporting of crime. Includes statistical tables and survey instrument.

789   Wood, Barry. "Keep Taking the Tabloids." *New Statesman & Society*
(31 July 1992): 14-15.
Reports on a mutually beneficial, but unethical, relationship which is
developing between "alternative" medical practitioners and tabloid
newspapers in England: the practitioner provides the publication with
sensationally lurid case histories in return for publicity. Only the pa-
tients are the losers. Britain's General Medical Council is taking disci-
plinary action.

790   "Young Princess Suffers a Bad Attack of *Sun* Spots." *British Journal of
Photography* (16 January 1992): 5.
Reports that British tabloid *The Sun* apparently retouched a photograph
of Princess Beatrice in order to exaggerate the signs of her chicken
pox. Discussion with newspaper picture editors includes the ethics of
retouching photos in specific circumstances and the issue of sensationalism. (The photograph in question is reproduced.)

FRANCE

Historical Overview

791 "Cheap Paper Pioneer." *The Editor & Publisher* (28 April 1906): 4.
Recounts the career of Emil de Girardin, founder of *La Presse* and "father of low-priced newspapers" in France. Refers to the *New York Evening Post* editorial which credits Girardin with liberating French journalism from political subserviency and printing all the news as it occurred, causing some to regard him as "a journalistic sensation-monger."

792 Conner, Edward. "Modern French Newspaper World." *The Editor & Publisher & Journalist* (17 May 1913): 21.
Describes the modern French newspaper scene including the nature of reporter's duties, standards of conduct, financial basis of newspapers, advertising agents, and the papers of Paris. Discusses the penny papers *Le Petit Journal* and *Le Petit Parisien*.

793 Fernsworth, L. A. "Paris Murder Trial Reporting a Riot of Passion." *The Editor & Publisher* (1 March 1924): 7.
Characterizes Parisian journalists' reporting of a politically-motivated murder committed by Germaine Berton, a 20 year old anarchist, as extremely emotionally-charged and departing greatly from the traditional factual model upheld by most reporters. While political partisanship complicates matters, it is maintained that the French are more inclined to base stories on emotional impressions than are other journalists, resulting in sensational newspaper coverage.

794 Freiberg, J. W. *The French Press: Class, State, and Ideology.* New York: Praeger, 1981. 320 pgs.
Provides an economic/political overview of the French press focussing on the journalistic implications of capitalism and class struggle. Chapter 9, "The Sensational Press" (pp. 213-226) views sensational journalism as a symptom of late capitalist society, characterized by depoliticization and crisis orientation. A content analysis demonstrating the "informational vacuity" of sensational journalism includes an examination of *France-Soir* and *Parisien Libéré*, the nation's leading sensational papers. Includes statistical tables.

795 "French vs. American Newspapers." *The Editor & Publisher* (17 December 1921): 32.
Editorial which discusses the comments of French journalist Stephane Lauzanne who credits American influence for the transformation of French newspapers from dry academic journals to popular news-con-

science sheets with plentiful photographs and prominent headlines. Notes that Lauzanne fails to comment on the sensationalism of French news stories and illustrations which, the editorial argues, would be considered libelous in America.

796   Smith, Richard Lee. "The Rise of the Mass Press in 19th Century France." *Journalism Quarterly* 53 (1976): 94-99.
Recounts the history of French "penny press" newspapers *Le Petit Journal* founded by Moise Polydore Millaud in 1863, and *Le Petit Parisien*, transformed into a popular newspaper in 1888 by Jean Dupuy. Maintains that the sensationalism of these papers both created a new mass readership and accurately reflected the opinions and attitudes of the masses. Comments upon the influence of the Dreyfus Affair on both newspapers, each of which handled the scandal differently.

GERMANY

Modern Practice

797   "Go East, My Sun." *The Economist* (6 April 1991): 64.
Reports that Rupert Murdoch will publish a British-style sensationalist tabloid, *Super Zeitung*, in East Germany.

HUNGARY

Modern Practice

798   Fuhrman, Peter. "Extra! Extra!" *Forbes* (19 February 1990): 54.
Tabloid newspaper owners Rupert Murdoch and Robert Maxwell have purchased rival newspapers in Hungary (*Reform* and *Magyar Hirlap* respectively). Though basically serious publications, Murdoch has begun to incorporate tabloid features into his weekly.

799   "Hungary: Red Tabloid Bares All." *Newsweek* (17 April 1989): 36.
Reports on *Reform*, a new popular Hungarian tabloid which resembles Western popular culture publications, a dramatic departure from the staid communist literature of recent decades.

INDIA

Modern Practice

800   Sarkar, R. C. *The Press in India.* Ram Nagar, New Dehli: S. Chand &
        Company, 1984. 320 pgs.
        Examines the growth and status of the Indian press. Chapter 7, "The
        Press and the Right to Privacy" (pp. 176-189) compares press limita-
        tions in Britain, America, and India. Chapter 12, "Review of the Work-
        ing Press in India" (pp. 279-306) includes a discussion of "rag journal-
        ism" (sensationalism) which is acknowledged as a significant problem,
        although not on a scale with the West. The author calls on the Indian
        Press Council to curb scandal-mongering journalists.

801   Weisberg, Jacob. "Bombay Diarist: Jew in the Crown." *The New
        Republic* (3 February 1992): 42.
        Reports on the state of housing and journalism in Bombay, as well as
        the books of V. S. Naipul. Indian journalists' penchant for understate-
        ment does not preclude their coverage of sex and violence, but rather
        adds a curious quality to their salaciousness. In addition, their matri-
        monial section is surprisingly explicit in detailing the characteristics
        desired in a mate.

ITALY

802   "Sensationalism Denounced." *The Editor and Publisher and Journalist*
        (2 December 1911): 2.
        Quotes A. Crespi of *La Vita Internazional* in Milan, Italy who finds it
        ironic that press freedom, thought to aid in abolishing causes of war, is
        now abetting public hysteria by publishing false, sensational reports.

JAPAN

Historical Overview

803   Altman, Albert A. " 'Shinbushi': The Early Meiji Adaptation of the
        Western Style Newspaper." In *Modern Japan,* edited by W. G.
        Beasly. 52-56. Berkeley: University of California Press, 1977.
        Traces the development of modern Western-style newspapers in Japan
        from the years 1866-1905, emphasizing particularly the years 1868-
        1873 when the process was in its early stages. Discusses the Popular
        Rights Movement beginning in 1873 which gave rise to newspapers
        with mass appeal.

804   Hanazono, Kanesada. *The Development of Japanese Journalism.* Osaka:
        The Osaka Mainichi, 1924. 110 pgs.
        Relates the growth of Japanese news reporting from the 17th century
        "slate impression" sheets. Chapter 15, "Commercialization of the press"
        (pp. 46-48) describes the movement to attract mass readership by run-
        ning sensational stories of crime, suicide and romance, and promoting
        contests. Increased influence of realism and materialism is also discussed.
        Includes reproductions of newspapers and new sheets through the years.

805   Sugimara, K. "Japanese Press Grew and Changed With Nation of Last
        Fifty Years" *The Editor and Publisher* (24 June 1922): 7.
        Traces the history of newspapers in Japan from their introduction in
        1867. From government sheets which included translations of foreign
        news articles, to political newspaper which accompanied the establish-
        ment of representative government in 1890, the "big" papers catered to
        the elite, while the "smalls—tabloids containing human interest stories
        aimed at the masses—developed separately. Gradually the "bigs" in-
        corporated human interest items in order to compete commercially,
        while the "smalls" included hard news to gain respectability.

Modern Practice

806   Morikawa, Kathleen. "The Popular Media: Self-Appointed Avengers:
        Japan Quarterly 39 (1992): 211-217.
        Reports on the popularity of Japan's *"Waido Sho"* ("wide" shows),
        daytime television programs which specialize in scandal, crime, and gos-
        sip. Posing as self-appointed champions of justice, these shows trample on
        human rights and privacy as they sensationally investigate their subjects.
        Japanese dislike of litigation means these programs rarely face libel charges.

RUSSIA

807   Bogert, Caroll. "They Came From Outer Space." *Newsweek* (23 October
        1989): 42.
        Reports that the Soviet media is taking advantage of "glasnost" to in-
        crease its popularity by publishing stories about UFO's, aliens, and faith
        healers. The world press reaction: "Soviets go Tabloid."

808   Walker, Martin. "Geroldoski: The Trash World of Soviet TV." *The New
        Republic* (19 & 26 August 1991): 16-17.
        Reports that Western commercialism is making inroads on Soviet radio
        and television where a variety of stations operate beyond control of the

government. Shows are produced featuring rock music, sex, games, sports, and western movies. Even Gostelradio, run by government-appointed Leonid Kravchenko, features tabloid television programming.

809   Wilson-Smith, Anthony, "Glasnost Enters the Twilight Zone." *Maclean's* 23 October 1989: 30.
Remarks on the sudden proliferation of sensational, tabloid-type news reports appearing in Soviet newspapers as "glasnost" proceeds. Included: numerous UFO and alien citings, an abominable snow man-type report, and articles featuring corpse-abusing gangs, and bizarre animals.

810   Young, Cathy. "Growing Pains." *The American Spectator* September 1991: 29-30.
Describes the status of the Soviet Union's newly-independent press which includes publisher Yulian Semyonov's *Top Secret*, a sensational tabloid. Although uncensored and gaining ground, the independent papers face a multitude of supply and distribution problems not experienced by the official ones.

PHILIPPINES

811   Lent, John A. "The Press Under Aquino." *Index on Censorship* September 1986: 8-9.
Surveying the status of the press under the Aquino government in the Philippines, the author identifies sensationalism and press irresponsibility as the most serious problems facing the journalistic community. Includes charges that past cronies of Marcos are purposefully spreading misinformation while masquerading as investigative journalists in order to discredit the Aquino government.

SPAIN

Historical Overview

812   Schulte, Henry F. *The Spanish Press: 1470-1966.* Urbana: University of Illinois Press, 1968. 280 pgs.
Surveys the history of Spanish newspaper journalism. Chapter 2, "The Franco Years: The Padlocked Mouth" (pp. 12-41) refers to the code of professional ethics for journalists created by the Spanish Federation of Press Associations and the Directorate-General of the Press (April 28, 1955) specifically prohibiting all sensationalizing of the news. Chapter 10, "The Federal Republic and Restoration" (pp. 203-220) credits a

series of sensational news stories ("The Crime of Fuencarral Street," war in Morocco and Cuba) with saving the industry from economic disaster. Includes information on Spain's first mass-circulation dailies, *El Noticiero Universal* and *El Imparcial* in the late 19th century.

MULTI-NATIONAL

813   Historical Overview

"Sensational Foreign News." *The Nation* 79 (1904): 494-495.
Supports the plea of Russian editor at a conference of international journalists in London who called for an end to sensationalizing international news. Such practice incites international prejudices. Comments on increased use of cable-transmitted news and its impact on the quality of information communicated.

814   Smith, Anthony. *The Newspaper: An International History.* London: Thames and Hudson, 1979. 192 pgs.
Provides an historical account of the development of the newspaper worldwide beginning in the 17th century. Chapter 6, " 'The Demon of Sensationalism' 1880-1980" (pp. 143-183), recounts the rise of populist papers with mass appeal, primarily in England and America, highlighting the contributions of W. T. Stead, Lord Northcliffe, and Joseph Pulitzer. A summary of the status of newspapers throughout Europe in the 20th century is also provided.

Modern Practice

815   Boissard, Justine. "This is Their Life." *The UNESCO Courier* October 1992: 14-16.
Reality television shows in America, France, Italy, and Britain are discussed. Critics, who consider such shows voyeurism, believe reality shows trivialize serious problems while exploiting emotional distress for commercial gain. Proponents point out that many reality shows are humanitarian (highlighting the heroism of emergency medical teams, e.g.) and democratizing (anyone can be a star).

816   Kassam, Shiraz. "Coups and Earthquakes Only." *World Press Review* September 1987: 64.
Reports that because two-thirds of foreign news in the 3rd World press originates in AP, UPI, Reuters, and Agence France-Presse news reports,

it suffers from "coup and earthquake" syndrome—only the sensational or amusing is reported. Worse than presenting the West with a false picture of the Third World, is the fact that the Third World is misrepresented to itself.

817   Lent, John A., ed. *Newspapers in Asia: Contemporary Trends and Problems* Hong Kong: Heinemann, 1982. 595 pgs.
Surveys the history and status of the press in nations throughout the Asian continent. Includes discussion of sensationalist newspapers in Burma, Hong Kong, Indonesia, Japan, Kampuchea, South Korea, Philippines, Singapore, Thailand, Taiwan, and Vietnam.

818   Östgaard, Einar. "Factors Influencing the Flow of News." *Journal of Peace Research* 2 (1965): 39-63.
Identifies sensationalism as a significant factor influencing reporting of news worldwide, resulting in depiction of a world which is more conflict-laden than reality would suggest. Also blames sensationalism for emphasizing the use of force, rather than tension-reduction, in solving world conflicts. Other factors discussed: simplification of news and identification with the audience. Complexity, lack of excitement or proper audience identification means information will not find its way past the "news barrier."

819   Picard, Robert G. *The Ravens of Odin: The Press in the Nordic Nations* Ames: Iowa State University Press, 1988. 153 pgs.
Examines the history and development of newspapers in Denmark, Finland, Iceland, Norway, and Sweden. Chapter 2, "The Nature of the Press" (pp. 26-42) discusses the relative absence of sensationalism common in the English and American newspapers. Indicates that the evening tabloids contain some sensational aspects, and that the press in Denmark appears most influenced by sensationalism (and Finland's press the least).

AUTHOR INDEX

References are to entry numbers.

SUBJECT INDEX

References are to entry numbers.